we had sneakers, they had guns

Freedom School.
Photographer unknown.

we had sneakers, they had guns

The Kids Who Fought for Civil Rights in Mississippi

Tracy Sugarman

SYRACUSE UNIVERSITY PRESS

Syracuse University Press, Syracuse, New York 12344-5160

First Edition 2009
09 10 11 12 13 14   6 5 4 3 2 1

All illustrations are courtesy of the author.

The paper used in this publication meets the minimum requirements
of American National Standard for Information Sciences—Permanence
of Paper for Printed Library Materials, ANSI Z39.48–1984.™∞

For a listing of books published and distributed by Syracuse University Press,
visit our Web site at SyracuseUniversityPress.syr.edu.

ISBN-13: 978-0-8156-0938-4
ISBN-10: 0-8156-0938-8

Library of Congress Cataloging-in-Publication Data
Sugarman, Tracy, 1921–
We had sneakers, they had guns : the kids who fought for civil rights in Mississippi /
Tracy Sugarman. — 1st ed.
p. cm.
ISBN 978-0-8156-0938-4 (cloth : alk. paper)
1. Civil rights workers—Mississippi—History—20th century.   2. Civil rights movements—
Mississippi—History—20th century.   3. Sugarman, Tracy, 1921–   4. Civil rights workers—
Mississippi—Biography.   5. Mississippi—Race relations—History—20th century.
6. African Americans—Civil rights—Mississippi—History—20th century.   I. Title.
E185.93.M6S887 2009
323.1196'0730762—dc22
2009004618

Manufactured in the United States of America

To Gloria
with love

Tracy Sugarman's art was first seen by a national audience in the pages of *Fortune,* the *Saturday Evening Post,* and *Colliers.* Publishers who commissioned him to illustrate their books include Simon and Schuster, Doubleday, Random House, and Time-Life Books. In an age of photography, Sugarman has continued to capture the disparate images of America with his pen and his watercolors. His reportage in words and drawings on the Seventh Avenue garment-center world of New York, his searing reportage for the *New York Times* on the Rikers Island prison, his documenting of the fascinating diversity of American corporate life, and his capturing of the lyrical world of the Tanglewood music culture and of the excitement of the Alvin Ailey Dance Group have all been preserved in his documentation. His paintings of the first rollout of the space shuttle *Columbia* are now a permanent part of the National Aeronautics and Space Administration Smithsonian Collection at the Kennedy Space Center, and his entire collection of art from World War II has been acquired by the U.S. Library of Congress.

Most significant for Sugarman has been his exploration of many of the areas in America where the struggles for change and growth are still being waged. His drawings of Appalachian life for VISTA, his dramatic drawings of the Malcolm X murder trial for the *Saturday Evening Post,* and his poignant coverage of marginal Hispanic American life in Texas for the Housing Investment Trust of the American Federation of Labor and Congress of Industrial Organizations have all contributed to ongoing dialogues in our society. But his recording of the civil rights movement in Mississippi in his book *Stranger at the Gates: A Summer in Mississippi,* published by Hill and Wang in 1966, marked the beginning of a searching fascination with a state that continues to challenge and intrigue him. The entire portfolio of his drawings of the "long, hot summer" in Mississippi is now a permanent archive at Tougaloo College. The present book, *We Had Sneakers, They Had Guns,* is a sympathetic journey into the past of the civil rights struggle in Mississippi with blacks and whites with whom he worked in 1964 and 1965.

In 1970, Mr. Sugarman partnered with filmmaker Bill Buckley to create Rediscovery Productions, Inc. In the intervening years their documentary film company has produced nearly forty educational films about social, political, and cultural challenges to American society. He continues to serve as artist, scriptwriter, and coproducer for Rediscovery.

contents

illustrations

prologue

Perhaps it is true that history is written only by the victors. Maybe in the long chronicling of winners and losers it has always been so. But in a much more intimate sense, I think every victor and every loser ultimately write, or rewrite, their own odysseys. I, too, am seeking my own clarity about the wheres, the whys, and the why-nots that composed my life, which laid out the road I've traveled. And I find myself increasingly searching the images in my rearview mirror. Most of my years I have spent searching the road ahead. There have been places to get to, crossroads to navigate, people waiting. But a singular image in the rearview mirror has repetitively drawn my eyes from my journey, nagging and insistent for my attention.

How achingly familiar, yet maddeningly unfamiliar, that receding landscape appears. Even the cherished places I once knew so well I could traverse them blindfolded. Even the shadowed, ominous corners that I continuously mapped to circumnavigate to get safely home. Even the battlefields that were so etched by fear and exaltation in my remembering. All jostle now for attention in a glass that often seems like a distorting mirror.

"But wasn't that . . . ?"

"But didn't I . . . ?

"But I knew . . . Didn't I?"

A white lacrosse ball bounces across the midfield stripe on a scrubby playing field. Two young bodies collide as they scramble to pick up the elusive ball. The scene has played countless times in my remembering, yet I watch, fascinated, as if it is the first time. The black youngster with the scarlet Geneva shirt finally snatches the ball, jukes to the left, twirls, and escapes the flailing stick of my Nottingham teammate. As he is dashing toward the vulnerable Nottingham goalie, the scene abruptly stops, like a jammed film. I can never remember whether the black Geneva player scored, whether it even mattered very much.

But I remember exactly, exquisitely, what took place on the sideline. I am seated on the Nottingham bench, a fourteen-year-old freshman, longing to get in the game, and dying for Coach Barrett to notice me. When the black Geneva player had broken loose and was racing down the field, I leaped to the sidelines and screamed to my pursuing teammates: "Get the Snowball! Get the goddamn Snowball!" I do remember the sudden hush on our bench just as I felt an angry hand grabbing my shoulder and twirling me around. Startled, I was inches from the furious face of Coach Barrett. In the sudden stillness he said, "Sugarman, that player has a name, and it isn't Snowball." Everyone on my team was staring, and I wished I was dead. And then the coach said, "If you were as good as he is, you'd be out there playing instead of on the bench. And if you were out there on the field, Sugarman, how would you feel if the other side started to yell: 'Get the Kike! Get the goddamn Kike!'?" Mercifully, the nightmare ends right there. But the agony of that confrontation in 1936 stays with me like a scar.

In all my fourteen years I had never before used a racial epithet. In truth, I had never even gone to a school that had black students. SNOWBALL? And in all my fourteen years I had never before been singled out as "someone other," someone different from all my classmates. KIKE?

As I was growing up in the 1930s, the only "others" in my insulated white middle-class world were not Negroes, who were only funny voices on *Amos and Andy*, the radio show my family never missed. The "others" in my world were the foreigners, the Jewish relatives, fleeing Germany, who often arrived unannounced at our door. Suddenly rootless in a strange soil, these unknown cousins appeared very different to my youthful eyes. Their speech was strange and hesitant, and their clothes looked coarse and odd. When I was told by my mother to take one of the newly discovered cousins, Bernhardt, to visit my sixth-grade class, I was embarrassed when he bowed stiffly to Miss Kelly and the whole class giggled. I was relieved when Bernhardt's family boarded the New York Central and headed to Cleveland. But until the searing and scary insights of that hot spring afternoon on the lacrosse field, I had never truly looked at what "the other" meant. It meant Negroes. It meant me.

I have rarely had to personally confront the racism that I see in my mirror. Nevertheless, racism has been a haunting and inescapable presence as I have grown up in America. Once seen and discerned, once acknowledged, racism has demanded that I respond. For me, there has been no sanctuary, no comfortable place to escape the questions it has insinuated into my life. Do I choose to look the other way? Do I "go along to get along"? Do I feel compelled to "stand up and be counted"? Why?

Whether on the scabby playing fields in the Depression years, on the sandy, bloody beachhead of Normandy, in the mud of the steaming Mississippi Delta during Freedom Summer in 1964, or in the green suburbs where I became a husband, a father, and a grandfather, the questions have rooted in each soil like a nettle. Racism has been the ageless evil in our nation's Pandora's box, and from the moment my startled eye first spied it beneath the lid, I have never been able to close the box again.

So I want to talk about racism. I want to talk about Mississippi. I want to talk about events I observed that turned into history. I want to talk about black people who didn't know white people and white people who didn't know black people but who shared a season of time, a long, hot summer, that some people now think of as mythic. But it wasn't mythic. Myths are populated by people who are bigger than life. I want to talk about people I met a long time ago in Mississippi who were not bigger than life, just more curious than some, more loving than some, more enlightened than some, more vulnerable than some, more lucky than some. I drew their pictures when they were younger and I was younger, and I wrote their stories in *Stranger at the Gates* more than forty years ago. I still want to talk about them. Those conversations were never finished. Those sketches were sketches, not a finished portrait. For me, Mississippi remains a remarkable work in progress.

introduction

In 1964, all hell seemed to be breaking loose in the American South. The nonviolent challenge to a centuries-old racial apartheid was being answered with state-sanctioned violence, the unbridled violence of the Ku Klux Klan, and the apparent collusion of the white establishment.

For me, who had been happily documenting the wonders of postwar American industry, invention, and education, the sudden revelations of a part of my country that recalled the horrors of fascism were sickening. Like so many veterans of World War II, I believed we had vanquished fascism twenty years before. I had been making drawings and paintings that celebrated our society. How, then, could such a good and diverse people permit such atrocities? In family council, we agreed that if a way could be found for me to go to the South to do my personal reportage, I should go. Perhaps my drawings could bring a better understanding to people in the North as to what was at stake. Few white businessmen, congressmen, clergy, journalists, or professionals across Dixie raised their voices in protest when the lynchings, the beatings, the burning black churches, the poignant pleas of preachers like Martin Luther King were news in every northern paper and featured nightly on television. In our household, the images of police dogs, hoses, and the four young black children who were killed in their bombed Sunday school classroom appalled and outraged all of us. We wanted to do something, anything, that would help to stop the cruel assaults on Americans who happened to be black for our whole society. If nonviolent protest were to be destroyed by fire and bombs, the alternative was unthinkable.

In the spring of 1964, we read that the Student Nonviolent Coordinating Committee (SNCC, pronounced "Snick"), an organization of young black men and women who had been inspired by the sit-ins of the early sixties, had issued a call to white students in the North to come join them in their struggle for the vote in Mississippi. Mississippi?

I could imagine Mississippi because I had read William Faulkner and Eudora Welty.

I could imagine Mississippi because every time I heard Billy Holiday singing "strange fruit hanging from the poplar trees," I wept.

I could imagine Mississippi because I remembered the lynching of fourteen-year-old Emmett Till because he flirted with a white girl in a Delta town.

I could imagine Mississippi because on national television I watched the white man who assassinated Medgar Evers walk free and proud down a Jackson street.

I could imagine Mississippi because I remembered the "Jew-baiting" of Mississippi senator Theodore Bilbo.

I could imagine Mississippi because I watched Mississippi senator James Eastland lead the charge against a bill that would stop lynching, and Mississippi senator John Stennis bottle up the bill that would guarantee Negroes the right to vote.

All those Mississippi imaginings. All those nightmarish images. How real could they be? It was twenty years since I had fought in the war that was supposed to have buried forever the insanity of "master race." Yet *"Segregation Forever! Integration Never!"* was being threatened on the very floor of the U.S. Congress. Fire hoses were being leveled at peaceful demonstrators who wanted only to register to vote, and police dogs were attacking black students who wanted to enter public libraries and to be served in public restaurants. If fascism had been buried in Hitler's bunker, you would never know it by watching the television news from America's South in 1964.

Those horrific images were inescapable and haunting, and they finally persuaded me to take my skills as a reportorial artist to Mississippi. I was determined to bring back real images of real people and real places so everyone could see American apartheid for what it really was.

In the summer of 1964 I became part of the civil rights movement. One thousand students from the North were volunteering to go to Mississippi to teach in Freedom Schools and to help register Negro voters, and I joined them at their orientation week in Oxford, Ohio. It was the first time since I was a part of the D-day landings in Normandy that I felt myself physically and emotionally involved with a life-and-death Invasion. What I learned during that remarkable week from the black civil rights workers from the Delta was how different this Invasion would be. Unarmed, with no possible protection from the local police, the local press, the local clergy, the local congressman, or the local leaders of the business community, we would have to face down the guns and hostility of a totally closed society. If there was to be any help offered, it would have to come from the black citizens of the Delta, among the poorest and least literate in all America. It was a sobering, frightening, and thrilling odyssey to begin, and I was determined to get started. I wanted to tell the story these young people were going to live for the next months, and do it in my words and my pictures. During that "long, hot summer" in Mississippi, I kept copious logs, made more than one hundred drawings in ink and wash, and took more than a thousand pictures with my Leica.

But it was a summer that never ended for me. The year 1964 was simply when my imagined Mississippi evaporated in the heat and passion of the struggle I witnessed in the Delta. For me, it was the very beginning of a journey of discovery that has continued to unfold for more than four decades. A place I had once only imagined has become a reality of flesh and bone and blood; of anguish and exhilaration; of courage I had never before witnessed; of hopes kindled, of hopes extinguished, of hopes incredibly reborn. It is the place that brought into my life some of the most memorable men and women, blacks and whites, whose hearts and brains and dedication transformed Mississippi forever, leaving behind a legacy of love, courage, and faith for the whole nation.

Part One

The Long, Hot Summer, 1964

Charles McLaurin

In 1963, Charles McLaurin walked warily into our lives, pushing through the lilacs that crowded the entrance to our yard. He stepped out of the shrubbery and paused for a beat. The brilliant May sun reflected on his dark glasses as he carefully surveyed the old, red colonial house, the green sweep of the lawn, and the pool that sparkled beyond. The Connecticut section of the *New York Times* was scattered around us on the lawn, and the giggles and shouts of Laurie and her friends in the pool were all that broke the comfortable silence. Our friend Oliver followed him into the yard, smiling as he shepherded the young Negro man to meet us.

"Hi, Sugarmans. This is the young fellow I called you about. Charles McLaurin, meet Tracy and June."

Oliver's call had come very early for a Sunday morning. The architect's usually cool voice had sounded constrained and husky. "You remember I told you about the New York doctors who were bringing those civil rights workers north for medical attention and a little breathing time? Well, four of those SNCC fieldworkers got here late last night, Tracy." He had paused, and his voice had lowered. "They're in the next room. We've been talking all morning, particularly with this kid, McLaurin. Listening, mostly. Christ, it's unreal, Tracy. Fucking Mississippi is unreal! Betty and I just look at each other and then look at these kids. McLaurin is nineteen! A year older than your son, Richard!"

The phone had become silent, and then Oliver had said quietly, "I think you and June should hear him. Can I bring him over after lunch?"

We rose to welcome them. June smiled and extended her hand to the young, watchful Negro. "Pull up those chairs and join us. We're just soaking up the sun. It's the first warm Sunday we've had." She nodded

3

to McLaurin. "You're probably used to a lot more sun than we get up here!"

"Let me get us all a drink," I said. "How about you, Charles? Can I get you a Coke?" When he hesitated, I said, "A beer? Anything?"

His eyes scanned the sun-drenched yard, and then held mine. A small smile revealed very white teeth, warming the serious young face that had seemed so immobile. "Yeah," he said. "Bourbon."

It started simply enough. A relaxed Sunday afternoon, talking quietly with this stranger from a strange land. It was the Sunday that we learned a little about Mississippi, the Sunday a friendship with Charles McLaurin was born that has lasted for more than forty-five years.

When he left we gave him a "liberated" German camera I had brought home from the war. "Try and get some pictures of what is really going on with the beatings," I urged, "and send them to the Justice Department in Washington. Maybe they can help."

He took off the dark glasses that he had worn from the moment of his arrival and shook his head, studying me closely. "No," he said firmly, "they won't help. The FBI has watched us get arrested and beaten, and instead of intervening they simply take notes." He smiled wryly. "Must be warehouses full of notes in Washington." He picked up the camera and thanked us. "We'll find lots of uses for this during the summer."

The friendship born that day deepened when we met on the March on Washington later that summer. McLaurin grinned and held up the German camera. "Got lots of pictures of Martin Luther King, John Lewis, Bayard Rustin, A. Philip Randolph . . . the whole march! And when I get back to the Delta, everybody is going to see them!"

In all the arrests, the endless days and weeks of outlasting time in Ruleville, Greenville, Greenwood, he had never been hit. The afternoon I had met him when he was visiting in Connecticut in 1963, McLaurin had joked about it: "Not me. I'm lucky, man!"

But now, in the spring of 1964, the highway patrol had beaten him. The SNCC staff workers had been forced off the road by the patrol as they headed for SNCC headquarters in Atlanta. They had beaten the driver and then herded the five young men to jail. The patrol had known the civil rights workers were heading east on the highway, and they had simply mousetrapped them. There was no charge, just arrest, "held for investigation."

One by one, the five Negroes were summoned from the cell. McLaurin was the last. From his cell he could hear the murmur of the interrogation, the angry shouting, the numbing sound of flesh striking flesh, the surprised gasps of pain. In an agony of terror, he watched his body, unbidden, move from the open cell. "I watched myself go. It was like it was happening to somebody else. I watched my feet move, one after the other, till I reached the top of the iron stairs."

"Down here, boy!"

He remembers looking down, the two policemen looking ridiculously tiny, their white faces turned up to McLaurin. Suddenly he was standing at the bottom of the stairs, and the two police faces filled the room.

"Boy," said the patrolman in a conversational voice, "are you a Negro or a nigger?"

McLaurin swallowed, his throat tight and parched. "I'm a Negro."

The patrolman slammed the back of his fist into McLaurin's mouth, splitting his lip. Tears betrayed his pain, and his mouth was full of blood.

"Boy," repeated the patrolman, his voice level and quiet, "are you a Negro or a nigger?"

McLaurin looked straight at the man. "I'm a Negro."

The patrolman at his side jolted him with a straight punch that exploded on the side of his jaw, pitching him in a thudding sprawl on the concrete.

"I felt no pain," he says, "but my teeth felt loose, and my mouth was a mess. As I lay there at the bottom of the stairs I knew they would keep hitting me until they killed me if I didn't say 'nigger.' That man had to hear me say it. He just had to. I got up and he said, 'Boy, are you a Negro or a nigger?' And I said, 'I'm a nigger.' He nodded, and I left the jail."

It was only a few months after his beating that I met McLaurin again. I had just arrived at the Western College for Women in Oxford, Ohio, and entered my first workshop of orientation, feeling very tentative and unsure of my role and my mission. As I found my seat, I heard a whoop and a loud laugh. Startled, I looked up at the beaming face of Charles, who was standing next to the blackboard.

"Mr. Charlie's all upset. He says run- and we ain't running"

1. Charles McLaurin.
"Mr. Charlie's all upset. He says run—and we ain't running."

"Well. Just look who's here! Hey!" We shook hands, and he smiled. "First the March on Washington and now here." He cocked his head and nodded. "Good to see you, man. So you're going to Mississippi. Do you know where?"

"Well, nobody special has invited me," I said. "Don't know a lot of folks that far south. Where are you going?"

"Ruleville," he said. "Senator Eastland's hometown. Like to get some folks registered for the next election." He paused and then said, "Might just be room for an artist to come along."

"Jesus, Mac. You must have lost the camera!" He had, and we both laughed.

Oxford

i t is still easy to remember the warm, beautiful moonlit evening in the heart of a bucolic Ohio countryside when I first met the young men and women who were going to Mississippi. On the moon-swept campus of the Western College for Women, a cool breeze lightening the evening air, they moved casually toward the lighted buildings beyond the green. The sound of young voices and a guitar drifted through the large open windows. I felt like I was joining a college weekend. Stepping into the harsh light of the Admissions Building where clusters of kids in bright blouses, shorts, and jeans were meeting for the first time and signing in for the next day's orientation classes, my old Panama hat and seersucker suit made me suddenly aware that I was seriously overdressed for the occasion. As I hurried to my dorm room to shed the noxious clothes and put on the khakis that I would wear for the rest of the summer, I heard one student as he nudged his companion and nodded toward me. "Dig the hat. He must be an FBI guy."

For the nearly one thousand students who went through the orientation sessions, the Western College for Women in Oxford, Ohio, in the spring of 1964 was the birthing room of their arrival and mine in the civil rights movement. The meetings between the white students and the very young but hardened veterans of the struggle in Mississippi were thrilling, frightening, and memorable. They were to spend a week together so that the assembled students could get some insights into the strange landscape of American apartheid. No two groups of young people could have been more different. With only a few exceptions, the SNCC organizers were black, some college educated, but most from the mean streets of Jackson or the tiny, impoverished towns of the Delta. Many of them had been trying to inspire blacks to try to register to vote for years. And for their efforts,

2. Rev. Jim Lawson at Oxford orientation, June 1964.

"There is a positive power in being good!"

men and women alike, the SNCC workers had been beaten, arrested, and constantly harassed by the local sheriffs and police. Most had never had a real conversation with a white person, and their suspicions about the students from the North were obvious.

Even after all these years later, that orientation week retains a surreal aura for me. More than four hundred volunteers, most of them white, were being instructed by a handful of blacks from the civil rights movement on the world of Mississippi that they were about to enter. It was a place we strangers could not really believe because there were voices we had never heard before.

The faces of the volunteers from the North reflected the wholesome good looks of those who have been spared the hardships of illness and poverty all their lives. Now they had come to perform the kind of good service many had heard about in their Friday-night or Sunday-morning church service. Eagerly, they held out their hands to the SNCC workers, and were often startled by the reluctant response. For the first time, many of the affluent children of the North were trying to relate to young people who were not only poor but black, and some were surprised by the cautious suspicion of the blacks. But many started to recognize that the partnership on which their lives might depend was going to take some major effort by each group.

The invitation of the SNCC leadership to the northern students was a bold and calculated move, but one whose success could not be guaranteed. Their lonely, painful struggle for equality had largely been ignored by the national press, and their pleas for equal protection under the law had fallen on deaf ears in a Congress dominated by southern senators such as Mississippi's Eastland and Stennis, or by a Justice Department headed by J. Edgar Hoover. Hoover was never persuaded that the civil rights movement in the South was not part of a communist conspiracy. SNCC knew in its bones that blacks in the South had no recourse when the night riders shot up their homes, burned their churches, or lynched their leaders. In order to gain the attention to these terrible inequities by those of conscience and power in the North, they had issued their invitations for volunteers on campuses across the country. Now those students had come, but would they stay when the night riders came again? Would

3. Oxford, Ohio, orientation, June 1964.
"Ain't gonna let nobody turn me 'round, turn me 'round."

they be able to share the impoverished life of the Mississippi blacks they had come to help, a life so distanced from anything they had ever known? And would the weary, battered SNCC workers, who had been sneaking onto plantations like that of Senator Eastland to try to register his black workers so they could vote, be able to work with the idealistic kids from the North? Much, they knew, would be learned in the next few days on this tranquil Oxford, Ohio, campus.

For two days and nights, the lectures and workshops mounted an unrelenting assault on the volunteers. I wondered uneasily if this perhaps was the real screening process. We were being frightened, and I sensed that this was a calculated strategy, a sharp, scalpeled insertion of reality intended to kill or cure. The terror and violence of Mississippi were detailed and dissected. The extent of police brutality was cataloged, and the unreal world of the barbarous newsreel and the tabloid spread was suddenly becoming our world. Even as we began to accept that that world was indeed real, it somehow widened the gulf that stretched between us and the fieldworkers.

The cool self-sufficiency of those SNCC people reminded me of the Royal Air Force (RAF) veterans of the Battle of Britain I had met during the war. We had come, fresh and eager from the States, trained, primed, and itching to find the war and win it. The young Brits had regarded us politely, nodded, and returned to the private society of those who knew because they had shared it together. No insult had been intended. They were glad we were there to win the war. It had simply ceased to be the same war they had fought alone. We had so envied the knowing grace of them. Each who had survived had been tested, purified of the doubts that nagged us as we waited for D-day. Even after we had fought our own war, we could never really know their world. The RAF veterans simply packed their neat duffels, and moved swiftly into the backwash of a war that had moved on. How could we Yanks know the pain and the nightmares that were packed in those duffels?

But here at Oxford the pain and the nightmares were being exhibited like a ghoulish display. There seemed to be a muffled drumbeat in those first days of that curious week. "They've got to know. They've got to know." The volunteers were now moving into the same battle as these quick, knowing fieldworkers. I watched the kids listening, and I knew they were wondering what I was wondering. "Am I good enough?"

My God, what if you really were beaten? What if they held you and smashed you? Could you take it and not cut and run? The SNCC kid this afternoon had said, "You've got to expect to be scared." Okay, we thought. What really frightens us? The dogs, maybe. Those terrifying pictures of dogs biting children in Birmingham. We tried to imagine

4. Black female student volunteer.
"You've got to expect to be frightened . . . "

being smashed, being bitten. And try as we might, we couldn't imagine being killed like Medgar Evers, the nonviolent head of the Mississippi NAACP. Not really.

But three hours before, a white minister named Ed King had tried to tell us about how vigilantes had tried to kill him. One side of his face was dreadfully scarred when they forced his car off the road. "Trust your instinct," he said. "When the feeling in the pit of your stomach says, 'Duck!' or 'Run!' trust it. It may save your life. It saved mine."

"Save your life!" Even the words sounded theatrical. Don't put us on, man. But as we watched the afternoon sun touch King's livid cheek, we knew it was so.

The first thing you noticed about Bob Moses was the spanking neatness of the blue overalls, the snowy white of the T-shirt. His body was compact and slim, and there was at once an air of modesty and dignity about him. His young face was alert and pleasant, and his eyes behind the glasses regarded the world with intelligence and a melancholy gentleness. As he moved slowly toward the front of the auditorium, we all knew some of his history. Born in New York City, educated at Hamilton College and Harvard University, where he earned his M.A., he had felt the need to come to Mississippi in 1961 to see what he might do to help in the struggle for civil rights. This scholarly young black American had stayed on, and endured. Bob Moses, we learned, was the man who had developed the strategy and logistics for the hazardous months ahead as the program director of the Mississippi Freedom Summer Project.

In the long, wretched winter months in the Delta he had fashioned a program so daring that it had alarmed even the seasoned young SNCC fieldworkers who had for years struggled against the worst part of American apartheid. They had learned to know intimately every corner of the Delta, every possible ally on the great plantations, every refuge where they could find shelter from the brutal police and the violence of the Ku Klux Klan. It took weeks of patient reasoning to convince them that unseasoned and untested white middle-class kids from the North could be of value to the movement. But Moses was determined to bring light into this darkest corner of the American conscience. No longer would the truncheon be swung in an isolated black cell against young men and women who were nonviolently demanding freedom. No longer would nameless black bodies be beaten, torn, and lynched by white men who walked freely on the street and bragged of their viciousness. And no longer would anonymous hooded terror be allowed to paralyze Americans who wished to vote like other citizens. When America's white sons and daughters would brave those everyday hazards endured by Mississippi blacks, Moses knew that the whole world would be watching.

The auditorium was hushed as he moved to the front of the stage. Many of the students had heard him before, at Berkeley, at Wesleyan, in Chicago, in New York, in Boston. "Don't come to Mississippi this summer to save the Mississippi Negro," he had said. "Only come if you understand, really understand, that his freedom and yours are one." Somehow the lonely sweetness of this scholarly man had caught them and drawn them to this Ohio campus. Now here they were, whites and blacks, come to bear witness to the lessons learned at the Friday nights and Sunday mornings of their hometown synagogues and churches.

Moses described the formidable challenges ahead: to create Freedom Schools for the children and the elderly so they could learn to read real books and learn real history, both of which they had long been denied in their segregated schools, and to help convince skeptical blacks that, despite the inevitable rage and retribution promised by the white establishment, they must find the courage to publicly stand up and demand the vote.

Bob Moses had clasped hands with death for three cruel years after he had come here from Harvard. He loved Herbert Lee and Medgar Evers, two of the civil rights leaders in Mississippi, and when they were assassinated by racists, he felt altered and lonely. The violence and the pain were scars he would carry privately forever, for they were an obscene offense to his gentle spirit. Of his own arrests and beatings he never spoke, but the savagery heaped daily on the heads of Mississippi blacks moved him to the calculating nonviolent action that would change the system that fostered it.

Even more than the revolting white violence, the boundless, numbing ignorance of the Mississippi blacks simply appalled and overwhelmed him. He knew that keeping the black population poor and unskilled was the weapon that had emasculated them, and made a mockery of progress and political sloganeering. Mississippi was a time-entrenched cotton society that had been built and perpetuated on the immense base of cheap black labor that was totally powerless. Now his voice in the darkening room was so quiet that I put down my sketch pad, my focus moving from the attentive young faces to the single still figure on the stage.

"Maybe we're not going to get very many people to register to vote this summer." The room was silent. "Maybe," said Moses, "we're not going to get very many people into the Freedom Schools. Maybe all we're going to do is live through this summer." He paused and studied the intent young faces. "In Mississippi," he said, "that will be so much!"

My eyes moved around the hushed hall, watching the students settling slowly back in their chairs. How many would leave, I wondered, after these wrenching sessions with Ed King and Bob Moses? Maybe while we would be at dinner some of these boys would toss their dirty sweat socks

5. Student audience.

"Politics without morality is chaos. Morality without politics is irrelevant."

into their knapsacks and quietly make their way to the Greyhound station in Oxford. And the girls? I had seen them talking earnestly into the phones that tied them to home. I wondered how many would say tonight, "Maybe you're right, Mom. It's not for me."

Moses's soft voice ceased, and the auditorium was silent as he quietly stepped back from the podium. The overhead lights dimmed, and the screen above the platform sprang to life. In the hushed darkness Mississippi ceased suddenly to be an abstraction. There, on the screen, brightly lit by an August sun, was Mississippi. A black girl, looking pert and resolute, walked down a dusty dirt road in the black quarter of a Mississippi town. The camera moved in, and her intent face filled the screen. "I want to vote so we can get some lights on our road, and get police protection."

A car passed behind her, a 1961 Ford, and the dust rose from the dirt road and caught the bright Mississippi sun.

Now the camera moved, and the television documentary dissolved to the massive bulk of a white registrar of voters. The gross indolence of the body was accentuated by the cranky baby face that lolled on the fat, fleshy neck. The effect was startling and ludicrous. Here was a parody of "massive resistance." This overblown baby of a man had denied the vote to the Negroes of Tallahatchie County for years, and he was somehow at once hateful and ridiculous. A snicker of laughter raced through the hall, and a quick "Shush!" followed as the audience bent to hear.

Now the cameras cut to the "Sanctified Quarter" of Ruleville, Mississippi, the side of the highway where a black slum of dilapidated houses was home to the Negroes in Ruleville. An elderly black man, his leather face etched and tooled by seventy years of work in the fields, was quietly describing the horror of shotgun blasts that had torn into his living room. He showed the couch where two young girls had been cut down as they watched the television. The hall was hushed, and a clearing of throats was the only sound that competed with the whirring of the overheated projector. "I had driven to Indianola and applied to register to vote." The old man's gaze into the camera was steady. "I aim to go back to Indianola and apply again. Shooting's not going to turn me around."

The camera panned to the elderly lady who was his wife. Her face was birdlike, and an absurd hat balanced on the top of her thin gray hair. The face and the voice conspired to conjure the image of an intent, bespectacled parrot, and her recital of the nightmare that had struck their home was lost as a nervous giggle ran through the darkened hall. Again an angry "Shush!" and all eyes stayed riveted on the real citizens of Mississippi.

The lights came suddenly on as the film ended. The blinking students began to stretch and move in their seats as an enraged young black strode down the aisle and leaped on the apron of the stage. His face was furious, and he quivered as he began to speak. "You should be ashamed," he growled. The students looked rapidly at their neighbors and back to the small intent figure that commanded the stage. "You could laugh at that film!" He stared at the students for a long beat. "Six SNCC fieldworkers left this hall when you laughed. They couldn't believe their ears, and neither could I." His voice broke, and tears glistened behind the glasses. With an effort of will he regained his control, and the words tore painfully from his throat. "I hope by the end of this summer you will never laugh at such a film again." The students looked stunned. What had happened? The dark figure on the stage was an accusing finger. Of what were they being accused?

At the end of the afternoon, I wandered into town, eager to collect my thoughts about the disquieting hour I had just witnessed. I shared the students' feeling of distress, the sense of loss that had so filled the auditorium. The realization that we had deeply offended someone important to us without intention or malice aforethought was very upsetting. When the lights had come up and we heard that the SNCC young men had walked out, we suddenly realized how insensitive our reactions had been.

At the bar in town I joined Jack Preiss, the young professor from Duke who was there at the orientation to facilitate communication between the two groups. Disconsolately, I asked, "What am I missing, Jack? What the hell did all that mean?"

"Think about this afternoon, Tracy," he said, his eyes once more seeking out the furious accuser on the podium. "The students watched a fat man who was against letting blacks vote in his district. They laughed because he looked grotesque and stupid. And when they saw a funny-looking little old lady who looked like a chicken, they laughed again. But when the lights came up and they heard that the SNCC boys had walked out, they suddenly realized how insensitive their reactions had been. They don't like to find out they're insensitive about anything. Certainly not about blacks. They were sure about that much . . . until tonight." He lifted his glass and swallowed deeply. As he lit his cigarette, he settled back on the worn bench, his head nodding. "Until tonight," he repeated. "The SNCC kids watched the same documentary, but they saw different things."

"How could they see different things?" I asked. "Okay, these students are not Mississippi blacks. Granted. But how different is their frame of reference about oppression or discrimination? After all, if they weren't sensitive to inhumanity, what brought them here?"

He shook his head irritably. He moved the beer pitcher to my side of the table and filled my glass. "How different? Listen. The SNCC kids didn't see a fat man who was against blacks. They saw a white man who was powerful, and he had hurt them. They knew this powerful white man, and they knew he would go on hurting them. This was no abstract injustice. This was the guy who said 'NO' after you had worked your tail off for months getting frightened people to the point of walking up this guy's county courthouse steps to try to register to vote. This was 'Mr. Charlie,' Tracy. This was no laughable fat man. This was the man you weep about. So when the SNCC kids heard the volunteers laughing, they couldn't believe it. 'They're laughing! What are they doing here?'" He paused and then plunged ahead. "And then they watched the lady from Ruleville whose house and nieces got shot up. She's not funny-looking to them. They helped her wipe up the blood off the couch and get her nieces into the hospital—the white hospital because they couldn't stop the bleeding. And they watched these students, mostly white, giggling at a ridiculous hat and a cackling voice. 'What are they doing here?'" His face pale, the professor wet his lips and ground out his cigarette. "These SNCC workers have taken it for so long they didn't think they were sensitive anymore. They thought that after the beatings and the grinding frustration, they wouldn't feel pain anymore. They were sure about it—until tonight. The students laughed, and they found their nerves were exposed." He stretched his arms wide and arched his back. "Like I said," he grinned, "it's classic." He slid along the bench and stood up. "But tonight tore it. At last we can really start talking tomorrow."

It was late when we arrived back on campus. We entered the foyer of the Administration Building and immediately sensed that something was different. The corridors were deserted except for two students who stood at the entrance to the lounge. They leaned intently against the doorjambs, listening, and seemed completely unaware of our approach. Preiss glanced quickly at me, and we moved swiftly into the crowd that filled the room. It seemed that everyone was there. They sat hunched on the floor, knees drawn up, silent. The carpet was filled with students, and each leather lounge sofa and chair was hidden by the crush of bodies. All attention was on the two SNCC fieldworkers who stood framed by the crowd.

The shorter of the two, a very dark, wiry youngster in his early twenties, was openly weeping, and his words twisted out raw and savage. "We love you—and we don't understand you. Sure, we want you to come with us, but we're scared for you. You don't know the score, and we're scared for you. You can't know. You can't know." The words were alive, and they moved into the hushed room like a high-tension wire, sparking, leaping, and lethal. "I was in the army. They taught me how to hate, and they taught me how to kill. But that's not what I need." His voice broke, and he blinked as the tears moved down the dark young cheeks. His hands were clenched tight against his thighs. "I need to love you. We're going to Mississippi together, and I need to love you."

Time vanished in the silent hall. No one seemed to notice that the clock had pushed past midnight, for a torrent of love, heat, self-confessions, hopes, and fears swept the room in a violent flood of emotion. When he finished speaking—the pulsing rush of tumbling words suddenly ceasing— the second youngster began. His eyes were dry, and his young brows knit intensely as he sought voice for his fear. He started to speak, the words beating like nervous fingers on a bongo. He spoke in a cadenced rhythm, his voice expelling in a sharp "hey" at the breathless end of each sentence. His eyes were troubled, and he seemed to beg understanding like a child, even as the staccato and stylized bop language made him sound worldly and citified. The students watched and listened, not quite knowing why they were not embarrassed by this public display of such profoundly private feelings. Instead, they felt a great surge of relief, and their gratitude flowed like a released spring. This stripping of cool pretense, this humble reaching out of hands for common touch, was a frightening but beautiful thing. For the first time they felt a real sense of communication with these SNCC workers who were taking them away from home.

I looked at the two SNCC fieldworkers. I had thought that they were young, but now for the first time I saw how vulnerable they were as well. They seemed a breed apart, isolated guerrillas, fighting a lonely battle for recognition and dignity (Look at me. I'm a man, too. Look at me!). They had been altered by their direct participation in the struggle, and this is what divided them from the kids listening. The volunteers were not removed from them by years, or even by race, for some of the students were black. They were removed by a searing experience that had stretched through three endless years, not two months with an exit waiting. Tonight their deep concern for these eager neophytes had swept away their defenses. The students' sense of exclusion and inadequacy was consumed in the heat of the confessional. The terrible intensity of the stated commitments began to forge a common bridge, for each in that room found an echo of his private fears. Preiss was alive with the moment, and his eyes glistened as he watched the tableau before us. It was finally happening. He knew that the two needy groups were starting to see each other for the first time.

This was the wonder, I thought, of SNCC. Two half-educated southern black kids had moved with a sure hand into a crisis that might have torn apart the whole fabric of the summer. Their instinctive sense of the right word and the right moment had illuminated the room. The simple honesty of their grief and fear had acted as a catalyst and transformed two suspicious groups into one. This was no prearranged tactic of the leadership. It was the kind of gut response that had kept them alive and resilient for three years. The room was on its feet now, arms around the shoulders of the nearest neighbor, and the voices were one voice, rising and filling the lounge, a fervent and plaintive song that must have echoed across the darkened campus. I watched these kids as they swayed and sang. Faces were streaked with tears and sweat, but their eyes were alive.

> We've been 'buked
> And we've been scorned—
> We've been talked about
> Sure as you're born
> But we'll never
> No, we'll never turn back.

The Ohio sky was a high delicate blue, and a sun-washed breeze played across the students and the SNCC fieldworkers gathered on the lawn beside the Administration Building. But few would remember the loveliness of that late June afternoon. What would be remembered would be the nightmarish Mississippi scenarios that were being enacted for the summer volunteers. The SNCC staff moved into their mock roles of white registrars, judges, sheriffs, and frightened field hands with a sureness that was startling. They enacted the rituals of denial and humiliation they had learned from childhood, and no one had to coach a response or prompt a line. It was an incredible theatrical experience for me. But this was the raw and unadorned, not a sublimation or transformation of life. This was the reality of the life of the black man in white Mississippi. It was an afternoon that assaulted your sensibilities and moved you to anger and shame. The dry, bitter humor, the sardonic shrug, the earthy contempt, the endless guile of half-truths, the limitless capacity to ingratiate, all these were revealed naked and unashamed during those remarkable pieces of theater.

Acting the role, a young black woman came to the "registrar" with her reluctant mother to try to register to vote. The quick dismissal by the registrar was sidestepped, and the young woman persisted in pressing for the registration form.

The registrar exploded with anger. "You get your goddamn nigger ass out of my office!"

Once more the agile maneuvering by the girl as she slid into a whining, feminine, ingratiating voice. "Mistuh Jameson, suh, don' you remembuh me? Emmaline? Emmaline Jones? And my mama here, Aunty Lou? Why y'all talk to me like that, Mistuh Jameson, suh? You knows us your whole life. Please, suh, just the regis' papuh and we'll be goin' home, Mistuh Jameson. How is Mastuh William and Miss Ann? My, what a pretty thing she is! Lawdy, I remembuh her chrisnen'."

The acrid, despised, and despising words hung in the air, words set to curry the scorning condescension and approval of a master. We watched the sly transformation that turned this bright black coed into a shuffling supplicant, a contemptible slattern using an ageless guile to ward off the blow of a white man.

We all stood as the sun edged toward the West, watching one last demonstration. The talk was muted, and kids shifted nervously in the crowd, full of the images they had witnessed. The wiry young fieldworker from the night before stepped quietly into the clearing. He held up his arms, and the murmur of the crowd ceased. "This is the way you protect your body," he said. His voice was flat. "The vital parts of your body are your head, your neck, and your groin. You can protect them best by curling up like a baby, your legs together, your knees pulled up to protect your gut and your privates, your hands and arms shielding your head and the back of your neck." The girl next to me sucked in a deep breath. The SNCC instructor stepped into the crowd and led a student to the open lawn in the center. "Let me see you protect yourself."

The volunteer assumed the position, and the instructor pulled back his sneakered foot, gently tapping the exposed areas of the supine student. "Your legs, your thighs, your buttocks, your kidneys, your back can take a kick or a billy club. So can your arms and your hands. Your head can't. Your neck can't. Your groin can't." The flat voice continued its dispassionate litany. "When your companion is being beaten or stomped while lying on the ground, you must protect him or her. You do it by shielding his head with your body. Your back can take it."

Once more the demonstration, and then still again. I became aware of the whir of the cameras recording this sober ritual of survival. Everything would be recorded for the great spectator public except the nausea and the outrage of having to learn the arts of protecting yourself from American police who were waiting to assault you. I lifted my eyes from the two figures framed by the crowd. The students beside me stood ashen-faced, staring straight ahead. Their eyes stayed riveted on the frozen tableau of a violence that until this moment had existed only in grade-B movies and tabloid spreads.

At the end of the orientation week, I raced home from Oxford for my son Richard's graduation from high school, my head and heart swimming with the images I had tried to capture. I wanted to share them with my family and friends. Something momentous seemed to be trembling, waiting to be born in 1964, but what? On the very day I had driven my son to visit colleges in New England, President Kennedy had been assassinated. As our car had moved up the deserted Merritt Parkway, the car radio played only dirges. The whole nation seemed to be weeping. Now I had returned briefly from Ohio being the messenger, bearing tidings of promise and aspiration, but also profound questions about the immediate future. With my son on the very cusp of an exciting adulthood, I watched as he struggled with all of us to find his moral footing in a hazardous landscape. We spoke our hearts, and each of us in the family felt resolved to face the present in his own way. We embraced, and I left for Mississippi.

In Oxford the orientation for the new batch of volunteers, teachers for the Freedom Schools, was moving ahead. Mrs. Fannie Lou Hamer, Bob Moses, and a group of SNCC workers were guiding them into the unsettling world of American apartheid they would soon be traversing.

On the very day I arrived in Mississippi, Andy Goodman, Mickey Schwerner, and James Chaney, three of the boys on the green my last afternoon in Oxford, were stopped by police while driving to investigate the arson of a black church near Philadelphia, Mississippi. They were arrested and "held for investigation." When they were released from the Neshoba County jail at night, they were said by the police "to be missing." No one ever saw them alive again.

Oxford still sounds like a clarion bell, its memory reverberating in each of us who was there in '64, for none more clearly than Martha Honey. She remembers her week in Ohio as the most formative event of her young life. With other students who were being readied to create Freedom Schools during that second week of the orientation, she heard the news of the disappearance of Andy Goodman, Mickey Schwerner, and James Chaney, and it electrified the campus.

"It's indelibly printed on my mind," said Martha. "I can still see the whole scene. When the word came that the boys who had just left Oxford were missing, the crowd in the hall got hushed, and Bob Moses and Rita Schwerner, Mickey's wife, came on the stage. And Bob said, very quietly, 'The boys' car is missing, and has been missing for ten hours. And we just don't know what has happened to them.' There was dead silence. And then Rita Schwerner spoke briefly." Martha hesitated, her eyes focused on the memory. She shook her head and continued in a soft voice. "I was in awe that a wife could be that brave, that she could speak so rationally about the disappearance of her husband, Mickey. It was like ice being thrown into our party. And right after they spoke, there was a long line of students at the public phones, everybody calling home. I don't know how many decided then—some did—that they were going home."

"And you?" I asked.

"It never occurred to me to leave. I think I simply couldn't believe the finality of what that disappearance meant, that those three young men, who were here last week, were dead. Nobody said 'dead' at Oxford. I was too young, too inexperienced, to believe that. It wasn't until I went to the Delta, after leaving Oxford, and was living with this marvelous Turnbow family, that I started to understand. I sat with the family and was watching the news on this little black-and-white television set. And when the broadcaster was saying that the three civil rights workers were still missing, Mr. Turnbow said, 'They're dead.' And I said, 'How can you say such a thing?' And he turned to me and said, 'Martha, they are dead.' And the fact that he said it so emphatically was chilling. This man, I thought, knows the truth. That's when reality really set in for me."

Linda Davis, now a Washington, D.C., judge, agreed that the Oxford orientation had been the crucible that shaped so much of her life in her career in the Justice Department and on the judicial bench. "I had been reading the newspapers up in Oberlin just before going to Oxford," she said, "and I was getting quite frightened and nervous about going to Mississippi. I probably came pretty close to backing out, but I did go to Oxford. And the very first day I was there, we all heard the report that Andy Goodman, Mickey Schwerner, and James Chaney, who had just left Oxford the week before, had disappeared in Mississippi." Her eyes widened at the memory. "What terror we all felt. But it was then that I met Fannie Lou Hamer, who had come up from Ruleville to meet with the Freedom School teachers. Watching her unflinching courage, her commitment to 'keep on keeping on, no matter what,' just made me fall in love with her. She was such a mesmerizing force that I determined to follow her to Ruleville."

The nature of a reportorial artist is to be curious . . . to explore . . . to uncover something out there. The resolve of Martha Honey and Linda Davis, two highly educated young white women, not to turn back but rather to deliberately put themselves in harm's way in an alien part of America for people they had never met, moved me profoundly. But they were not exceptional. Hundreds of summer volunteers crossed from the North into every corner of the Magnolia State, and it was clear that burning churches and kidnapped civil rights workers were not going to deter them. They had come to stay. It was an odyssey that has few if any rivals in American history. I was determined to find the different sparks that had fired their individual missions.

In the very act of seeking, one sometimes finds something so profound, so true, so inspiring, that you, yourself, are altered. From that moment on, you begin to see in a different way. When I went to Mississippi to make drawings of what was happening, I was in every sense simply one more of the "strangers at the gate." I was convinced that Mississippi was not the America I had grown up in, not the America I had fought for in World War II, not the America I had heard about in sermons and Fourth of July speeches. What I would find, as did all the volunteers, was that my experience in this small corner of darkest apartheid America would forever help illuminate my way as I sought fresh insight about the South, about my country, and about myself. What would emerge, troubling, clear, and surprising, was the conviction that in a thousand ways, Mississippi is America.

The Delta

i picked up a Hertz car in Memphis and drove due south into the Mississippi Delta, heading for the first meeting with Charles McLaurin in Ruleville. I would need it for my reportorial work, and Mac had told me how invaluable to the movement my car would be. There were not many wheels in the black community, and Indianola, the county seat where people had to apply to register, was thirty miles from Ruleville.

A bright, open-faced young activist whom I had met and liked at Oxford, Dale Gronemeier, rode in the shotgun seat beside me. By the time he had arrived at the orientation, Dale had already amassed an impressive series of civil rights credentials. On the long, harrowing drive I learned that in 1959 he had authored the National Student Association's resolution condemning loyalty oaths while still an undergraduate at Illinois State University. As a graduate student at Northwestern University, he formed the Northwestern Student Forum to bring civil rights and civil liberties speakers to the campus. And for two years he was a member of the Board of Directors of the Chicago Committee to Defend the Bill of Rights. Though I was easily twenty years his senior, Dale appeared to me to be a seasoned veteran of the civil rights struggle, and a good companion for this neophyte for the trip to the Delta.

Dale's careless attitude of repose was deceptive, for his eyes were quick and alert, scanning the road carefully ahead and searching the road behind for any approaching vehicle. I studied the rearview mirror and saw only the sunbaked two-lane highway stretching north toward Memphis. The sun was at its height, and the road shimmered and wavered in the heat. I pumped the gas pedal, and the Chevy raced down the deserted pavement.

26

6. Rev. Bruce Hanson, National Council of Churches.

"He looked worried and concerned in Oxford. He still looked worried six weeks later in the Delta."

"Take it easy," Dale cautioned. "There's a car coming toward us, and the Mississippi Highway Patrol must be moving up and down this route."

My eye moved once more to the mirror, once more to the road ahead, once more to the shivering needle of the speedometer. Once more I eased to fifty-five, and for the first time was beginning to feel the tension in my neck. The car approaching moved out of the overheated light and turned out to be a green Ford pickup truck. Two white men wearing wide straw farmer hats studied our license and squinted at us as the truck whooshed by. As I read my mirror, the man next to the driver turned and watched us move away.

Dale sensed my concern, and he leaned silently across the seat for some moments, watching the Ford grow small in the distance. "They're gone," he said finally. "But watch your speed."

"I'm watching my speed. Christ, I've never watched my speed so carefully in my life. I'm getting a stiff neck watching my speed." I turned to look at Dale, who gave me an innocent smile. "What the hell difference does it really matter if I'm going fifty-five or seventy-five?" I demanded. "If the Mississippi Highway Patrol decides to arrest me and they say I'm going seventy-five, then I'm going seventy-five."

We looked at each other and laughed. "You're right. Seventy-five!" Dale said. And I floored the gas pedal.

When we reached the shade of Fannie Lou Hamer's pecan tree in a sweltering Ruleville, we scanned the sweaty, bedraggled volunteers who had been checking in and were hailed by McLaurin's hearty, "Hey, man, you made it! Grab some water in the kitchen, and I'll take you to your new home. Jim and Rennie Williams are expecting you."

We stepped gingerly on the two short planks that crossed the shallow sewage ditch, and made our way across the small front yard. I followed Dale Gronemeier as Mac held open the screen door. We stepped into the warm shadow of Mrs. Williams's living room. As we moved, blinking, inside, she wiped her hands on the striped apron that was tied around her ample middle. Mahogany skin glowed in the dim light of the room, but a bright reflection from the doorway was caught on the panes of her glasses. The lens of one was cracked horizontally across the center, but the fracture could not disguise the wide-eyed humorous appraisal she was giving us. Her head tilted back, for she was quite short, and she took my extended hand with a warm smile.

"Why, I'm so glad to meet you! Won't y'all come in and set down for a while?" She pulled some rockers near the open door where there was a chance for a whisper of a breeze. "How have you been, McLaurin? I ain't seen you since you're back from Ohio." She gave a sly sideways smile at Mac, full of playfulness and affection. "Don't hardly seem the same without McLaurin holdin' meetin's at the chapel. Girls been askin' for you, McLaurin. 'When's McLaurin comin' back?'" She watched him flush with embarrassment, and her head rocked back, hooting with laughter.

"We're havin' a meetin' tonight," he mumbled, and then grinned, "We'll sing up a storm, even without Mrs. Hamer!" His head turned toward the door leading to the bedroom. "How are you, Mr. Williams?" A spare, bald, bright-eyed man of seventy-nine stood quietly in the doorway. His bony old man's chest was visible beneath his white underwear shirt, but his arms and hands still showed the corded, cabled muscles of a young man. A small paunch on his wasting frame seemed out of place.

"This is my husban', James," said Mrs. Williams in a tender voice. "These are the gennemen who are going to stay with us, Jim."

His brown feet padded unshod across the aged linoleum in a slow old man's walk, and he shook hands silently with Dale. When he reached me, he took my hand in his, and I felt the worn and calloused skin press mine with a surprising gentleness.

"I'm very pleased to meet you, Mr. Williams. It's very generous of you and Mrs. Williams to open your house to us this way."

His head shook slightly, and I saw tears start behind his wire-framed glasses. He opened his mouth in a vain effort to speak, looked deeply into my eyes, and shook his head. His eyes dropped, and his hand slowly released mine. He made his way from the room in the same silence with which he had entered.

It wasn't until I was unpacking my sketchbooks later that evening that I heard Mr. Williams approach my bedroom. "Come on in, Mr. Williams," I called. He paused at the door.

"I'm sorry I couldn't welcome you befo', Mr. Sugman." His voice was an old man's voice, gentle, a little uncertain, and he made an effort to

7. Mr. James Williams, sharecropper, church deacon, courageous host.
"A sweet dignity, a gentle man."

8. The Williams bedroom.
"My bedroom in Mr. Williams's house."

control it. His bright eyes blinked, and he continued. "I was jus' so filled up, meetin' you and Mistuh Dale in my house. I couldn't talk." His voice grew stronger, and he stood very straight. "It's a fine, Christian thing, a fine thing that you all have come here." He shook his head wonderingly, and his glance moved to my plaid suitcase on the bed. "McLaurin told us you have a family at home." His voice quavered, and he cleared his throat. "It's a fine thing, your coming," he said huskily. His bald head was nodding as he left the room.

Goodman, Schwerner, Chaney

all the talk that first morning was of the missing students. The news of their disappearance had flown through the Sanctified Quarter, our neighborhood, and when Dale and I reached the chapel for the first meeting, the kids were standing in knots around the steps.

"Gee, I had lunch with Andy last Friday!"

"Which one was Schwerner? The kid with the beard?"

"Yeah. He had his wife with him at Oxford. They've been running a small community center over in Meridian."

"It looks lousy. Not even a trace of their station wagon."

"Chaney's from Meridian. James knows the score. That's why it looks lousy. He didn't get lost. What do you think, Mac?"

McLaurin stood on the first step, his hands deep in his pockets. His eyes were troubled. "They say in Jackson that the three of them were picked up for speeding, 'held for investigation,' and released at ten thirty at night. That's the story that they got from the Philadelphia sheriff." He shook his head vehemently. "Mickey Schwerner wouldn't have left a jail in Philadelphia at ten thirty at night." Abruptly, he wheeled and went up the steps to the chapel.

Mac leaned against the rickety pulpit, and his voice patiently spelled out the pattern of the days and nights ahead. "The cars you'll hear moving through the quarter at night are vigilante cars. They work out of the Billups Station over yonder. They don't know what we're doin' yet, so they're gonna keep movin' through the quarter to find out." He studied the intent faces before him. "So it's time we got our security operating. Dale, you move over to the Hamer house and set up communications. Three of our people are missing; probably they're dead. We've got to be careful, and we've got to keep in touch."

"Goodman, Schwerner and chaney are missing."

9. Student volunteers at the meeting.
"Goodman, Schwerner, and Chaney are missing."

He stopped, and the dark glasses swept the rows of seats. "From now on, call Gronemeier at the Hamers' when you get home at night. If you see cars or trucks movin' through the quarter, get their license plate numbers and pass them to Dale. Stay away from windows if your light is on, and be careful. If there is any trouble, call in, and we'll pass the word to the rest of the Sanctified Quarter. Dale will be in touch with Jackson, and he'll relay news in and out of Ruleville."

10. Communications center at the Freedom House.

"Have your local families call us immediately if you're not home at the expected time . . . "

He paused as a green pickup truck moved slowly past the chapel and stopped as a white police truck came alongside from the opposite direction. The bed of the truck was a wire cage. The door swung open, and a large black and brown police dog paced back and forth on the tailgate. The two drivers spoke briefly, their faces turning toward my Chevy and the windows of the chapel. The policeman noted my license number, and the two trucks moved silently down the road.

McLaurin turned from the window. "Mayor Durrough, the police, the vigilantes—they all know you're here. They're worried sick about it." He slapped his hands sharply together and leaned toward the group. "So startin' right now, we're gonna start working on getting these people in Ruleville to sign up and go with us down to Indianola to try and register." His voice hardened. "No police dog's gonna change that." Nor Andy. Nor James. Nor Mickey.

I settled into a corner of the tiny platform that held the lectern in Williams Chapel. The shabby church was alive that first night of "mass meetings" in Ruleville. The walls were bare but for a number of pennants proclaiming "Banner Offering Class," and a poster-sized book of illustrated Bible stories that hung from a clothes hook in the rear of the hall. Behind the pulpit was a threadbare American flag draped across the window. A single poster showing children facing fire hoses in Birmingham proclaimed "We Shall Overcome." But there was a pulse of expectancy as the folks from black Ruleville began to fill and then overflow the wooden theater seats that served as the pews. The green-seedling promise of that hot night remains fresh in memory more than forty years later.

The students who had been arriving from the Oxford orientation looked fresh and alert, their faces beginning to flush in the crowded sanctuary. They looked tentatively about them and smiled. The Negroes seated near them returned their smiles shyly and dropped their eyes. A group of elderly women sat in the front row, fans from the local funeral parlor moving steadily in their hands. Their faces were damp with sweat, and their dark skin shone in the light of two naked bulbs that lit the room. Two rows behind were filled with teenage girls, their bright cottons in pastel pink and yellow lighting up the front of the chapel. They put their heads together and smothered giggles, their eyes darting around the room, missing nothing.

11. First student meeting in Ruleville.
"When it's dark, you should be in your houses. When you're not working, you should be out of sight."

The boys drifted in and out of the doors, uncertain whether to stay. They would stand briefly in clusters at the back of the room, looking uncomfortable. A scattering of middle-aged and elderly men sat fanning themselves near the exit in the rear, their eyes moving with guarded curiosity as they surveyed the gaggle of white faces standing with Charles McLaurin. Certainly in remembered history none could recall as many whites in this sanctuary or, indeed, on this side of Highway 41.

For black Ruleville, that meeting was a breathtaking event in the brown and even pattern of their days. Here was youth—smiling, kind, smart youth! And not just the scrubbed whites, whites like they had never known, but their own. Their glistening eyes would settle on John Harris and Charles McLaurin, and you knew that these were their very special knights. These were the new folk heroes of the Delta, a place where young black men had rarely been permitted to become heroes.

McLaurin called the volunteers to the front, and they ranged across the slightly raised platform. Their presence brought a vicarious sense of certainty and well-being to the impoverished little hall, and they seemed handsome and impregnable. McLaurin's dark glasses moved from the stage to the suddenly hushed seats. "I'll let them introduce themselves to you."

"I'm Dennis Flannigan, University of Washington."

"I'm Gretchen Schwartz, Swarthmore College."

"I'm John Harris, Howard University."

"I'm Len Edwards, University of Chicago."

Their voices continued to ring out, their vitality seeming to fill the church. Together they reflected an unharried America. Their open faces seemed to reflect the kind of radiant confidence that comes through the skin of the nation's favored children. Their faces were flushed with heat, and their fresh shirts and blouses were beginning to spot with sweat. No one but they knew the fear and the wondering, the nagging questions with which they had lived the last weeks. As they met Ruleville, they searched the audience. For the first time the enormity of their commitment stood visible. They read it in every face that looked toward them. It was manifest in every youngster's unblinking gaze and in every moist eye of the adults. It was in the old, mended clothes, on the peeling boards, the rickety, splintered chairs. Help us. Oh, can you help us?

The students' eyes shone as they scanned the hall. My God! Where are the men? All these women and children. Old women! Jesus, don't let them expect too much. How happy they seem that we're here. Smile back! God, we're really here. In Ruleville. Mississippi!

From the moment he stood to quiet the applause, McLaurin was in charge. His neat, compact body moved with agile assurance, and his voice throbbed with repressed excitement. He slapped his strong hands loudly together, and his words rang like a summons through the packed room:

Go tell it on the mountain!

The audience took up the cadence and responded in a joyous surge of sound:

Over the hills and everywhere
Go tell it on the mountain
To let my people go!

Mac moved like an oiled cat, building effortlessly from instruction to exhortation. The songs seemed to free him, and he winged his words intuitively, sensing the responses, building to his message naturally.

"Tomorra we start signing folks up here in Ruleville. We're gonna knock on every door. And then we're going into Drew and Shaw, even Indianola! Mr. Charlie's not goin' to like it, but we're goin'!"

A kind of inevitable logic worked through the text and the singing, and the "mass meeting" became a created whole. A unity of purpose and a sharing of aspiration grew almost visibly in the humid hothouse of Williams Chapel.

Ain't gonna let no-body turn me 'round
Keep on a'walkin, keep on a'talkin,

Marchin' up to Freedom Land.

The crowd surged up the aisles to the front of the chapel. The boys from the rear were among them, and the men who had sat tentatively on the side were now arranging themselves in the human chain. Arms crossed and hands reached out to neighbors. The old women, tears running down their cheeks, clutched hands with old friends and "these nice young folks who've come to help us."

We shall overcome
We shall overcome.

The hands clasped tighter, and the anthem soared through the windows.

We shall overcome.

Across the highway at the Billups Gas Station, a cluster of white men stood framed in the pool of light that shone flat and white over the pumps. They silently drank their Cokes, listening in silence to the exuberant singing. When the singing ceased and the noisy meeting hall began to empty, people inside began to step into the darkness of the unlighted Negro quarter. As they started up the dirt road to their homes, they halted abruptly as a darkened pickup truck, its motor roaring, careened past the Williams Chapel, causing the startled crowd to leap backward. Silent now, they watched as the truck wheeled with squealing tires onto Highway 41 and then turned immediately into the Billups Station. The driver swung quickly from his cab and strode to the Billups office. He held the door open as the watching men filed in. His eyes rested for a long moment on the chapel, and then he slammed the door tight.

The Lindseys

a t the edge of town I wheeled the Chevy under the overhang at the gas station, rolled past the tanks, and stopped in the knife edge of shade thrown by the building. I moved to the rear of the car and with a paper towel started to wipe away the scrawled FREEDOM NOW! that some kid at the Freedom School had left on my dust-covered hood. Go live with teenagers, I was thinking. Jesus! That's all I need in the Delta—a sign! Two white women stood watching from the office door. The taller was blonde and pretty. She tossed back her hair saucily and called over to me, "You don't look like the others."

Her chin was up, and she threw the words like a dare. I finished wiping off the trunk as I watched her. She was young, late twenties, I thought, and she was very pregnant. Her companion seemed taken aback that the blonde had spoken to me. She was tiny and looked embarrassed. Her fingers fussed with her linen purse. I wiped my hands on the towel and walked slowly across the soft asphalt. I stopped directly in front of them and said, "Beg your pardon?"

The blonde flushed, but stood her ground. "I said you don't look like the rest of them!"

I grinned at her. "I'm just like the rest of them. I'm twenty years older than they are, but I'm just like the rest of them!"

She giggled, and the tension seemed to ease from her shoulders. The sunburned skin around her eyes crinkled, and she stole a quick look at her companion. Her face swung back to mine. "Take off your sunglasses," she commanded. "I've got questions to ask you, and I want to see your eyes."

Obediently, I removed the glasses and squinted down at her in the noon glare. "What would you like to ask me?" I inquired.

"Well, what are you doing here in Ruleville?"

"I'm spending the summer making drawings. I'm covering the kids who came down here to work. I'm an artist."

She cocked her head with interest. "Who are you bein' an artist for?"

"CBS."

Her eyes were steady now, and the playfulness had been turned off. "Would you answer me honest—would you really talk with me?"

A trickle of perspiration moved down the small of my back, and I was aware for the first time in days that I was stained with sweat and dust. There was an agreeable feminine radiance about the woman, and she made you remember that you were a man. I smiled at her and nodded. "Sure. Let's talk. What's bothering you?"

She pouted and tossed her hair back. "We can't talk here!"

I looked about the deserted station elaborately. Teasing, I said, "Why not?"

"Oh, for heaven's sake!" she exploded. "This is a gas station!" She paused uncertainly, and took a breath. She glanced quickly at her companion, and then seemed to make a private decision. Her eyes were challenging as they moved to my face. "Would you come to my house?"

Her friend's eyes widened, but she remained silent.

"Well, now. That's the first invitation I've had from the white community since I arrived!" I said lightly.

She flushed. "Now don't start that!"

"Before I accept your kind invitation, you ought to know that if I come, I'm liable to jeopardize your position in the community. When I drive out of the quarter," I said, "I'm often followed."

The blonde shook her head in annoyance. "Don't be silly. Everybody in Ruleville knows me. Just come."

"Thank you. Can I bring some of the kids I'm living with? You'd like them."

"Heavens, no!" Her eyes were so wide in horror that I burst out laughing.

"When would you like me to come?" I asked.

"One thirty. Emily, you come, too." She smiled at me. "My name is Bette Lindsey. What's yours?"

Back at the Freedom House in the Sanctified Quarter, Jerry Tecklin stared at me. His thick notebook of local information lay open on his lap. "The Lindseys are important people. Bette Lindsey is married to Lake Lindsey, a family that reaches way back in Mississippi. His daddy was a very big wheel in the Delta." He closed the notebook. "You're really going to their home?"

I nodded. Jerry picked up the Ruleville phone book and wrote down the address and the phone number. "If you're not back by four thirty, we'll come looking for you."

The Lindsey house was adjacent to the highway, five minutes north of town. I parked the car at the dead end of the small road and looked about me. It was a new neighborhood, pleasant and unpretentious. The modest house suited the street. As I climbed from the Chevy, the aluminum screen door swung open, and Bette Lindsey waved cheerily. "Hi, Tracy! Come on in."

The living room was cool and inviting. The slipcovers were bright, and the furniture was simple and comfortable. Lake Lindsey rose from the corner of the couch and met me in the middle of the room. He was a large, taciturn man, six foot three, perhaps 220 pounds. I noted the heavily muscled arms and the belly that was beginning to paunch. He looked like a former athlete, probably a tackle or a fullback who had never been really lean. His face was set and his eyes still.

"Bette told me about you, Tracy. I'm glad to meet you. I'm Lake Lindsey, and I'd be obliged if you'd call me Lake." We shook hands, and he nodded to Bette's morning companion. "You've met Em?"

She smiled shyly, her eyes alert. "We met Mr. Sugarman at Sandy's gas station." Her voice was light and musical. "Sandy is my brother, Mr. Sugarman."

A Negro maid brought coffee. She caught my eye and swiftly looked away. It was Ora May. She and I had met at the very first voter registration meeting at Williams Chapel. Without another glance, she noiselessly disappeared back into the kitchen. Bette sat, Buddha-like, on the floor, filling our coffee cups. Her eyes were bright, and one could see that she was curious and excited. She handed me my coffee. "I'm glad you came, Tracy."

"I appreciate your inviting me here. It's nice being in a room like this again." I set the saucer carefully on the edge of the coffee table and looked at the Lindseys. "I'd like to talk with you. But I don't think we can talk honestly if I don't level with you to start with."

Lake Lindsey sat stirring his cup, and his eyes were careful. I cleared my throat, and started again. "I told Bette at the gas station that I was covering the Summer Project down here for CBS. That's true. But I don't want to misrepresent myself to any of you. I'm not just a reporter who happened to get assigned to Mississippi." Lake sipped his coffee, one heavy arm draped across the back of the couch. "I'm here because I wanted to be here. I believe in what these kids are here to do. I told CBS I was coming, and then they said they would show my drawings. You all deserve to know that. I'm not neutral."

Bette's eyes were level over her coffee cup. She put the cup down, and her face was serious. "I told Lake I had invited you home because there were questions to be answered. You're living with these people, Tracy, and we'd still like to get some answers. Lake?"

He hiked himself forward on the couch, and his elbows rested on his knees. His resonant voice rolled quietly across the room. "Bette's right. We would like answers. We suspected you don't share our point of view." He hesitated for a moment, and then plunged ahead. His face darkened, and his voice took on a timbre. "Maybe you can tell us how these kids can presume to come into our state, not knowing our people or our customs, and tell us how to live our lives." His voice was more troubled than angry.

"Well, Lake, I went through the orientation course with them in Ohio, and all I can say is that they're not here to change your way of life. They're here to help the Negro in Mississippi change his way of life. They think they can do it in two ways. The first is in teaching him the responsibilities of citizenship—the importance of voting. The second is by enriching his education so he has some sense of American history, and his own history as well. These kids are here to work in the Negro community, not the white community."

Bette sniffed loudly. "Thank goodness! I never saw such a filthy bunch of people! Where did they find these creeps?"

I looked at her face. Her nose was wrinkled with disgust. "At Harvard," I said dryly. "And Swarthmore. And Stanford. And Reed. And Howard." She flushed but did not reply. "Look, Bette, these kids aren't 'creeps.' For the most part they're middle-class kids from our best schools. They're the only ones who could steal a summer without working. The 'filthy kids' you're talking about are just like all the kids who have been hanging around our house with my teenage son for the past four years. This is not the sandal-and-beard contingent, the Beatniks. These are the idealistic youngsters who want to help right what they think is wrong. You drive in to pick up your maid in the quarter, and you pass these boys and girls working up and down the unpaved roads. You think: 'Jesus, what filthy kids! How scruffy!'" My voice had grown angry, and I paused. I put down my coffee cup and stared at Bette's troubled face. "Think about it," I said softly. "When it's dry, the roads are dusty. When it's wet, they're muddy. You don't pave roads in the Negro section of Ruleville."

"There's no excuse for being unclean," Bette said sharply. "No excuse for looking crummy."

"I won't offer excuses, but I can give you reasons, Bette. And they have nothing to do with the moral fiber of the kids we're talking about. I wonder if you know that only 30 percent of the Negro houses down here have adequate bathing or toilet facilities. In the house I'm staying in, there is one cold water tap and no sink. It's hard in hundred-degree heat to keep clean and shaven with cold water in a tin basin. Most of the kids do their laundry in kettles over fires in the backyard. Bette, we're living the life your Negroes live all the time." She sat silent, her fingers picking at the edge of the rug. "There's one other reason. These kids are scared. They wake up scared, they go to church scared, they do their jobs scared, and they go to bed scared. And the next day they do it all over again. These are kids who never had to worry about pickup trucks with shotguns, and wagons with police dogs."

She lifted her eyes from the rug and picked up her half-empty coffee cup. As Bette replaced it on the table, Ora May moved silently into the room to remove the soiled cups and saucers. Bette pushed her hair back from her ears. Her eyes were kindled. "I saw Len Edwards, the congressman's son, on television the night you all arrived in Ruleville. He looked like such a nice, clean-cut kid I wanted to bring him home to meet Lake and see our kids. See how we really live. How we really are." She narrowed her eyes, and her voice was cutting. "The very next day I

saw him walking down a road in Sanctified Quarter with a nigger girl!"
I watched Ora continue to load the tray. Her hands moved from the table
to the tray without a missed beat. "I could have killed him!" Bette's hands
clenched, and she beat a fast tattoo on the rug. The maid stepped carefully
around her and left the room. Bette's chin came up, and a mischievous
grin touched her lips. She shook her head. "No. I couldn't have killed him.
But I wanted to!"

Lake stormed at the northern press. "They crucify us!" He had pounded
his fist into the palm of his other hand. "And they lie. I saw a northern
paper that said whites had burned down Williams Chapel in the Sanctified
Quarter!" His eyes searched my face. "Now, you know that isn't so. Hell,
if we wanted to burn down that church, we would have done a better job
than that! The truth of the matter is that our white fire truck got out there
in ten minutes and put out the fire. And at two in the morning!"

"I'm not going to defend bad journalism, Lake, whether it's in the North
or in the South. If you say you saw the story, I accept your word. But over
twenty churches have been burned to the ground already this summer,
Lake. And that's not an invention of the northern press. If you're suggesting
that Negroes set fire to Williams Chapel, I'm telling you that you're wrong.
You don't know me, and you don't have to believe what I tell you. But I
know the Negroes in the quarter don't have the money even to repair the
damaged steps from the fire, or repaint where the bags of gasoline singed
the walls. And I know they're heartsick and frightened by the arson."

Emily had listened attentively, and at this point her thin voice piped
across the small room. "Well, the Yankee papers certainly do manage
to give Mississippi a black eye every chance they get! You'd think we
invented violence down here!"

"You're wrong," I retorted. "Mississippi gives Mississippi a black eye.
What do you think the *Look Magazine* editor is going to write when he
was chased last Wednesday night from Ruleville to Greenwood, thirty
miles, by a carful of whites at ninety miles an hour? I know this guy. He
was scared to death! He doesn't have to invent a story about Mississippi,
Emily. All he has to do is tell the truth!"

Bette's lips curled in a tight, private smile. She said softly, "Nobody
was going to hurt him."

Lake Lindsey warmed to my challenge. His large body was poised on the edge of the couch, and he would reach for arguments and responses. "I wish I was better educated so I could say better what I want to get out." When he would bait me with the high rate of illegitimacy among the Negroes, I would point out the impossibility of middle-class values among people who were eking out a marginal existence. He would frown, and thrust ahead. "I was too smart to go to college, Tracy, so I can't answer you the way I'd like to."

He clung to the image of the childlike, irresponsible Negro as if it were an act of faith. "I know them. They don't want to learn. We build schools for them, and they don't use them!" I pointed out that he could hardly criticize the Delta Negro for caring little about an educational system that spent only seventy dollars a year on his education. "What if the Negro kid does stay in your inadequate Negro high school, Lake? What if he doesn't drop out? What's he going to do in Ruleville after he graduates?" Lindsey hunched his shoulders and shook his head. "I'll tell you, Lake. But you know. There are two factories in Ruleville, and they don't hire Negroes. So he graduates to chop cotton."

Bette's voice was silken. "I told you that, Lake. I told you!" It was a slap that occurred often that afternoon, but Lindsey was not listening to her.

His face was grave, and his eyes winced in concentration. "What bothers me most is you people trying to register everyone to vote! Hell, Tracy, what would happen to this state if we let everyone—anyone—vote?"

"Well, what's happened to your state not letting everyone vote? By almost every measurable standard, Lake, Mississippi is fiftieth of fifty."

"But it's ridiculous to think that every nigger who can make his mark should decide how to run this state," he exploded. "It isn't race, it's education! Why, there are whites on my place that I wouldn't let vote!"

I stared at him. "You wouldn't let vote? It's not up to you, Lake, to decide who's qualified to vote. The Constitution sets those qualifications. But in Mississippi qualified Negroes have been deprived of their vote, and unqualified whites have been registered. I know, because I know who I've taken up those steps at the Indianola courthouse to try and register. And you know, because you live here."

Bette nodded, her face turned toward her husband. Lake stared back. Finally, he cleared his throat, and his words were low. "I'm not going to pretend that what you're saying isn't so, Tracy. There should be a standard for everybody. But I know that if they give the vote to unqualified people, there's going to be trouble—real trouble—in the Delta."

"But Lake, this is 1964. There are Negroes who've gone all over the world in the military service, and come back to Ruleville. You can't tell them they can't vote! Some white registrar with a grammar school education can't deprive people who are better educated than he is because he doesn't approve of Negroes voting! I've taken Negroes down to Indianola who finished high school, and the Man still won't register them. And what about the older folks, the ones who never had a school to go to? They may not read or write well, but they know what the score is in Ruleville. Can you fail to educate people and then penalize them for being uneducated?"

Lindsey's gaze was level and unblinking. "There'll be trouble. Real trouble." He shook his head in exasperation. "What's so hard to explain to you—to people like you—is how much we care for our niggers. You think we're heartless because we segregate our society. I tell you that the nigger prefers it that way, same as we do. We know each other. It's worked out for a hundred years this way." His voice trailed off. When he began to speak again, I strained forward to hear. "I've taken nigger kids out of my field, and driven them to school. Who put them in the field, Tracy? Me? Hell, no! Their folks. Bette can tell you. The football weekend we gave up at Ole Miss so I could stay at the bedside of one of the sick nigger children from the plantation. I drove him to the hospital in Mound Bayou. The kid's mama didn't care, and Christ knows who the kid's pa was." His eyes were bright. His voice lifted. "They're not responsible people, Tracy. They're children themselves. They chuck responsibility every chance they get. But we know them down here. They're good-hearted folks, most of 'em, good-hearted as most whites I know. Better than some. I've been raised next to them, and I know them." The room was silent. A flush of embarrassment touched his heavy, boyish face. "In a way I love them. I don't suppose you can believe that."

Bette and Emily had nodded agreement as Lake had spoken. I knew that he had echoed the great thesis that underpinned the "Southern Way of Life." I nodded as well. "You're wrong, Lake. I do believe you. I think you're a good man, a compassionate man, and I believe you. What I don't believe is that your love has helped them. Or Mississippi." Lake leaned back in the couch, wiping his mouth with the back of his hand. "You say you love your Negroes. I say you don't respect them. You don't now, you never did, and as a result they often don't respect themselves."

I pointed at the comfortable room we were enjoying. "If you couldn't provide for Bette and your kids, if you couldn't earn enough even to feed them twelve months a year, you'd despise yourself. Maybe you'd even drink, like so many of the Negro men do out in the quarter. It makes their inadequacy easier to bear. Did you ever wonder why the Negro woman is so often the backbone of the family, Lake? Because she can usually find steady work. If the white southerner respected the Negro, he'd see that he learned skills so he could be a stable member of society. Instead, he thinks he's being noble when he goes down to the jail on Monday morning and bails out his 'boy' so he can get back to chopping."

The lemon-yellow rectangle had edged across the rug as the afternoon had raced away. Now it had moved up the wall, touching the frames of the two oil portraits of the Lindseys. I thought of the sepia photographs on the Williamses' wall back in the quarter, so different in feeling from these two smiling "young marrieds." I wondered if they had been painted on their honeymoon in New Orleans.

The door from the kitchen opened, and Ora May stepped into the room. She stood silent, waiting for Bette to notice her. Bette smiled when she saw her, and waved her closer. "Ora," she said, "say hello to Mr. Sugarman. He's"—she paused for a beat—"visiting in Ruleville."

Ora turned to me with a polite smile and nodded. "I hope you enjoy your stay, Mr. Sugarman." She turned back to Bette. "Is there anything I can get for you before I leave, Mrs. Lindsey?"

"Just help me up off the floor, Ora. After seven months I feel like a truck that's run out of gas."

Ora May helped her to stand and then paused before leaving. "Good night, Miss Emily. Mr. Lindsey." She nodded in my direction and left the house.

The room was cool and quiet, and we could hear her steps on the walk outside. Each of us seemed to be savoring the moment, deep in our own thoughts. When she spoke, Bette's voice sounded almost plaintive in the quiet room. "Seven months," she said. "Just two months to sweat out till I bring our new little baby into Mississippi." She paused and then seemed to rush ahead. "Into what in Mississippi, Lake? Into what, Tracy?"

Her fingers were tightly clasped, and her eyes were fixed on something outside the room. When she spoke again, her voice echoed a deep sorrow. "Emily and I were teaching a Sunday school class at our Baptist church, Tracy, when someone rushed into the room with the news. 'Someone blew up a Sunday school class in Birmingham, Mrs. Lindsey! A nigger Sunday school!' Em and I just stared at each other, thinking we must be going crazy. No. It was true. Four little girls were just blown to bits. At Sunday school." Her face looked stricken. "My God, Tracy, where does it all end?" She stared at Lake. "Where? Where do we even start?"

When she turned to me, I could only shake my head. "I wish I had the answer, Bette. I wish someone did." Her eyes held mine. I wanted to answer but was struggling to find the words that could help. "I guess you start where you are, where you and Lake can make a difference. Maybe right here in Ruleville." I told them about the Negro high school and the overcrowded classrooms and facilities, about the lack of vocational courses. "Why not start there? If you were turning out electricians and carpenters and roofers instead of just cotton choppers, the whole Delta would benefit. These folks could bring their kids up in clean houses and with pride. Those kids are going to be neighbors of your kids, Bette."

She nodded, her face down. Her voice sounded hesitant and muffled. "You can't know. It's so hard. I can't stand their touching me, shoving against me." Her face came up, and her eyes were wet and wide. "What can I do?"

"I can't help you, Bette. The world keeps turning, and I guess we have to turn with it. It's easy to get panicked by change unless we look at it realistically. The kind of social integration that you find so hard to face is not going to happen suddenly. Most Negroes in the Delta can't afford to go to restaurants and motels. Besides, they're much more interested in jobs

12. Summer volunteer George Winter in Drew, 1964.
"Do you want your kids chopping cotton for three dollars a day?"

and education and the vote than they are in integrating country clubs. No. The kind of integration that you're going to have to cope with soon, like it or not, will be when four frightened little colored children come to the Ruleville grammar school. Everybody in Ruleville is going to get all upset. But after all, that's all they are. Four frightened children."

The phone rang twice. Bette listened and said that I was wanted on the phone. George Winter's drawl crackled through the phone. "Hey, man, where are you? We've got to go register some folks in Drew." There was a pause, and the Okie voice continued quietly. "You okay?"

"I'm just fine. See you in ten minutes." I walked to Lake and extended my hand. "I've got to go." We shook hands, and the Lindseys followed me to the door. "Thanks for your hospitality," I told them. "I hope we see each other again. It was a good afternoon."

There was a quality to that afternoon. Perhaps it was the mutual wonder that we all shared, the remarkable happening that had allowed this kind of conversation. Not once in the hours together did rancor or personal hostility sour the talk. The intervening days were to witness pain and change. The search for Andy Goodman, James Chaney, and Mickey Schwerner, the three missing civil rights workers, was throwing an ominous shadow across the Delta and far across the country. There was a steeling of resolve on the part of both the Negro and the white community. But in that tragic summer of violence and martyrdom, I look back to the shaded living room of the Lindseys as a tiny island where, for a brief moment, one could seek understanding.

Blacks, Whites, and Whites

the few times when most of us in the Ruleville project spoke to whites at all, it was at arm's length, most often in an official encounter or in a highly charged confrontation. Ours was a reality of "them and us," a besieged garrison mentality. What made it more bizarre for the student volunteers was that the "them" were whites who were dangerous and the "us" were whites who felt very much part of the black community. The attention and energy of most of the white volunteers were in finding ways to be useful to the black community that had courageously opened their homes and hearts to us. But reality refuses to be boxed and cataloged so neatly. Only an audacious person like Bette Lindsey would dare to try to bridge the awesome divide. That kind of courage in the Mississippi white community in 1964 was singular. In all the conversations I have had in more than forty years with civil rights workers who worked in the Mississippi Delta, I have yet to hear of one unfettered and open white-and-white relationship other than the one that began for me with the Lindseys of Ruleville. Born on that steamy afternoon in 1964, it has been a friendship of candor and trust that has survived and blossomed over four decades. With their help, I came to recognize that stone faces and bravado are often merely facades, and the truth one can discover behind the masks is often more revealing if one is patient. That, of course, is much easier to comprehend in the cool light of years of reflection.

With the exception of the Lindsey family, Jack Harper, the Sunflower County chancery clerk, and Sheriff Bill Hollowell were the only whites with whom I ever conversed. They were studiously polite, but totally uncommunicative. I sensed their unease about the fraught scenario that

13. A worried black woman.
"What are we going to do after you folks go back north?"

was being played out during the overheated summer. They were constantly being reminded by the national media and the federal agents in the state that three of our civil rights workers were still missing. And every day seemed to bring news of another burning of a black church, or another attack on a Freedom House. They were vividly aware that Mississippi was being seen by most of the nation as a barbarous society that was unable or unwilling to protect American liberties. There was much we might have wanted to say to each other, but it was to remain a wordless dialogue of unspoken fears and unrealized hopes.

The truth about white resistance, of course, was more nuanced and complicated than we were then able to understand and accept. In a time of conflict, it was equally impossible for Mississippi to realize the wide diversity that existed within the civil rights movement. It is possible now to have the searching dialogue that was almost impossible then. My few encounters with the Lindsey family were aberrations, opportunities for candid social engagements that were as rare as they were revealing.

Translating visual images into tangible realities on paper or canvas has defined my professional life. The stark and dramatic imagery of those first days and nights in the Delta made their way into my reportage in sweaty drawings and feverish logs as I sought to capture the immediacy of the racial interaction I was witnessing. What became clear to me only much later was that my spilling sketch pads were focused almost exclusively on the interaction of the blacks who had long been exploited and the young and ardent whites who had come to help them. What was missing was the invisible elephant in the room, the white community that ordained the life of the Delta. We moved in the shadow of their omnipotent power, tactically moving to outflank their barriers and strategizing to escape their punishment. But almost without exception, the whites who came to Mississippi and the whites who were already there passed that summer like ships in the night. We whites peered at each other from both sides of a racial, hazardous highway that had for centuries separated blacks from whites in Mississippi. To work synchronously with any hope of being effective, we had to adapt. On our side of the divide we had to learn to see each other in ways that we could never have imagined. It was a revelatory experience that changed all of us. But it was a focus that was essentially parochial, for on our side of the highway that severed Ruleville like a moat, we were alone together.

How to explain the close-stitched fabric of that summer that lines our memories still? How to describe the warp of the black humdrum of their life that was suddenly our life, and the woof of our whiteness that became a shameful brand every time we examined the despairing houses we shared or watched the furious white faces in the threatening cars that robbed our nights of sleep? Close-stitched, smothering, inescapable, black and white together, how would we survive? How could we be of help? How would we be altered by life shared in that overheated cocoon? We learned not just to look, but to see. And we learned not just to listen to the voice, but to hear the person inside.

seven

Drew

We're going to Drew." McLaurin's voice was tight as he looked around the group of us gathered under Mrs. Hamer's pecan tree. "We'll pull off the highway next to the school and park near the church. Go in twos, and fan out through the neighborhood on that side of the tracks. I'll work on the far side of town. At seven, sharp, we'll meet back at the cars and head out of town together." His dark glasses scanned the group, and his voice was solemn. "We don't want to be in Drew after dark."

An almost gut-wrenching fear of imminent, hair-trigger violence was what we all felt every time we ventured into the ugly mill town of Drew. Linda Davis, who came to know the Delta so intimately, always said it was the scariest town she ever saw. And it was a town where we almost always struck out. It was never for lack of trying.

At five, we parked our three cars beside the church's vacant lot, and tension moved into the streets as we stepped from the cars. Mills and businesses had just closed, and a stream of workers drove down the dirt road toward the highway beyond. As they drove slowly by, one could read the shock and indignation on their faces.

"Okay," said Mac briskly, "get goin'."

Many of the workers, spotting our integrated group, had apparently abandoned all thought of driving directly home. Instead, they circled slowly through the Negro quarter. When they would come alongside a student, they would lean from the window, spitting curses and abuse. We were Drew's first "invaders," and they lost no time in reviling the volunteers as they made their way through the broken fences and up the dirt paths that led to the Negro homes.

56

14. Charles McLaurin addressing group.
"You don't want to be in Drew after dark."

A pickup truck moved nervously down the roads, driven by the Drew chief of police. McLaurin had notified Sheriff Hollowell that we planned to go to Drew that night. Hollowell said that peaceful canvassing would be tolerated, and had passed the word to the local police. The presence of the chief seemed to restrain the circling whites whose fury was clearly building. At any moment, I felt, they would climb from their cars.

By six thirty I started walking slowly back to our parked cars. A gas truck turned the corner as I approached. The driver viciously swung the wheel as I moved to the side of the road to let him pass. Startled, I leaped back as the high fender grazed my thigh. The face in the cab was livid as he shouted, "Sonuvabitch!" I was too astonished and breathless to even notice his license number.

The students started to congregate as the minutes dragged slowly past. The stream of cars continued to edge by us. Suddenly, a green Plymouth stopped dead in the middle of the road, blocking the exit to the highway. In moments, a half-dozen cars were lined along the road. I glanced nervously at my watch. Six forty-five. The cars idled their motors, and the angry faces stared through the settling cloud of dust. A woman sat impassively as her husband leaned from the green Plymouth.

"You chicken bastards!" His voice sliced the silence, a ragged, grating yell. "You goddamn nigger-lovin' sonsuvbitches! What are you doin' here?" The southern singsong cadence of his speech rose to a scream, and his face was florid. "I said: What are you white niggers doin' down here?"

The students stood silent, turning from the strident rantings of the infuriated man, or shifting nervously, watching with mounting alarm as the string of halted cars grew larger. The face of the woman in the Plymouth was pale and shut as her husband continued his torrent of abuse.

Larry Archibald, a gangling, lanky, suddenly tall youngster, stepped from our knot of civil rights workers. A tentative, struggling red mustache made Larry appear even younger, and his voice cracked as he spoke in a sudden silence. "But, sir, we're just down here to help these people to register to vote!"

I saw the raging man in the Plymouth reach for his door handle as his incredulous face stared at Larry. "You're what?"

I reached quickly for Larry's arm. "Cool it, Larry! Shut up!"

Larry looked suddenly flustered and hurt. "But . . . " He stopped abruptly, and turned away from the car.

We held our breath, for we all sensed that the moment the first car door opened, every car would empty. But the man's rage had spent itself in obscenity. With a screech of tires in the dirt, the Plymouth lurched forward and moved to the highway. The line of cars raced their motors and edged past us, the faces of the drivers unforgiving, staring.

With relief, we saw McLaurin turn the corner of the church. The mask of his sunglasses hid his eyes from the hating faces in the cars. He moved jauntily down the walk. "Time to move out," he sang, and climbed into the front seat of my Chevy. I wiped the sweat from my eyes and glanced sideways at Mac as I turned the key in the ignition. He was studying the crowd of Negroes on the far edge of the road. His eyes brushed past the children who were now edging close around our cars, and lingered on the knots of men and women who stood watching. Now that the last mill worker's car had moved to the highway, the Negroes appeared on their porches and behind the short dusty hedges that edged the street. McLaurin smiled broadly and waved gaily. As we started down the road, his voice rang out loud and clear. "We'll be back!"

At three o'clock on the very next day, volunteer Jim Dann was picked up by the Drew police chief. He was told that he was breaking a city ordinance by distributing leaflets that announced the first civil rights meeting to be held in Drew. Dann fought to control his temper, for his contempt for Mississippi police was matched only by his inability to disguise it. Indignation edged each word as he responded, "There is no city ordinance that prevents me from handing out leaflets to people on their property. That's what I was doing."

The chief pursed his lips, pondering the technicalities. Abruptly, he motioned to his waiting car. "Let's go," he commanded. "The mayor wants to see you."

15. Jim Dann, now a teacher, giving a deposition after his arrest in Drew, 1964.
"They called me a nigger-loving communist and then arrested me!"

"I wasn't really arrested," he reported later, "just 'picked up.' They were trying to frighten us off."

"Did the mayor give you a hard time?" I asked the still furious Dann.

He cocked his head, brow furrowed. "Well, he said that 'livin' with niggers was un-American and anti-Christian,' and that anyone who did 'was a communist and a disgrace to the white race.'" Dann, who had interrupted his studies for a Ph.D. in history to come to Mississippi, had had to suppress a desire to smile. He shook his head at the memory now, and laughed aloud. "What really bugged the mayor," said Jim, "was my answer to the 'great question.' He actually asked it! 'Would you want your sister marryin' a nigger?' When I told him I wouldn't mind, I thought he'd have a stroke." The police had released him with a warning, and he was with us when we returned to Drew later that afternoon.

McLaurin had not yet been able to wheedle the use of the church in Drew from the frightened pastor, so he had called for the meeting to be held in the churchyard. Jim Dann's leaflets had raced through the Negro sections, and now people lined the street. Teenagers had gathered in the churchyard, but the men of the quarter stood silently across the road. In the middle of the street, I saw the police chief's car and the police pickup truck. Two additional policemen on foot stood facing the churchyard. An ominous hushed watchfulness held the block.

Mac moved as though no one was there but us. As the students grouped around him in the yard, he started a spirited. clapping. His voice slapped at the silence in the street:

We are soldiers in the army,
We've got to fight although we have to cry.

The youngsters around McLaurin joined in the singing, and the rhythm reached out among the silent watchers.

We've got to hold up the freedom banner,
We've got to hold it up until we die.

The song surged, building ever louder. We are soldiers . . . in the army . . . we've got to fight. . . .

A few women, one carrying a baby, crossed the road and joined the singers. Kids, who only ten days before had raced away when we made our first forays into Drew, were now jiggling and clapping around the students. They giggled as they noted the flushed faces of the police, and they watched McLaurin with wide and wondering eyes. The sound, swelled by the numbers, beat against the rows of silent men. When the music ended, McLaurin began to speak to the crowd in the churchyard, but his words were winged to the hushed street.

"We're havin' a peaceful meetin', on church property, and the police there are tryin' to harass us. What are they afraid of?"

The chief stepped from his car, and the patrolmen on foot moved beside him. Arms folded, they stopped twenty feet from the churchyard. McLaurin moved through the crowd on the lawn and stopped on the edge of the sidewalk. His words were boldly directed at the black men standing silently on the other side, and he ignored the phalanx of the law that stood between.

"What they're afraid of is that you're gonna rise!" His voice rose. "That you're gonna say, 'I'm a man! Treat me like a man!' Now we're havin' a meetin', and they're afraid you're gonna cross the road and join us . . . like men! That you're gonna act like men, not boys! And they're afraid of that! Are you gonna let them see that you're afraid? That you won't join these kids and women?"

The burning words seemed to hang in the silent street. The chief stood impassive, his eyes glued on the young Negro whose voice was lashing the men. The police about him shuffled nervously, their armpits damp stains on their shirts, their lips dry. But no one moved across the road.

McLaurin abruptly turned his back, and started a clapping chant. I saw there were tears in his eyes, but his words soared out:

Which side are you on, boys?
Which side are you on?

Three of the Negro girls from Ruleville who had come to work with us in Drew picked up the verse. They seemed to hurl it at the men who stood silent.

Oh people, can you stand it?
Tell me if you can,
Will you be an Uncle Tom
Or will you be a man?

The crescendo of sound infected the kids up and down the block, and more kept spilling into the churchyard. Volunteers Mike Yarrow, a white, and Fred Miller, a black, moved through the youngsters, handing out freedom song sheets. The surging, excited crowd had moved onto the sidewalk when the chief pushed his way into the chanting kids and grabbed Yarrow and Miller.

"You're under arrest for handin' out leaflets on a public street without a license," he intoned, and pushed the young men toward the waiting pickup truck. As the tension and the noise riffled the crowd, the chant rose louder:

Don't "Tom" for Mister Charlie,
Don't listen to his lies
'Cause black folks haven't got a chance
Until they organize!

Now the chief and the two police moved swiftly back into the singing, swaying youngsters. Volunteers Gretchen Schwartz, Charlie Scattergood, Landy McNair, and Jim Dann, all whites, were hustled toward the truck, arrested for "blocking the sidewalk." The song ended on a ragged note, the excited chatter stilled.

John Harris, a black volunteer from Howard University, was being led toward the truck by a policeman. He paused as he moved to climb into the cab of the truck. He turned his angry face to the Negro men who still stood rooted. "If you register and vote, you won't have to elect stupid public servants like this one!" He climbed in beside the furious cop as Gretchen and Charlie began to sing and clap:

Ain't gonna let no po-lice
Turn me 'round,
Turn me 'round,
Turn me 'round. . . .

16. The first arrests in Drew.

"Which side are you on, boy? Which side are you on?"

Mac had removed his sunglasses. He stood on the edge of the grass, and he spoke to the silent men across the road. His eyes were wide and young, more vulnerable than I would have imagined. His voice was imploring, urgent. "We want all the responsibilities of citizenship. Not tomorra! Now! Not next year. Now! You're payin' first-class taxes, but you're lettin' Mister Charlie keep you second-class citizens! If you stay there, if you don't sign up to go down to vote in Indianola, you're sayin' to the white man, 'Don't treat me like a man. Treat me like a boy!'" His voice was hoarse, and the tears shone in his pleading eyes. "We've got to stand up."

He moved past the motionless police and into the crowd of sullen men. From one to another, he moved, a stubborn gadfly, cajoling, shaming, holding out the Freedom registration form that no one would sign.

I ached for Charles. And I wept for the silent men.

I was worried when the angry police had driven John Harris to jail. "Accidents" had happened too often to outspoken Negroes in Mississippi jails. But he had merely been penned with the rest of the male students in the single concrete cell that was the Drew jail. Gretchen, to her fury, had been separated from the men, and sent to jail in Indianola. It had seemed a needless risk to leave her jailed alone, so we had pooled our money and bailed her out before dark. To Gretchen, it was male chauvinism, and she had been furious with all of us.

Once in jail, John had taken charge. "According to that cop outside, we're going to be arraigned at nine tomorrow morning. When they ask how you plead, you say, 'Not guilty.' And you sign no statement till you've been allowed to see your lawyer." He paused, glancing at the sweaty kids crouched around him. "Just hope the lawyer gets here before the hearing."

The excitement of the afternoon fled with the last light. Darkness closed on the tiny blockhouse, bringing with it the first apprehensions. They could watch the cars move slowly past the little stockade. Word had flown through Drew that seven of the "mixers" were over in the jail. Only a tall wire fence, topped with some strands of barbed wire, separated them from the road. Harris measured the distance. No more than twenty feet, he fretted, an easy lob if someone wanted to throw anything from a passing car.

It was a long, uncomfortable night. Sleep was fitful, and they thrashed awkwardly in the cell, trying to get rest. The exhilaration that had sustained them was chilled in the early morning damp. John stared at the pale salmon sky that was framed by the barred window. He remembered McLaurin pleading with the men to cross: "You say to the white man, 'Don't treat me like a man. Treat me like a boy!'" Mac's voice filled his ears, and surprising tears burned his eyes. Those poor bastards, he thought. Those poor, poor bastards.

By eight they had been moved to the police station. As they filed in, John sought in vain for someone who could be a COFO (Conference of Federated Organizations) lawyer. His face brightened as he saw Gretchen and me hurrying into the station. The chief, looking choleric and angry, was about to start the proceedings. Harris caught my eye. Soundlessly, he mouthed the words, "Where's the lawyer?" I shook my head and opened my hands. We had phoned SNCC headquarters in Jackson, and they had promised someone would be there. I glanced at the clock. It was nine o'clock.

The chief stared distastefully at the camera that hung from my neck. "Nobody allowed in here except the prisoners," he said curtly. I stepped to the door and almost collided with the two breathless COFO lawyers as they bolted into the station. I grinned at the students and stepped outside into the heat of the morning. My tire had been slashed, and the gathered crowd of whites watched with amusement as I struggled to change the tire. I was soaked and filthy by the time the door of the police station swung open, and the chief led the boys to the two cars parked next to mine. I reached quickly for my Leica and stepped into the road as the chief approached.

He stopped short, and the boys halted abruptly behind him. His face was angry and red, and he poked a stubby finger in my direction. "Don't take one damn picture if you don't want to lose that camera!"

I lowered the camera and stepped aside as he led the prisoners across the hot pavement. Jim Dann winked as he opened the police car door and climbed in. The boys all appeared disheveled, but only John Harris looked haggard and upset. The two cars pulled out and moved down the shaded avenue, turning left finally to meet the highway that ran south toward Indianola.

The seven arrested students had been released on bail at noon, and by four forty-five that afternoon the nonviolent assault on Drew was renewed. We loaded three cars with voter registration people and a half-dozen kids from the Ruleville youth group. Volunteers Ellie Siegel and Chris Hexter, excited and curious, climbed into the rear seat of my Chevy. For the first time, Freedom School teachers were going to a voter meeting.

Newly deputized whites sealed off both ends of the street that faced the churchyard. They sweated under riot helmets, and carried billy clubs and sidearms. They looked worried and tense, and their eyes kept moving to the hundreds of Negroes who lined the street and milled in the church-yard. The deputies made me think of the kids who came green from boot camp during the war. I shuddered at all the lethal hardware that hemmed in the restless block. The singing started the moment we stepped from the sidewalk.

Woke up this morning with my mind
Stayed on freedom!

The singing was strident. Nervous. The chief and the police regulars once again dominated the center of the road. Their eyes were riveted on McLaurin as he worked the crowd to shouted response. Voices rang with excitement and enthusiasm. "Oh, YES!"

The mounting din broke suddenly as the chief stepped forward. His drawling voice could be heard easily as he spoke with a slow, deliberate enunciation of each word. The demonstrators were trespassing, and if they did not wish to be arrested for trespassing, they must leave the church grounds immediately.

McLaurin's reply was sharp and immediate. "We have permission from the deacon of the church to hold an outdoor meeting on the church grounds."

The chief shook his head. "That permission has been withdrawn by the deacon."

A growl of resentment sounded in the yard. McLaurin led the angry crowd swiftly into the empty lot that bordered the churchyard, and the meeting resumed with a rush of sound. Chanting soared as more young people from the road joined the demonstrators. The chief retreated to his car and used the radio. Minutes later, another police car pushed its way through the cordon of helmeted deputies, and an elderly white woman was escorted from the car and led over to the agitated police chief. The woman's face was pale, her mouth set in a thin, colorless line, and her eyes were alarmed.

"This is the lady who owns the property you are on." The chief's voice was flat and hard. "She wants you off."

McLaurin's frustration and rage exploded. His hoarse voice slashed at the police. "These police aren't used to having Negroes standin' up like men! They're not used to having Negroes refuse to run when they say 'Run'!" The tense crowd responded at every sentence, closing tightly about the taut figure of the speaker. "They don't want anything that's gonna change a system that lets them get rich, and leaves you workin' cain't to cain't [can't see because it's too early in the morning to can't see because it's too late at night] for three dollars! They don't want change because when you stand up, you're gonna change the things that keep you second class!"

The police edged closer to the walk. The chief's hand rested on his holster, and his voice shook. "I'm telling you all for the . . . ," but McLaurin's furious voice interrupted.

"They don't want us to demonstrate peaceably. The U.S. Constitution says we have a right to assemble peaceably, that we have a right to request a redress of grievances. But these police say 'No'! They say no, and we're supposed to stop. They say no, and we're supposed to turn around!" He shoved his way through the churning crowd toward the edge of the lawn. "If they want to force us out of the churchyard, force us out of an empty lot, force us into the street so they can arrest us, then we'll go! We'll all go into the street! And we'll fill all the jails!"

"Yes! Yes! Oh, yes!" Clapping and chanting, they surged across the lawn and into the street. McLaurin turned for a moment, and signaled to John Harris to take over. John nodded understanding, and deliberately stepped back on the lawn to avoid arrest. The police herded the stream of clapping and singing Negroes down the dusty ghetto road toward the jail.

The song rocketed around the quarter as they moved on. "WOKE UP THIS MORNING, WITH MY MIND . . . STAYED ON FREEDOM!"

Ellie Siegel, Gretchen Schwartz, and five of the local girls from Ruleville were arrested and sent into segregated cells in Indianola. Chris Hexter, McLaurin, and fifteen other members of the Ruleville and Drew youth groups were sent to the county farm prison in Moorhead.

I returned to the Freedom House in Ruleville, and we started the tedious process of gleaning bail money from our scattered supporters in the North. It was a draining exercise that had to be constantly repeated during that long, hot summer, but one that had to be done swiftly and successfully if we were to protect the kids who were languishing in the Mississippi jails. By eight the next morning, the Western Union key started to chatter in the back room of the Ruleville Rexall Drugstore. The money orders from California, Illinois, Washington, and Connecticut were arriving.

A sulky-faced white boy wrote out the checks, and petulantly called out the names. "Heidi Dole. Len Edwards." The staccato gossip of the key continued. "Linda Davis. Jim Dann."

By eight thirty the total had reached forty-five hundred dollars, and the clerk was pale and angry. He stared stolidly at the students, refusing even to acknowledge their "thank-yous." He looked like he had been made an unwilling conspirator, trapped into aiding and abetting criminals whom he abhorred. Linda and Heidi stood near his counter. By any standard, they were very pretty young women. This morning, their color high and their eyes dancing with the thought of the ransom for their jailed friends that had arrived, they looked radiant. I leaned against the tobacco counter and watched the young clerk. What did he see when he looked at them? I wondered. His pale-blue eyes were flat and opaque. It was the look I had seen on the faces of New Yorkers as they stepped around a sick drunk who lay inert on the subway steps. It turned inward, away from the offending stench, shutting out the sight with a flick of the lid.

Sheriff Hollowell counted the money carefully, totaled the amounts, and filled in the proper forms. "Get the girls," he said to the deputy, and moments later the young women filed into the room. Hollowell turned from Dale, who had been handling the bail transaction, and nodded toward the women. His voice was neutral. "Have any of you been mistreated in any way?" The girls shook their heads in the negative. Their faces showed the strain of the day in Drew and the night in the Indianola jail, but they looked unharmed. The sheriff turned back to Dale. "I'll notify Moorhead that you're coming. You can take the girls now."

Gretchen stretched her arms in the sunlight and lifted her face to examine the tiny window of the second floor cell. "That's where they put Ellie and me," she said. "Man, even in jail they segregate."

The segregated quarters had not really separated them from the Negro girls. They had called to each other, and late into the night they had sung together. Ellie pushed a strand of hair from her forehead. "Ugh! Do I need a bath! Let's get the boys and go home."

The long, low buildings of the county farm lay sweltering in the sodden heat of noon. The jailer stepped outside to watch our cars move into the yard. His narrow shoulders hunched against the brightness, and the deep, shadowed eyes looked ferociously from the tight ferret face. "You just stop. Right there!" He spat on the lifeless sod of the drive. Without another glance, he crossed the yard and disappeared into one of the low buildings. Ten minutes later, the boys stepped from the building. They looked exhausted and filthy. Squinting in the blinding light, they climbed into the cars.

"Are you all right?" I asked.

Jeff Sacher, looking pale and ill, grinned weakly. "We're all right. It's just that I'm allergic to the hay in that sty. I'll be fine once we're out of here."

The white boys had shared one section, the Negro boys another. But the heat and the rank, nauseating offal of waste and despair were democratically shared. A drainage ditch near the screenless windows sent clouds of insects into the odorous cells.

Jim Dann said, "It was a menagerie. We had lice, mice, chiggers, mosquitoes, flies, and the skins of two snakes that had once lived there."

"It was just so damn dirty, and so damn hot," said Jeff. Angry welts of bites and scratching covered the skin of most of the boys. Sacher's eyes were puffy and inflamed, but his voice was vibrant. "For a while the jailer kept a fan going, and it helped a little. But late last night a call came through from New York senator Kenneth Keating's office in Washington. Keating, a Republican, wanted the local authorities to know that he knew

17. Volunteer Jeff Sacher.
"I don't know where these blacks get their courage, no matter what!"

one of his constituents was being held in Moorhead. The jailer was sore as hell, and he turned off the fan."

A Negro youngster from Drew leaned from the seat near the door. He shook his head admiringly at McLaurin in the backseat. "You should have seen McLaurin," he chuckled.

I caught Mac's eye in the mirror. He looked unruffled and fit. "What did you do, Mac?" I asked.

"I didn't do anything," he smiled. "I just curled up on the cot. The kids kept askin', 'When are we gettin' out?' and I couldn't tell 'em because I didn't know. So I curled up on the cot and slept. All the time I was there I just slept."

eight

Freedom School

alongside the highway that bisected the black quarter stood an ancient house of gray, unpainted wood. It stood on the corner of a dirt road that met the highway. This, I had been told with great pride by McLaurin, was to be our Freedom House, and the home of our Freedom School. I stood surveying the wreck, appalled at the state of hopeless disrepair. Grinding, relentless poverty had stamped it indelibly, and the generations of families who had lived there had been unable to bring anything to the old frame house. It stood, dispirited and broken, a lonely survivor, and still so close to the highway that any torch from a passing car could turn it to ash.

I tramped through the building, slapping the swarms of mosquitoes that rose as I entered. Rotted bedding, blackened and cracked windows, and walls that were stained and mildewed from years of seeping rain and snow spoke a wordless, nauseating language of hopelessness. I was sickened by it, and made my way quickly back to the sagging porch. My heart sank when I realized that the Freedom School teachers would be arriving on the following day. What the hell had McLaurin been thinking when he rented this wreck?

But a restorative burst of energy moved into the quarter when the bus arrived from Oxford. The young women climbed out, creased and tired, but full of zest for the work ahead. I watched with amusement as the young "veterans" like Jim Dann and Charlie Scattergood jumped to help get them settled. The laughter and high spirits of a college weekend echoed through the dusty quarter as the Ruleville Negroes peered out from their stoops at the girls from up north.

The assault on that incredible relic of a house that was to be our Freedom School could have been mounted only by the energy of the dedicated

18. Arrival of volunteers at the Freedom House.
"A Community Center is a state of mind!"

young. They invaded the musty interiors with brooms and mops, pails and soap, and emerged bearing the old accumulated filth. A pile of bedsprings and rags, old bottles and broken chairs, rose in a corner of the yard, an odorous monument of neglect. Brigades of buckets swabbed out the grimy corners, and light moved into the rooms through shining windows. The kids' laughter mingled with the clatter of broken glass being swept, and "Who swiped my Tide?" and "Jesus! Just look at that toilet!"

One of the girls was tying a bandanna around her hair and saw my look of disgust at the pile of accumulating filth. She smiled and stooped to grab a bucket of suds. "Don't you know," she said, "that a community center is a state of mind?" and disappeared through the torn screen.

If Mark Twain had wandered over from his Mississippi River, Liz Fusco, the minute, bright-eyed "schoolmarm" of the Freedom School, would have grabbed his arm and marched him up to her class of black kids and said,

19. Students unloading lumber.
"Man! A buck and a half for twelve feet! But we got shelves for the Freedom School!"

"This man is the best storyteller in the world, and you're the best audience he'll ever have!" But of course, Twain had long ago gone to his great reward, probably raising hell in heaven. So the best that Liz could do was introduce the kids to his wonderful inventions, Tom Sawyer and Huck Finn and Nigger Jim, and she did it with a gusto and delight that moved like magic through the pack of children that huddled on the sagging, shaded porch of the Freedom School around *The Adventures of Huckleberry Finn.*

The Freedom School had gotten started that morning at eight fifteen. Seven elderly women eagerly responded as Linda Davis began the exciting journey that would teach them to read. "These are sounds," she said. "I'll say them, then you say them. We'll go slowly. There's no hurry. Now. Ah! Ah! Ah!"

The women peered through their glasses or squinted as the sunlight touched the sheet that Linda held in front of them. They cleared their throats and very softly repeated back. "Ah. Ah. Ah."

20. Books arrive at the Freedom School.

"We've got encyclopedias—and Twain and Faulkner—and picture books—and a whole pile we've labeled 'crud'!"

"You're doing fine," said Linda with a broad smile. "Ay! Ay! Ay!" Absorbed now, they answered back. "Ay. Ay. Ay. Ay."

In the next room, a dozen four through seven year olds were discovering the delights on the freshly papered bookshelves. Heidi Dole, her pretty face animated with pleasure, was handing books to the bright-eyed youngsters. They would curl up on the floor and excitedly thumb through the volumes in search of pictures and color. A world beyond the Delta began to unfold, and a wonderful silence fell on the room.

Heidi's gentle voice said, "These books are yours. We can find all sorts of things in them. You can always come and use them here. And, if we take care of them, you can even take some of them home to read. In your own homes." She tucked her feet under her, and picked up a book. "Why don't you all gather around, and we'll read this one together."

At two in the afternoon the sessions for the school-age children began. In groups of three and four, teachers led their students to areas of the lawn where they might discuss and question without interrupting the progress of another group. Books, pencils, and papers sprinkled the hard-packed yard with confusion and color. The excited talk of the enthusiastic teachers mingled with the suppressed excitement of the Negro children. I watched the young teachers starting to probe, gently urging their wide-eyed kids to ask, to be curious, to dare to try. The youngest children were quickest to be fired. Their surprised laughter and exclamations showed contact was being made. The older boys and girls smiled shyly, seriously frowned, or dropped their eyes. No white teacher had ever taught them, and the northern speech sounded hard and strange to their ears. Few teachers in the understaffed and ill-equipped black Ruleville school had ever reached out to them with such ardor and trust. It was new, but not uncomfortable. They watched from lowered lids, said little, and noticed everything.

I laughed as I moved through the clusters of kids. America's most fortunate and verbal children were teaching her most deprived and least-verbal children, and the results were sometimes hilarious. Words that had been useful back at Swarthmore or Stanford like *dichotomy* and *incongruous* were suddenly embarrassing and pompous when offered to the bewildered children. But as I watched I realized that most of what the eager

21. The books from Oxford, Ohio, in Sunflower County, Mississippi.
"Ohio books for the Magnolia State."

teachers were saying was striking sparks. Even during that first afternoon, one could hear the vocabularies becoming simpler as common ground was gratefully sought and found. At last, the self-doubting that had badgered so many of the teachers since those daunting days and nights at the Oxford orientation was being removed in the actual confrontation with the Mississippi children. Finally, they were beginning to do what they had come so far to do.

22. Lucia Guest teaching typing at the Freedom School.
"A new world in an old Delta."

The Freedom Schools that the civil rights movement brought to Mississippi were ambitious and courageous, the teachers eager to plant seeds of curiosity and love of learning. But they could only dampen an arid soil that had been parched for three hundred years. It was shocking for me to realize that, at age forty-three, I was only beginning to perceive the vast desert of educational deprivation that existed in my country.

To me, the world of the Negroes in Mississippi that I was discovering in 1964 was as shocking as it was unimaginable. Those who had survived that desert did so from tiny oases they discovered in their churches, in their poverty-stricken Jim Crow schools, or in their mothers' nurturing kitchens, often thirsting for more intellectual nourishment that might one day burst them free. The students who first timorously, and later joyously, flocked to the Freedom Schools were the children born of a peculiarly

23. Freedom School nutrition class.
"Fred Miller's nutrition class at the Freedom School."

American serfdom. For the most part, they were the products of a Mississippi education for Negroes that intended their future labor to be productive for the Mississippi landowners, and equipped them for little else. They were the children and grandchildren of black sharecroppers, men and women who perpetually had survived only on the desperate margins of hunger, victimized by plantation owners and the vagaries of drought and flood. All were the remnants of a dehumanizing system of denigration and slavery that had seeded bitter harvests of ignorance, cynicism, and resignation.

But how to explain the tender compassion, the fierce bravery, the wry humor, the keen intelligence that, astonishingly often, managed to survive even in the darkest corners of American apartheid? How does one account for the Negro men and women whose indomitable spirit transformed that daunting summer, and whose often humble lives seemed to ennoble that time and that place? As the summer drew toward its end, each of us "outsiders" had to wrestle with the realization that by leaving Mississippi, we were leaving friends who had become incredibly close, and abandoning, perhaps forever, that precious part of our lives when we had been made magically colorblind. We knew that all our efforts could be only marginal in helping to change Mississippi because we were, after all, "strangers at the gate." When we said good-bye, it was with pride but with a sense of regret that we couldn't do more. For the kids that I observed, the "long, hot summer" had been a selfless devotion to hard and thankless work. They had put themselves in harm's way for others, not themselves. For some, like Linda Davis, Len Edwards, and Liz Fusco, leaving was too high a price to pay, and they remained to carry on the work so laboriously begun.

Fannie Lou Hamer

When we had all arrived in Ruleville from Oxford, we had assembled with Charles McLaurin in the shade of Mrs. Hamer's pecan tree. "Sorry Mrs. Hamer isn't here to meet you. She's up north meeting the teachers, singing, raising funds for the movement," Charles told us. "Be back tomorrow, Vergie," he called to Mrs. Hamer's little girl who sat on the porch step. "She's gone a whole lot of the time," he said, his voice lowered. "Hard on her husband, Pap, and Vergie."

That summer of 1964 I came to know Mrs. Hamer, and I recall the very first time I saw her. With a decided limp, carrying her suitcase, and shining with perspiration, she made her slow way up the path to her porch. At the step, she turned to watch the excited chattering of the volunteers on the lawn, and her large head turned slowly to look at the gas station across the highway where a tight knot of whites was standing on the pavement near the pumps, silently watching. And she knew now that the night riders would be coming again. When you had grown up in the Mississippi Delta, you knew it. You knew it in your bones. They came whenever a black stood up and said, "No more." And she had done that. And now the students were here, and the faceless men at the gas station knew they were here. So now the unmarked trucks with the shotguns would be coming again. Every night during the angry times, in the early years of the movement, they had moved ominously through the quarter where Fannie Lou Hamer lived. She'd watch them from her darkened porch and sip a long glass of cold water. They were long, lonely nights.

Frowning, she turned to the porch and broke into a wide grin when she saw Vergie. She dropped her valise and opened her arms. "Hey, baby!"

The child leaped from the step and rushed happily to embrace her. "Mama! Mama! You been away so long!"

Perhaps because our ages were much closer than those of the other volunteers who arrived in Ruleville, she felt comfortable in sharing her thoughts and concerns with me. I felt equally at ease sharing mine with her. It was the cement that bound our friendship that lasted until her death in 1977. The time we spent together in Mississippi and on her trips north at our home in Connecticut was a rich gift to me and to our life as a family. To me she was the bravest, most formidable single person I met during my years with the Freedom Movement, and the most memorable.

Extraordinarily bright, passionately Christian, and devoted to freeing both blacks and white Mississippians from their tragic legacy of racism, she had become the voice and the soul of the struggle. When this seventh of twenty children of a black sharecropper's family grew to lead the nonviolent fight against the repression, she became the target for every kind of economic and physical violence.

"Although I get threats," she told me, "I still feel great, knowing for the first time in my life that I can stand up with dignity. I feel more free than some of the worst segregationists down here. Because I can go to bed and sleep. But they're restless because they're studying up another scheme, and wondering what they can do next." And then her great mahogany head tilted back, and a deep, rumbling laugh echoed across the scarred porch with the torn screen. At last the unfettered laughter ceased, and her large yellow-tinged eyes locked on mine. She nodded. "With dignity, Tracy."

For daring to register to vote, both she and her husband were banished from their plantation home where she had served for seventeen years as the head timekeeper. They were declared "unhirable" throughout the Delta for her presumption. Their home was attacked by faceless night riders who fired and fled, and their church, Williams Chapel, was torched shortly after we volunteers arrived. And after being stopped on the highway while returning from a civil rights conference, she was arrested. In that Winona jail, she was beaten nearly to death.

In a summer when the whole nation's attention was riveted on the lynching of Andy Goodman, James Chaney, and Mickey Schwerner in the

Delta, the muffled rage of the Mississippi blacks was given voice by Mrs. Hamer. "We are sick and tired of being sick and tired!" No one grieved more deeply for the three young SNCC fieldworkers than she. Her powerful preaching and singing reached far beyond tiny Ruleville, where it could skewer a timid preacher or confound a racist mayor. It echoed in the halls of Congress, where debate raged on the Civil Rights Bill and the Voting Rights Bill, and even in the White House of Lyndon Johnson, who was worried that too many passions were being aroused and his southern political base could be challenged. Within the striving and struggling civil rights organizations, the singular trumpet of Mrs. Hamer was heard and honored, an inspiring reminder that even simple folk can speak truth to power and help change the world.

We would often talk long into the night on her dilapidated porch, or when I was sketching her as she worked with the volunteers or the elderly women who were learning to read at the Freedom House. Watching her calm resolution, I found it difficult to comprehend. The indignities I watched her endure were a daily diet of abuse and intimidation, though they never appeared to slow her down. I was amazed that she never answered anger with anger.

"How can you not be bitter, Fannie Lou?" I protested. "These Mississippi police and Klansmen would like you silenced, even dead."

"I won't hate them, Tracy," she told me, "because then I will be just like them. I don't hate. A child has to be taught to hate, and I was raised in a church and a home that taught me not to hate, but to love."

On a furiously hot Sunday morning, I picked up Mrs. Hamer to drive her to church. "Where do you want to go to church today, Mrs. Hamer? I promise to drive slow."

She grinned. "Well, Tracy, there's a little country church between here and Drew that I've been meanin' to visit. A nice little minister who I'd like to talk with. Is that too far?"

I laughed at the calculation in her eyes. "No, ma'am, it's not too far."

One look at Fannie Lou Hamer's purposeful mien must have convinced the young country pastor that he was in for a trying morning. He quickly concluded his reading from scriptures, smiled tentatively, and welcomed us. "I'm right pleased that Mrs. Fannie Lou Hamer has joined our service

24. Fannie Lou Hamer showing new voters how to register.
"You are free, black, and twenty-one, and you have every right to vote!"

this mo'nin'. We are happy to see you." He cleared his throat and plunged ahead. "Would you like to say a few words to the congregation?"

Mrs. Hamer rose majestically to her feet. Her magnificent voice rolled through the chapel as she enlisted the biblical ranks of martyrs and heroes to summon the congregants to the Freedom banner. "We want to be free!" she thundered. "We can protest these wrongs by register-ing to vote. I want to know, right now, how many people will go down to Indianola on Monday morning?" She halted, scanning the wide-eyed congregation. "If you're afraid, me and my daughter will go with you. 'Cause we need people to go NOW. We need people that's going to trust God NOW. We need people to work for freedom NOW. Not tomorra, but we want freedom NOW!"

Suddenly her rhetoric ceased, and a silence rushed into the room. Her finger trembled as she pointed to the shaken minister on the pulpit. Fan-nie Lou Hamer's voice was commanding, but its passion came pure from her committed heart. "And you, Reverend Tyler, must be Moses! Leadin' your flock out of the chains and fetters of Egypt, takin' them yourself to register—tomorra—in Indianola!"

Drawing Conclusions

e very night before going to sleep in the stifling back room of Jim and Rennie Williams's house, I would struggle to write down my impressions of that day before falling deep asleep. The incessant heat, the tension generated by every confrontational crisis, and my strained focus on every drawing simply drained me and left me exhausted. Page after page in my tattered notebooks would spill over with the excitement and emotion of what I was observing. And in my sketchbooks I was recording the images I was determined never to lose. Old women learning to read for the first time. Young wide-eyed black neighborhood kids, kidding and laughing with the white volunteers. The volunteers, black and white, who refused to let fear dictate flight from the hatred and violence that threatened them. Instead, without fail, they continued to do their jobs every day with affection, humor, and dedication. White deputies and white registrars at the Indianola courthouse. Blacks in the Mississippi sun, waiting permission to mount the courthouse steps. Peaceful demonstrators in the hostile streets and the incensed response of the police who came to arrest them. Mrs. Hamer singing "Ain't Going to Let Nobody Turn Me 'Round" in a voice so loud and compelling that the Klan just across the highway could hear it, too. And drawings of Charles McLaurin, looking cool and confident behind his black sunglasses, laying out the strategy for the day, reminding us to be careful, excitedly leading the freedom songs in our little Williams Chapel that made us feel braver. By summer's end the sketchbooks were sweaty and stained. But on the pages were more than one hundred drawings of that time in the Delta. Drawings I could carry back north.

The Mississippi I had imagined was an exotic mixture of William Faulkner's *Intruder in the Dust*, Billy Holiday's "Strange Fruit," B. B. King's Delta

"We lit a lamp here in Ruleville - and it's shining its light in the whole Delta!"

25. Charles McLaurin at Williams Chapel meeting.

"We lit a lamp here in Ruleville—and it's shining its light in the whole Delta!"

blues, and Howard Fast's *Freedom Road*. The truth I would learn over that "long, hot summer" was far less exotic. Recording and drawing the lives of the blacks I lived with in Ruleville, I came to know how banal evil can be.

When I would sketch the Ruleville on the black side of Highway 41, my pad would fill with images of unpaved roads that turned to mud with each rain and became baked and rutted in the interminable heat. When I drew the pathetic house I lived in, no better or worse than all the others in the quarter, it was a dwelling with an iron roof that trapped the damp heat of the Delta until long after dark. I could only imagine how porous the flimsy walls and floor must be when the cold winds of winter would sweep across the cotton fields. Black Ruleville was unsanitary trenches rather than sewers, and unlit streets at night that robbed the blacks of any protection from anonymous night riders who wished to harass or intimidate.

When I would cross the highway into white Ruleville, the streets were paved and well lighted. The houses were as proudly maintained as in any comfortably middle-class neighborhood of Rochester or Seattle. Old trees spread their shade over spacious and green lawns. It seemed that every day the drawings in my pads were a shocking reminder of what American apartheid really looked like.

The first time I helped McLaurin carry apprehensive blacks to Indianola to have them try, yet once again, to get registered, I made a series of drawings of the event. I sketched our Ruleville neighbors as they walked silently toward the imposing courthouse. From time immemorial, this courthouse had been a symbol of the implacability of white power. As they waited permission from the angry armed deputies to mount the steps, they stood, uncomplaining, in the stifling heat. Finally, a few at a time, they were allowed to wait in the shade of the tall white columns of the courthouse porch. While the silent tableau was unfolding, I moved out on the broad lawn of the courthouse to start a drawing of the structure that soared above me. Curious deputies began to drift over to watch this "outside agitator," distracted from their vigilant surveillance of these "uppity niggers" who were only out to give them "trouble." Mac quietly sent a smile in my direction.

Facing the courthouse was the Indianola jail where all of us knew McLaurin had been so savagely beaten for "making trouble." "Are you a Negro or a nigger?" This part of Indianola was where real power was

26. Cotton fields in Ruleville.
"The view of white Ruleville from black Ruleville."

wielded, and those who were powerless would usually move swiftly past. But today they stood patiently in line, right across the street.

Historians will make their ultimate judgments about what was most significant about the Mississippi summer of 1964. As an intimately involved reportorial artist, I was never that coolly removed from the intensity and heat to be able to argue persuasively that I was capable of historical objectivity by summer's end. I would never have tried. I confess to having been much more interested in capturing what I read as the truth of a situation than donning a mask of feigned dispassion. I thought, and still believe, that there were moral imperatives being contested that summer in the Delta about which one should be passionate. Each day and night of Freedom Summer had simply drained me as I raced about the Delta, scrambling to seize those moments that so demanded my most searching attention. With my words, my photographs, and my sweat-stained

27. Going to register at the Indianola courthouse.
"Speaking truth to power in the Mississippi Delta."

sketches, I was seeking merely to preserve those precious pieces of time with integrity. But the images I recorded were the images my eyes saw, the images my hand drew, and the images my heart felt. What they all might contribute to an honest depiction of that slice of American history would have to be determined later by the scholars.

It was the human drama that totally captured me from the first moment of racial confrontation in Ohio in 1964 to the last moment of my reportage in the Delta in 1965. The sheer audacity of the Summer Program that against all conceivable odds would face down a centuries-old fortress of apartheid was stunning to witness. In 1964, I simply could not take my eyes off the young and old blacks and whites, who, unarmed and in sneakers, were putting their lives on the line for an ideal. They are the people I put in my sketchbooks, and they are the American images I will treasure in my head forever.

Indianola

for weeks, the volunteers had been walking the dusty roads of Rule-ville, Shaw, and Drew, building support for the voter registration drive. It was tedious and dangerous work, but it slowly built understanding and momentum. More and more local black high school students were joining in the forays into hostile or indifferent neighborhoods. The example of the older college volunteers opened their hearts and minds to exciting new possibilities for lives that could stretch far beyond the Delta cotton fields.

For Charles McLaurin, the ultimate prize would be to carry this activity into the heart of Indianola, the very birthplace of the hated White Citizens Councils. It was his dream to find a safe building that could accommodate both a Freedom School and a community center where political organizing for the vote could be held. The day he found the empty Negro Baptist school only one mile from the courthouse, he was ecstatic. "It's great!" He gazed at the prize with a smile and opened his arms wide. "It's not only great," he exulted, "they can't burn it down. It's brick!"

Once the building was secured from the church elders, three of the volunteers and a handful of Ruleville teenagers made tentative probes for the push into the county seat. When the Ruleville students found their Indianola counterparts, they were often asked: "Where have you people been? We've been waitin' and waitin'!" I was able to sketch the first outdoor "Freedom Meeting," which was held on a street corner in a driving rainstorm because the Indianola youngsters' enthusiasm was so unquenchable. Only two weeks later, when McLaurin's leaflets announcing MASS MEETING AT THE BAPTIST SCHOOL TONIGHT! hit the streets, every black and every white in Indianola got the word.

28. First outdoor meeting in Indianola.
"It rained, and we all stayed!"

Worried about the safety of the women and children who might show up, our Ruleville chaplain, Rabbi Al Levine (our third cleric during that summer), decided to pay a "clerical visit" to Sheriff Hollowell to ask for police protection. When Hollowell surprisingly agreed to the request, Levine thanked him and asked that the police not come into the meeting, but remain outside "to discourage any intruders."

Hollowell replied, "They will be outside. I don't expect any trouble."

Levine looked skeptically at the sheriff. He knew that all of us expected trouble, that we were certain the Indianola whites would not sit still for such "outside agitation." That morning McLaurin had said to me that he didn't think more than a few local blacks would dare to show up at a civil rights meeting.

During the extraordinary meeting in that poor Negro Baptist church that night, I found myself an avid participant. There was no way that I could dispassionately make drawings to record the happening. We were still arranging the benches in the hall when the first kids began to drift into the yard from the surrounding neighborhoods. By seven o'clock, groups of teenagers and young women were crossing the yard from the street, their heads bobbing animatedly. By seven thirty, the entire hall was packed with an exuberant crowd of 250. The walls were lined with people who could not find seats, and clusters of children leaned in every window. The elderly sat scattered through the crowd, their eyes bright with excitement and wonder. For the first time in the summer, I noticed a large group of the middle-aged. Husbands and wives, some with tiny children in their arms, chatted quietly, waiting for the meeting to begin.

John Harris leaned against the wall at the front of the room. "McLaurin's on the way from Ruleville," he said. "Probably driving like mad!" He looked at the hundreds of blacks in the room and grinned. "I hope I can see his face when he walks in!"

The high Delta sky was lavender with dusk when McLaurin came across the porch and made his way slowly through the noisy congregation at the door. His dark glasses swept the crowd. He was shaking his head as he made his way around the packed benches to stand next to me against the wall. Harris had seen him, and with a wide grin led the crowd into song. They responded with a rush of sound, and the exultant voices lifted in unison:

BLACK AND WHITE TOGETHER,
WE SHALL NOT BE MOVED!

McLaurin's eyes were wet, and he grinned like a foolish Buddha. His fist rubbed the end of his nose, and he wagged his head in joyous disbelief. As the song swept the hall, his voice sounded harsh and shaken in my ear. "Man! This is INDIANOLA! Do you realize that? INDIANOLA!" His voice broke, and his face shone with pleasure. "I thought there'd be ten people here! Look at them! In Indianola!" For Mac this was the happiest, most incredible moment since he entered the movement. Five times he had been jailed in this town! Here, now, was the reality of every fantasy he had dreamed during the lonely, frightened nights in the Delta. His tough, compact body moved with the powerful urgency of his words.

JUST LIKE A TREE THAT'S PLANTED BY THE WATERS,
WE SHALL NOT BE MOVED!

John Harris let the song subside. He sensed that the familiar music had eased the strangeness that always accompanied a first meeting. His boyish face was smiling, and he nodded approval to the eager faces. "I'm going to introduce you to one of the persons who has been leading the freedom fight here in Mississippi for . . . " The voice stopped abruptly. An angry murmur had started near the door. Harris resumed, his voice uncertain. "Well," he said, "we've got an unwanted guest in here."

People rose from their seats, and benches scraped shrilly on the wooden floor as the crowd strained to see. A woman next to me whispered along the row, "It's Slim!" An alarmed cry sounded and was repeated around the hall. "Slim! It's Slim!"

McLaurin moved swiftly along the wall toward the huge black policeman who had shouldered his way into the center of the room. I touched the arm of the woman who had first spread the word. Her frightened eyes swung toward me. "Tell me," I said fast. "Who is Slim?" Her chin rose, and her eyes were angry and black. "He's a killer. He's killed two blacks in Indianola."

An ox of a man with a heavy, dull face and enormous hands, Slim stood like an animal at bay. His jaw was lowered, and his eyes stared furiously at Al Levine, who blocked his path. The noise was shrill in the hall, and Levine's quiet voice was drowned in the surging sound. McLaurin reached the rabbi's side as he was repeating slowly what he had already said. As if to a slow child, Levine patiently explained that police were not needed or wanted. "Don't you understand? The sheriff promised us that the police would stay outside." The policeman's eyes seemed not to comprehend, and the great hulk stood as if rooted to the floor.

McLaurin's voice rasped through the excited babble. "This is church property. You have no right to be here."

Slim's yellow eyes shifted from the rabbi to McLaurin, and they narrowed in recognition. His thick neck strained at the blue collar, and one heavy hand moved slowly to rest on the holster. The oxen slab of face was shining from the steamy heat of the room. The small eyes studied

McLaurin. Silence had suddenly surrounded the two men. Slim's voice could be heard clearly: "I'm stayin' right here."

McLaurin turned and pushed his way through the agitated crowd to the front of the heaving room. The nervous whispering ceased as he raised his hand for attention. The chunky body balanced on the balls of his feet, and his whole attitude was taut and controlled. Ignoring the policeman, he addressed the back seats and benches of the room. "Before we start here, I'd like for you to know that this is church property. We've got an agreement with the sheriff that says we don't have to put up with any policeman inside. Now it's up to you whether you want him here or not."

Feet scraped on the floor as everyone stood, and a wave of noise roared through the room. "GO! GO! GO!" The children had frightened half-smiles on their faces, but they screamed the word louder and louder. "GO!" It seemed that every throat in the crowd was unleashing its accompaniment to the barrage of sound that assaulted the policeman. I watched the fury on the faces of the old men and women. They were yelling "GO!" to a Mississippi policeman for the first time. They cut the air with the word they had never said aloud. "GO! GO! GO! GO!"

McLaurin fought his way through the stamping, chanting crowd to the side of Levine. Slim's eyes were wide and staring as the crescendo of noise broke about him. McLaurin pointed to the door, and his vibrant voice scissored through the din. "YOU GOT TO GO!"

The policeman's great head rolled, and his tongue licked at the heavy lower lip. He stared at McLaurin. "I could kill you!" he growled, and heaved the heavy service revolver from his holster. As the crowd eddied about the tableau, someone saw the dull glint of the .45 that was leveled at the rabbi and screamed.

Slim stood transfixed. His eyes were wide and frightened now, as the shouting, lurching crowd pushed from the rear. Only then did white-helmeted policemen elbow their way past the entrance and into the tense and throbbing room. A moment later they had wrestled the sweating, humiliated Slim through the crowd and onto the porch. The cries from the room followed them. "GO! GO! GO!" And now there was derisive laughter as well. Tomorrow every black child in Indianola would know that a bully cop had been faced down.

McLaurin edged to the front of the hall. As he made his way clear of the milling people, he was greeted by applause and relieved laughter. He stood, face alight with excitement, waiting for silence. Slowly, the aroused crowd settled back on the benches. Slim stood just beyond the open doors, on the porch. The light spilled across the enraged face and touched the white helmets of the Indianola police as they clustered in the dark beyond the step. The metallic chatter of the police car radios sounded lifeless and lonely. In the long, hushed room, McLaurin's voice sounded almost conversational. "I'm not unmindful tonight that many of you are here against the will of your folk. Kids are here against the will of their parents. Women are here against the will of their husbands. And many men are here against the will of their wives. And I understand why they were all against your comin'. People have been killed in Mississippi for comin' to a Freedom Meeting! But I know something's happening, something's changing. For better than two years we've been trying to get a meeting in this town so the people of Indianola could say out loud—in public—what they've said over the years as they crouched under their beds, prayin'. Say out loud that they were tired of being pushed in corners. Tired of the way they were living. Tired of havin' Mr. Charlie tell them when to move, how to move, and where to go! But now something's changing. You're not askin' Mr. Charlie when and where and how. You're here—tonight—attending a Freedom Meeting! In INDIANOLA!" He swallowed hard, and there was a timbre to the voice as it rang out. "To me that's a great thing! A great thing!" His eyes were shining with the pride in them. He gestured toward the door where the huge policeman moved restlessly. His voice was ripe with scorn, and he hurled his words at the glowering man who ceased his pacing back and forth to listen. "I'm not unmindful of the fact that right here in your city we have a policeman who should be pickin' cotton!"

The silent tension was torn with hooting shouts and screams of laughter. The faces were full of contempt and mocking. "Not unmindful," he cried, "that right here in your city you have a policeman who is not qualified to be a policeman!" Two police mounted the porch and stood with Slim, staring at McLaurin. McLaurin's voice fell, inviting the confidence of the rapt crowd. They strained forward to hear. "You know," he said almost casually, "once when I was arrested up in Leflore County, a white official told me something. He said, 'If a white policeman shoots a Negro, you have a racial crisis. But if a Negro policeman shoots a Negro, you don't have a racial crisis.'" He stopped, and every eye turned to the door. For a long moment there was complete silence in the room. Then McLaurin's throaty voice spat out the words: "And that's why they hired Slim!"

A single breath seemed to suck through the audience, and then was expelled in a sighing, "YES! OH YES! YES!" A roar seemed to fill the space, a wild mixture of relief, laughter, scorn, and admiration. Tears stood in the eyes of the oldsters, unbelieving half-smiles on the lined faces. They watched this boy—this David—come to battle. And they cried.

When the room quieted again, McLaurin shifted his tack. Never again did he so much as glance at the policemen near the exit. His voice was full, and he spoke with confidence. "For years I've known that we aren't the scary type of people. Our ancestors killed lions! They ate the meat of animals that would tear men apart! We're the same people that fought on foreign soil in two wars and in Korea! We're not afraid! We weren't afraid to go over there and shoot people who never did the things to us that these white people in Mississippi have. We weren't afraid!" He stood motionless, searching the wide-eyed faces of the youngsters who bunched along the walls. Softly, he asked the question. "Then why don't we shoot the white folk here?" The voice stopped again, and he took a half step closer to the teenagers. His voice spoke softly to them, and their heads nodded gently. "Because in this movement we don't hate. We love. Because even in Mississippi we're Americans. Born here. Raised here. That in this movement we are going to win by being nonviolent. Because soil out there is enriched with the tears, the blood, the bones, and the sweat of our ancestors. We own this country as much as anybody else. America is sacred to us. America is a land that we want to live in." His voice was vibrant with hope and full of the wonder of the moment. He leaned toward the children, and his young voice was joyous. "What's happening today is real. Not something you're reading about. It's happening RIGHT HERE! You are doing things that people before you would not have dreamed of doing. You are HERE! You won't say, 'I heard about it.' Or, 'Somebody told me.' You'll say, 'I WAS RIGHT THERE! I SAW IT! MY FEET WERE IN THAT PLACE WHEN HISTORY WAS MADE!'"

I think often of that meeting in Indianola. In a way it seems like a microcosm of the whole Mississippi summer. All the elements were in that room. The barely suppressed violence of the police, the thrilling awakening of a people who for a hundred years had known the nightmarish sleep of the hunted, the bone-weary, dusty kids from the campus who knew that something private and profound had been stirred deep in them, altering them forever. And the young Mississippi blacks, like McLaurin, making themselves say it, making themselves do it, making themselves be brave for all of us.

For Mississippi blacks, political powerlessness was the strangling reality that had chained them to the soil, robbed them of progress, and denied them even hope for change. Ever since the betrayals of Reconstruction, real political power for the blacks had been denied. But with the coming of the movement's vibrant black leaders like Bob Moses, Fannie Lou Hamer, John Lewis, Jim Foreman, Charlie Cobb, Charles McLaurin, and Amzie Moore, the dead hand of "gotta be like it always was" began to loosen its grip. In its place was a new, sometimes frightening, but exuberant fervor that challenged each Negro to dare to dream. But for the civil rights workers trying to empower long-subservient Negroes, it was a grueling and often heartbreaking struggle.

twelve

The Civil Rights Bill

late one afternoon I sat rocking in Mr. and Mrs. Williams's doorway. The carillon in the Baptist church across the highway was sounding for vespers, and the old, beautiful hymns winged through the weary quarter. I wondered if the Baptists knew or cared that the Negroes who couldn't enter their church doors were enjoying their music.

A loud peal of laughter and a raised scornful voice broke my golden reverie. Baby Sharon scrambled across the room and leaned against the locked screen door, peering to see her grandma. Mrs. Williams came trudging down the street, carrying on spirited conversations with the neighbors who sat on their porches or stoops. "Oh, yes, ma'am! I just did see it on the television! Glory be!" Her great laugh rang up and down the dirt road. "Oh, my, yes! All them senators gathered 'round! And repasentatives, too! An' then Presiden' Johnson signed the bill!" She was at the step now, and her voice was etched with acid as she glared at the house next door where a timid schoolteacher had refused to work with the movement. "Now some scared folks can stop bein' scared, and stand up! It's the law!" A broad grin lit her face as she spotted Sharon and me in the doorway. "Presiden' Johnson has signed the Civil Rights Bill!"

The day following the historic signing was a big day for Ruleville. At least, it was a big day for the churning black community that made its way unseen through the days of white Ruleville. Len Edwards's father, the congressman from California, drove into the Sanctified Quarter by himself. Having called Len from Memphis earlier that morning, news of his coming had leaked via the telephone central to the office of Mayor Durrough. His Honor had immediately placed calls to Len, who failed to answer the suddenly interested mayor's request for information. "Why

99

29. Mrs. Rennie Williams and her granddaughter.
"Now you hush, Sharon!"

should I answer his calls?" asked Len indignantly. "Last week he was saying that we set Williams Chapel on fire!"

It was a long and frustrating day for the mayor. Not receiving hard information as to when the congressman was to arrive in his little town, he stationed himself at the entrance of the quarter. He had sat for hours and failed to recognize Congressman Edwards when he moved into the quarter in a rented car. Worse still was the arrival of three more congressmen early that evening, sweeping up to Williams Chapel behind the flashing red lights of the county sheriff's escort! All four congressmen had been enthusiastic partisans of the Civil Rights Bill, and they were touring

Mississippi to show visible support for the civil rights workers and the Negro community who had long been cheated of equal access to public places. That evening in the scarred and steaming Williams Chapel, the Civil Rights Bill became poignantly alive for the men from Washington. They spoke but briefly, for they were moved beyond words by the naked love and trust that surged from the audience. In that strange summer, the Mississippi Negro was finally finding allies. Not one of the five Mississippi congressmen had ever come to address the Negroes in Ruleville. But here, in Williams Chapel, were Len Edwards's own father and three other congressmen from California and New York!

I watched the black and white hands reach out as the heartbreaking "We Shall Overcome" soared from the tiny church. I wondered if the white folks across the highway, tucked behind their spacious lawns, walking the broad, shaded avenues, could hear the anthem, could know that the hoarse and passionate voice that led the singing was that of Ruleville's Fannie Lou Hamer. I wondered if they got the news that four congressmen had visited Senator Eastland's Ruleville today. And I wondered if Mayor Durrough would tell them. For me, those human dimensions were the essential text of the summer. But there was also an unprecedented political scenario that was being played out across Mississippi, confrontation by confrontation, that was to reach its climax at the Democratic National Convention in Atlantic City.

It seemed to me to be wonderfully appropriate that in a summer of David versus Goliath, a mewling political infant, the Mississippi Freedom Democratic Party (MFDP), was to confound the best-laid plans of the president of the United States, and change the habits of the Democratic Party. If 1964's summer was to witness the nation's first interracial lynching of Andy Goodman, Mickey Schwerner, and James Chaney, 1964's autumn was also to witness the first major challenge to racially exclusionary delegations at American political conventions.

Birth of a Party

the struggle to politically empower the Mississippi Negro was begun in countless lonely battles over the many years since the Emancipation Proclamation. But it would not be until 1964 that the battle would be joined on a national stage and carried "live" into the living rooms of America and across the world.

With the passage of the Civil Rights Act, a new energy surged through the black community. Mississippi Negroes, now guaranteed access to public accommodations, felt emboldened to try new stratagems for gaining the vote and finding a political voice. But in a state that was essentially a citadel of one party, the Democrats, Negroes remained blocked from any meaningful participation in its deliberations. The platform of the Mississippi Democratic Party in 1960 stated defiantly: "We believe in the segregation of the races and are unalterably opposed to the repeal or modification of the Segregation laws in this state." Those few Negroes who made their way into the Democratic Party found themselves utterly powerless to advance the cause of equal rights. The long frustration created by the blatant racism was the long, slow fuse that finally burst into flame in April 1964. Hundreds of disenfranchised blacks and a handful of courageous whites created their own organizing tool for building political change. It was the Mississippi Freedom Democratic Party.

The MFDP became the mechanism through which the historically powerless could learn about the political system, and observe how their decision making could affect their lives. When the MFDP worked with the civil rights workers that summer, they enrolled 55,000 blacks and a handful of whites on their rolls. It provided striking evidence to refute white establishment charges that Negroes didn't care about voting.

In July and early August, the MFDP held precinct meetings in twenty-six counties, followed by county conventions in thirty-five counties where 282 delegates were chosen to go to a state convention. The state convention chose a challenging delegation of men and women that was racially integrated, and was pledged to support the progressive platform of the national Democratic Party. Among the 68 delegates who were chosen to go to the National Democratic Convention in August were Fannie Lou Hamer, Lawrence Guyot, and Charles McLaurin, all civil rights veterans. Four of the delegates were white, including Rev. Ed King, the Tougaloo chaplain. While working to register black voters with Medgar Evers in Jackson in 1963, King had been forced off the highway by racists, and had been badly scarred in the accident. A native Mississippian, born in Vicksburg, his was a lonely but insistent voice in the MFDP convention challenge to the seating of the all-white Mississippi "regular" delegation.

"There are not many white people openly working this way in Mississippi," he told the credentials committee of the Democratic Party at Atlantic City. "We have four white delegates in our freedom delegation here. There are more who would like to have supported us but could not do so for fear of their very lives."

When Governor Lawrence, the chairman of the credentials committee, appeared skeptical, King straightened in his chair and said with barely concealed emotion, "I know many Mississippians in the last several years, more than 100 ministers and college teachers, who have been forced to leave the state. This nation is being populated with refugees from the closed society in Mississippi."

When challenged that the MFDP delegates were not really representative of the whole state, King replied with anger that it was fear of white violence that had limited the delegation. "We were not able to hold a county convention in Neshoba County or a precinct meeting in Philadelphia because the church we wanted to meet in was burned to the ground." His voice faltered, and then rose in the hushed meeting room. "Three of our workers were murdered in Philadelphia." His gaze was steady as he confronted Governor Lawrence. "We do not apologize to you for not being able to hold a county convention in Neshoba County, Mississippi."

King's testimony underscored a political truth that could no longer be ignored by the political delegations from every corner of the country. In a state with 435,000 Negroes of voting age, there was not a single Negro delegate, and not a delegate among the "regulars" who was willing even to offer support for the platform offered by the national Democratic Party. An incipient movement of support for the MFDP challenge seemed to be growing, and the national media began to focus on this unforeseen revolt that might unravel the convention that was about to mount a challenge to the Republican candidate, Barry Goldwater.

The emotional climax of the quixotic challenge occurred when Fannie Lou Hamer testified as a witness before the credentials committee. Before banks of reporters, photographers, and television lights, Mrs. Hamer presented her case. No more passionate and ardent voice could have articulated the sorrow, pain, and longing of the Mississippi Negro than Fannie Lou Hamer's that riveting afternoon. All over America, the world of the oppressed, beaten, and victimized black American was suddenly standing naked in this half-educated black woman's images. "Is this America?" Thrown off a plantation for daring to vote, beaten nearly to death by Winona police, pleading for the right of Mississippi Negroes to have a voice at last in the nation's conversation, Fannie Lou Hamer touched the conscience of millions of Americans. "All of this," she concluded in tears, "is on account we want to register, to become first-class citizens. And if the Freedom Democratic Party is not seated now, I question America. Is this America, the land of the free and the home of the brave where we have to sleep with our telephones off the hooks because our lives are threatened daily? Because we want to live as decent human beings in America?"

Fannie Lou Hamer's testimony precipitated a storm of support for the MFDP. And the effect was felt sharply at the White House. A furious Lyndon Johnson decided to intervene with a use of political power that would validate his candidacy for the presidency, and silence the rump challengers from Mississippi. He believed that by signing the Civil Rights Bill in 1964, he had earned the thanks and support of the black community, and now he was demanding political payment.

Joe Rauh, who had been serving as legal counsel for the MFDP challenge, became the target of the assault from the White House. Rauh had long worked with Senator Hubert Humphrey within the Democratic Party, and had served as a legal representative for Walter Reuther, the United Auto Workers president. In his recollections of the events of the Mississippi challenge, Rauh wrote, "Johnson had seen the television and Mrs. Hamer calling for representation, and he called Humphrey and Reuther, and told them in essence: 'You tell that bastard goddamn lawyer friend of yours that there ain't gonna be all that representation shit at the convention.'" Rev. Ed King, a national committeeman on the MFDP during the frantic negotiations with the Democratic Party, recalls, "As Mr. Humphrey reported things from President Johnson, the president said, after hearing Mrs. Hamer speak to the credentials committee, that 'we can't let that woman ever speak at a Democratic Convention again. Therefore, she shouldn't be a delegate.' So the president of the United States decided for the black people of Mississippi that they could not have Mrs. Hamer as a leader."

Now the pressure built quickly on Rauh to abandon the MFDP. Unless he stopped the fight, he was informed by a Johnson aide, Hubert Humphrey would not be selected to be the running mate with Lyndon Johnson. Reuther, who believed it was vitally important for labor to have Humphrey in the role of vice president, confronted Rauh. "You will be blamed for Hubert's not being vice president if he doesn't get the job."

Alarmed that the public rebellion could cost him the political South, Johnson summoned civil rights leaders who still sought present and future assistance from the White House. He demanded that they work out an immediate compromise that would allow the convention to proceed. Joe Rauh and the leadership of the MFDP now had to resist the pleadings of Martin Luther King, Andy Young, Walter Mondale, Walter Reuther, and, most important, one of the civil rights movement's oldest allies, the senator from Minnesota. Hubert Humphrey asked for the MFDP's trust and urged that they accept a compromise that would award them two delegate seats. Four years hence, he promised, there would be a truly representative delegation from Mississippi.

Mrs. Hamer replied, "We didn't come all this way for no two seats, since all of us is tired." Ed King recalls, "Humphrey was a really good speaker. But he was up against Mrs. Hamer. She said to him that if he compromised right now on this issue, the right of the people to speak for themselves, he would never be strong enough again to stand up for peace in Vietnam, or for any of the social issues that he said was what the Democratic Party was about. Humphrey argued with her, and she finally said, 'Senator Humphrey, I am going to pray to Jesus for you.'"

In the end, the MFDP rejected the compromise, and the Mississippi "regulars" were seated. It was a bitter disappointment for the Mississippi blacks, and signaled the moment in time when many of the SNCC leaders lost all illusion that the established political parties could be trusted in their pursuit of equity for poor and minority Americans. For some, Atlantic City proved that white liberals could not be trusted, that an integrated civil rights movement had betrayed them. Black separation would lure many away, and "Black Power" would become a rallying cry that moved from the South into the ghettos and barrios of the North.

If the battle had been lost, surely the war had not. Political change in American society often comes in tiny increments, in small movements that move the goalposts back a fraction. Rev. Ed King, reflecting on the monumental struggle at the 1964 convention, says: "We left the Democratic Convention confident that we had won a victory, that never again would all-white delegations be allowed at a Democratic Party Convention."

The dispirited delegation returned to Mississippi, fearful of their future. Most had never dared to dream that high, and now they were coming home to dead-end jobs and the leaden promise of lean provisions for the winter ahead.

"Sick and tired of being sick and tired," Mrs. Hamer told Pap and Vergie. Sick of fighting a war with no power but your own convictions. The memory of the past weeks lay heavy on her usually ebullient spirit. She was tired, bone tired, of trying to sustain her small cadre of disinherited with so few victories. Her sudden emergence into the nation's consciousness created demands on her time and strength that seemed endless. The sagging little house on Lafayette Street in Ruleville was now a destination for politicians from the North, for preachers in the South, for educators, reformers, even revolutionaries. Now there were invitations to campuses, to antiwar conclaves, and to pulpits across the country. She recognized the emblematic importance of those appearances, and the speaker's fees were necessary for her continuing work as she began to dream of creating a Freedom Farm to sustain the poor in the Delta. Fannie Lou Hamer longed to return to her family, yet her days were spent in exhausting travel, her nights in crowded halls of strangers, often ending in lonely rooms.

When I saw her before I had to return to Connecticut at the end of that summer, I was startled by her exhausted appearance and melancholy demeanor. It had been a cruel period of testing for a gallant and very weary warrior. As I embraced her, I said, "Come see us in Connecticut. It's a good place to hide for a little."

A warm, familiar smile eased her broad face. "I'll try. Now you take care."

Leaving the warm embrace of our little garrison in Ruleville was unbelievably hard. One by one my companions of the summer were moving out, and I hungrily scanned the faces that I had come to know so well. Jim Dann, Heidi Dole, Ellie Siegel, Dale Gronemeier, John Harris, Chris Hexter, Linda Davis, Liz Fusco. I had captured them in my sketchbooks, but now they were heading out of the Delta and out of my life. They were browner now, burned by the Delta sun as they had trudged the roads of Ruleville, Drew, and Indianola, and seared by experiences that they had never imagined they would know back in their buffered world at home. As they hugged their black friends in farewell, there were tears on every side. If the hallmark of the "long, hot summer" appeared to those beyond Mississippi to be courage in the face of fear, the youngsters making their reluctant way to the Trailways bus terminal knew otherwise. The summer had not been about hate or about courage. It had been about love.

As they waved from the bus, they were no longer the young and vulnerable men and women I first met in Ohio. Their eyes had seen too much terror that was frightening. But many had also known trusting interracial comradeship for the very first time, their lives graced with unimaginable friendships that would endure. There were so many new feelings about their society and so many new political aspirations to be examined and sorted out that they would carry with them back to the North and the green oases of campuses and graduate schools. Only later would they learn how they had been altered, how skewed and strange so much of their remembered pre-Mississippi life would appear. In a lot of ways I felt that they had become family. Would I ever see them again?

In the sweat-stained, crumpled notes of my 1964 Mississippi log I find the words I scribbled as I departed the Delta at the end of the long, hot summer: *The state's legacy of race hatred has crippled all her children, black and white, and stunted her growth. Any moral resolve for new beginnings remains hidden. The killers who murdered Andy and Mickey and James are still out there, uncaught and unindicted. The killers of Rev. Lee and Medgar Evers still walk the streets, unchallenged. The unspeakable violence has stained the state with guilt. For the Mississippi Negroes, the promise of victory, of even rudimentary justice, may be all they'll know for a long time.*

When I left Mississippi in 1964, I assumed I would never likely return. I was eager to shake the dust from the summer and reenter my life as a husband, father, and illustrator. But as so many of the summer volunteers were learning, I, too, found that life cannot be so easily parsed. The steaming racial turmoil throughout the South was continuing to bubble, and movement confrontations with the southern establishment were commanding front pages every day. As people just home from Mississippi, the summer volunteers were constantly being asked to speak to a newly intrigued public. As my drawings of the '64 summer were being aired on CBS-TV and used in magazines such as the *Saturday Evening Post,* I too was being sought out as a speaker by colleges, community groups, and churches. We all felt the need to bring out the whole story of injustice and sacrifice that we had seen and to build support for the friends we had left behind.

The ominous communiqués we would receive from SNCC headquarters in New York told of ongoing harassment and violence in Alabama, the Carolinas, Louisiana, and Arkansas, and from Mississippi came word that night riders had attacked the homes of our coworkers in Indianola with firebombs and burned our dearly won Freedom School to the ground. Linda Davis, who had stayed on through that fall and winter, barely escaped the flames, and Jim Dann and John Harris were only doors away when the firebombs were lit. And Charles McLaurin was once more being held on invented charges in the Indianola jail where he had been previously beaten. Byron de la Beckwith, the man who boasted of having killed

Medgar Evers, still walked the streets of Jackson a free man. Our battle in the Mississippi Delta had helped move Congress to pass a Civil Rights Bill guaranteeing public accommodations to all, but the Voting Rights Bill that would ensure the ballot for all was being held hostage in a senatorial committee by Senator Eastland. The fall and the winter of 1964 and the spring of 1965 were harrowing reminders that the work begun had far to go.

Our home became a stop on the underground railway of the civil rights movement, as leaders such as Julian Bond, Ivanhoe Donaldson, Andy Young, and Mrs. Hamer paused during their efforts to raise vital money for lifesaving bail bonds. Our community responded vigorously, and we were able to enlist the talents of musicians such as Leonard Bernstein, Isaac Stern, and Tossy Spivakovsky, actors such as Burt Lancaster, and painters and illustrators from the area who contributed their work in order to raise the necessary funds for the struggle. It was an exciting and rich experience for my whole family, and early in the spring when my son, Richard, a freshman at Brown, took a leave from the university to answer a call for volunteers from Martin Luther King in Selma, it came as no real surprise.

Richard worked as a carpenter as the heroic march advanced day by day on Montgomery, helping build the platform for the great King rally when they reached the capital. Shortly after his return to Brown, he asked our blessing to go with SNCC to Arkansas during the summer. We struggled with the decision because it was a situation fraught with the possibility of Klan violence. Violence against the movement across the Mississippi River in the Delta was as savage as anything in Mississippi. But Arkansas did not have the sometimes protective shield of an omnipresent news media that we had in 1964. The violence was anonymous and often unreported. SNCC outposts in Arkansas were often totally isolated. It was a family decision not easily made. Only after being assured that this was a mission he felt morally compelled to do, not simply because his father had gone in '64, we took a very deep breath and gave him our blessings. We were proud of him, and scared to death.

On my return from the Delta in '64, I began to slowly translate my creased and tattered logs written in Mrs. Williams's overheated bedroom into a memoir of the summer. *Stranger at the Gates: A Summer in Mississippi* began to emerge. Mrs. Hamer generously permitted me to use a wise and thoughtful rumination about the meaning of Freedom Summer that she had shared with me to serve as an introduction to my book. But as winter moved into spring, I felt the need to return to Ruleville and the Delta for a perspective on what remained from the "long, hot summer." It now makes me smile to recall that once more I would go as an observer, only to find that the battle I had joined in no way had been consummated, and that I was there, once more, as a participant.

Part Two

Return to the Delta

June 1965

t wo work-shirted youngsters placing colored pins in a wall map looked curiously at me as I entered the MFDP headquarters in Jackson. A third was talking excitedly into a phone.

"Tractor drivers! Yeah. You're sure they were tractor drivers? Great! We'll check you later." He scribbled on a pad and called across to the others. "Five tractor drivers in Indianola are out. Jesus!" As he hurried across the room to the map, the boy noticed me for the first time. "Can I help you?" he asked shortly. When I told him I was headed back to the Delta after being north almost a year, and was simply "reporting in," he leaned against the battered desk and grinned. "You were here for the 'long, hot summer,' huh? Well, we don't have the same security setup as last summer. It really isn't necessary. If you've got Mississippi plates on your car, that's enough. You should have no problems." He handed me a form to fill out stating where I would be staying "for the records." When I finished, I joined the three young men at the map. The area near Shaw held clusters of pins. Pins at Tribett, a few at Cleveland, a scattering of pins at Indianola.

"What do they mean?" I asked.

"Blue pins stand for cotton choppers," one replied. "White pins for truck drivers, and red pins for tractor drivers who have walked off the plantations."

I stared at him. "What do you mean, 'walked off'? On strike?"

He nodded. "On strike." He waved his hand at the Delta. "Almost a thousand of them. And it looks like it's just starting."

"But are they organized? They'll get clobbered if they're not organized. Do they have a union?"

He nodded again. "They organized it in Shaw. Months ago. Before the planting started. They call it the Mississippi Freedom Labor Union." The week before I returned to the Delta, a hundred people, the families of members of the new union, had been thrown off the Andrews plantation in Washington County. The union members, who had twice before requested $1.25 per hour, confronted Andrews at five thirty on the morning of May 31, and informed him that they were striking. He had responded by summoning the police, ordering the families off the plantation, and dumping their household goods along the highway. It was the beginning of an unwinnable struggle that would continue in the months ahead.

When I returned to Ruleville, I headed directly to Fannie Lou Hamer's home. I knew that my old friend would be in the thick of this latest struggle. I found her sitting in the shade of the pecan tree in her front yard. Her face was wet and shining with perspiration, but she reached out and embraced me with a great hug. A grin lit her mahogany face, and she examined me at arm's length. "Connecticut ain't spoiled you much," she said. "I'm real glad to see you here again!" She silently handed me the chilled bottle of water at her side. "You look like you can use this." Almost a year had passed since last we sat together in Ruleville. The frame house seemed wearier, and she, too, seemed more melancholy than I remembered. Perhaps it was the contrast. Last summer this yard had echoed to the racket of young people. The screen door would bang against the warped frame, and Mrs. Hamer's deep contralto voice would be calling out urgent organizing orders to the students, or impatient rallying calls to the neighbors. It seemed then that Dale Gronemeier's typewriter was always clacking on the sagging porch, and the only phone was constantly ringing in the kitchen. Now we sat alone, and the house drowsed in the afternoon sun. Here in the deep shade of the pecan, the color of the zinnias was vibrant, mocking the painful white glare that shimmered in the quarter. I squinted at the heavy, damp figure of Mrs. Hamer. Her face in repose seemed sadder, and the lines between her heavy brows deeper than I recalled.

I recognized Joe McDonald's truck as it bumped its way up the rutted road, and a long brown arm waved from the dusty cab. Fannie Lou's face lightened. She smiled and shouted a greeting. "Hi, Mr. Mac!"

30. Seal's Grocery on Highway 41.
"Downtown in black Ruleville."

I nodded at the receding truck. "I was just thinking how different it seems now. Last summer when a pickup truck would turn down there at the highway, we'd all start sweating!"

Mrs. Hamer's yellowish eyes narrowed as she watched the dust settle in the hollows of the road. "We've gone through a whole lot of suffering in Sunflower County, and last summer those students suffered with us. But you're right, Tracy. It is different now."

"But now you've got the strike," I said.

"But now we've got the strike." She cocked her head. "I gotta go to speak in a church in Shaw tomorra. About the strike." Her eyes twinkled. "You want to carry me down there?"

Her innocent voice made me laugh. "Of course," I answered. "How else am I going to find out what the strike is all about?"

As we drove through Shaw, I pointed to a field beside the highway. A white family, mother, father, and children, was chopping between the long rows of cotton. No Negro laborer was in sight. The family never looked up, but intently pursued the weeds that were threatening the fledgling crop.

Dust swirled about them as the wind whipped across the black tableland. The first drops of rain stained my dust-covered windshield.

"Come on, rain! Rain for the strikers!" Mrs. Hamer cocked her eye at the black sky. "If it rains good, those weeds are going to multiply. Come on, rain!" The sky cracked, and a ragged sliver of lightning lit the road.

"You must have a direct line upstairs, Mrs. Hamer!" I laughed. "Here it comes!" I slowed the Chevy as the rain beat against the car. In seconds, the hollows between the rows of green were awash.

"It's only right," said Mrs. Hamer with satisfaction. "Those strikers've got guts, and they need all the help they can get."

"The Mississippi Freedom Labor Union is going to have a tough time organizing," I observed. "From what I read, the last strike down here was in the early thirties, and it was broken fast. Do you think the union should be a part of the Freedom Democratic Party?"

Her expressive face became thoughtful. "No," she said slowly. "Anything the MFDP can do to help the union keep going is important. But the party was organized because people couldn't have anything to say in the government. The union was organized because people couldn't get paid fair for what they were doin'. This union will give thousands of folks the chance to say: 'We want more for our work, or we're not gonna do it.' And that's somethin' that we've wanted to say all our lives!" The large face turned to watch the water cascading the fields. She grinned and tapped my knee with pleasure. "Oh, my! Look at it rain!"

Finally, the rain slackened, and we rolled down the windows of the car. A freshet of rain-fragrant air poured in. Mrs. Hamer's spirits were bubbling. "It's catchin' on, Tracy! I think the union will spread more and more. Five hundred people have walked off here in Washington County alone. Last week it was only eighty! It's catchin' on because folks are catchin' on. Even in areas where civil rights workers have never even been. They're goin' out on strike because they're tired. Tired. And I know how tired you get when you work from sun to sun for three dollars."

"It seems to me," I said, "that take-home pay must seem more important than a vote to lots of people down here who have never voted."

Mrs. Hamer's rich voice was low and intense. "At first. Maybe, at first. But once those folks come off the plantations on strike, they'll find out what's been goin' on. They want to know! They've found the strength to walk out on strike because they're hungry for something. When the MFDP tells them what their vote means, what it can do in support of their fight against the Man for a livin' wage, there'll be a whole lot of people who never cared about voting before that are goin' to become registered voters." Her voice was buoyant and confident.

I wheeled sharply in front of the church where she was scheduled to speak. As I pulled on the brake, I turned to grin at her. "From your lips to God's ear," I said with feeling. "I do know that you have a direct line upstairs, Mrs. Hamer. Look at those puddles!" I looked at this extraordinary woman whose faith and will had helped to turn the whole state around, who had kept her "eye on the prize," year after grinding year. "It's really been amazing, Mrs. Hamer. In one year you've had the birth of the MFDP, the congressional challenge in Washington, the Voting Rights Bill, and now the Mississippi Freedom Labor Union!" I shook my head. "Everything is new!"

The great brown face shone with pleasure. She tapped my arm, and her smile widened. She nodded. "Everything! Everything is new. And all of it is great!"

The hall was crowded with men and women of all ages. As the moderator posed a question, hands were raised by people eager to testify. The room was warm and hushed, more like a church meeting than a labor rally. The people strained to hear, silent and watchful. Only some of the old would interrupt with exclamations of "Yes! Oh, yes!" At the conclusion of each testimony the crowd would applaud enthusiastically. These were the families on strike. Their language was ungrammatical, quaint to ears tuned to the careful cadence of educated speech. With biblical images, they exhorted each other to "Be like Silas! Be like David!" They were full of homely advice on how to save their money for the lean weeks and months that stretched ahead.

When Mrs. Hamer rose to speak, her hoarse voice echoed through the hall. With passion she enlisted the biblical ranks of martyrs and heroes, summoning those still timid among them to rally to the Freedom Labor Union banner. Her rolling, building battery of quotations and allusions from the Old and the New Testaments stunned the audience with its

31. An elderly black tenant farmer.
"I remember the fever and the water was everywhere before they drained the fields."

thunder. "Pharaoh," she cried, "is right here in Washington County! Israel's children are building bricks without straw . . . at three lousy dollars a day!" Her voice broke, and tears stood in her eyes. "We're tired. And we're tired of bein' tired!"

As I looked at the intent faces of these sharecroppers and tenant farmers, betting their lives on this fragile challenge, daring to "speak truth to power," I thought that pioneers facing an ominous future must have congregated like this. These poorest of America's poor were building their courage in concert from hidden mines of heart and spirit.

"I can eat fish," said an old man. "An' if they's no fish, I can eat berries." He smiled. "An' if they's no berries, I still got two teeth left to gnaw grass with."

Return to the Lindseys

"Come the day after tomorra," Bette had said on the phone. "You can meet our new son. He arrived in November." I had wondered how she would sound. At Christmas I had sent them my card, a sketch of black and white kids racing across a meadow, and I had speculated about the Lindseys' reaction. Bette's voice was warm. "We got your card at Christmas, and we certainly appreciated hearing from you." I smiled. Noncommittal but not hostile. "Come about ten."

Bette led me through the new sunken living room. Two masons were chipping bricks for the raised Bermuda fireplace, oblivious to our passage across the room. "Did you notice I'm using Negro workmen?" she whispered. Her impudent grin lit her sunburned face as she led me onto the new patio. The year that had passed had done nothing to harness the irrepressible qualities of Bette Lindsey. Lake Lindsey unfolded from the wicker chair with the gracelessness of an overgrown boy. He held out his hand and smiled. "Glad to see you again, Tracy. Meet Dick Milburn."

A slim man in his late thirties stood at his side. He stepped forward, his head slightly extended in a frank and searching sweep of my face. "I'm happy to meet you," he said amiably in a gentle voice. "Bette and Lake had told me about you. I hope you've found the Delta interesting." His smile was disarming.

"I certainly have. That's why I've come back."

The conversation moved lazily through the heavy July air. The three had recently returned from a holiday in Yucatán, a celebration of the birth of young Kevin. "Dick is the only person in the whole world who could persuade Lake Lindsey to fly away from Ruleville on a vacation," purred Bette. She fondled the memories of the Yucatán like an excited child. Her eyes flashed, and an evil grin lit her expressive face. "Dick had told me that when we got to Mexico I should respond to any question in Spanish (which I do not understand—not one single word) by saying, 'No, no, no.' I'll tell you," she giggled, "one look at those Latin men, and I decided to say, 'Si, si, si!'"

Milburn's shoulders shook with silent laughter, relishing the story. Lake mopped his neck with a moist handkerchief, his narrowed eyes restlessly moving across the great glaring expanse of the sky. "It's damp as hell," he muttered, "but not a real rain in three weeks." He leaned forward, his thick arms making small, moist stains on his khaki pants. "Tell me, Tracy, what do you think about this Mississippi Freedom Labor Union?"

"Oh, no," groaned Bette. "I want to talk about the Yucatán!"

"I never heard about the union till the other day," I said. "What do you think?"

"Damn, damn, damn," muttered Bette and went to tend the waking baby.

Milburn stirred his coffee, listening attentively. Lake's eyes were bright. The face that had seemed so indolent in repose now was alert. "A dollar twenty-five an hour is going to hurt the niggers. Hurt them bad. In the end they'll be the ones to suffer. The plantation owners will have to let two-thirds of them go if the union insists on that kind of money." He tapped my knee. "Take my place. I've got more tenant families than most around here, almost thirty. If I have to pay a dollar and a quarter, I'll have to run twenty of them off my land. I'd hate like hell to do it, too." The wicker chair creaked as he leaned back, surveying the pearl brightness outside. "What's going to happen to those families? Just forget them? Let them starve to death?" His chin dropped to his chest, and his troubled eyes sought mine. "I've known most of those folks all my life."

"I don't know the answer," I said. "Maybe the government will have to subsidize people like they subsidize cotton, Lake. Come in and teach these folks some modern skills. Hasn't automation been pushing the Negroes off the land anyhow?"

Milburn, nodding quietly, set his coffee down. "That's true. These Delta towns have become the way stations north for the people being automated out. This union is just going to speed up the process." He relit his pipe and smiled at me over the flame. "I just read in a conservative magazine I'm sure you would not approve of, Tracy, an analysis of the problem the world faces trying to feed an exploding population. I assure you that within fifteen years the crisis will be very real. We're going to have to become very much more productive as farmers. My farm is a regular stop for the U.S. State Department tours for visiting agricultural people from all over the world. They're all looking for answers on how to speed up production. One of the answers is that stoop labor must be replaced with more efficient means." He tapped out the pipe and absently sucked on the stem. "The old plantation system created a monster of cheap, unskilled labor. It worked then. But it's got to go now, or it will strangle the South."

Bette had been standing in the doorway, listening attentively, her eyes moving from Milburn to Lake. I realized that Dick Milburn had tacitly been made their spokesman. Articulate and well educated, he spoke also with the authority of one who had proved himself a success in his sixteen years in Mississippi. Only a year before, Lake had struggled to explain and defend his point of view, apologizing for his own limitations. But he had honestly tried to describe his deep concerns about what would happen if change really came to the Delta. Now change, with passage of the Voting Rights Act, had come, and it was no longer "whether I would allow my niggers to vote." It was now worry that this new black dynamic would threaten his economic sinecure. He was struggling to keep his footing in this newly strange landscape, and he looked for help from people like Dick Milburn. His was a different voice than he had been weaned on, a voice that resonated less from the past. It was quiet, controlled, pragmatic, and urbane. And it spoke of the future, of a New South, and of a world that reached far beyond Lake Lindsey's Sunflower County.

When Milburn invited me home for lunch, I accepted gratefully, pleased to have the chance to talk further with this thoughtful man. Bette shook hands at the door as we left. Her eyes mirrored the annoyance she felt that the conversation had moved to talk of the Delta. "I wish we had time to really talk . . . about skiing resorts, and travel, and New York. It seems that in Ruleville, Tracy, we never get to talk about interesting things like that. We talk about small-town things . . . about whether the rain is going to come in time for the planting . . . and about each other! My, don't folks here love to talk about each other!" She brushed back a lock of damp hair, and her eyes became mischievous. "If they run out of things to talk about, I just walk to the Rexall Drugstore in short shorts, and they start all over again!"

Milburn held open the door for me as I stepped into the large, cool, and unfashionable rooms of the old house. He nodded toward the brightly flowered slipcovers of the living room furniture and made a face. "It's not very chic and not even my own sorry taste. I rent this place furnished. Been doing it for almost sixteen years. You remember bachelor quarters? Well, this is a cut above. But my housekeeper, Olivia, keeps my body and soul together." He crossed to the hall and stuck his head around the door leading to the kitchen. "Olivia, come see who our guest is for lunch."

A round, composed face appeared in the doorway as Olivia Waters calmly surveyed the new luncheon guest as I was being introduced. When the matronly, confident woman stepped into the room, her eyes narrowed and then smiled. "I do believe I saw Mr. Sugarman once at Sunday service last year. You were with Rennie Williams. Now, isn't that nice that you've come back to Ruleville!" She turned to look at Milburn. "This house is too quiet, Mr. Sugarman. Just Mr. Richard and me most of the time. I'm glad he asked you to come." Her words were unadorned and unapologetic. The affection beneath the words was accepted and understood. "Let me go set a place," and she moved swiftly down the hall.

"Like I said," laughed Milburn, "body and soul!" Richard's pride in his cotton operation was obvious as he moved about the den he used as an office. With enthusiasm he explained the organization of his nine hundred acres. Full-color photographs of planting, of snowy harvests, of green vistas that stretched to the Delta horizon, of combines, of tractors, of foreign visitors were spread before me like a family album.

"The plantation looks beautiful, Richard. Particularly these pictures at harvest time. I've never been here for that."

He nodded. "It is beautiful. It's not the Kodachrome!" He scooped up the pictures and bent to slip them into a drawer. As he settled back in his leather chair, I was struck by the sudden seriousness of his expression. His fingers drummed against the edge of the desk. "But it's not a plantation. It's a farm. I dislike the word *plantation*." The distinction seemed to be very important to him, as if the acknowledgment would somehow make him vulnerable. "It's just a farm. A damn good one, too." His face suddenly softened, and he smiled. "Even though my friends, the Lindseys, have called me "the gentleman farmer from California" all these years to kid me, I'm not a 'gentleman farmer.' I work too damn hard for that!"

Luncheon was served by a smiling Olivia, and Milburn was a gracious and relaxed host. Afterward we settled to talk in the living room as rain began to spatter against the windows.

"Lake finally got his rain," I said, watching the furrows in the fields rapidly becoming puddles that seemed to stretch forever.

He nodded, stuffing his pipe. "I never realized how important weather was till I started farming in the Delta." He smiled. "Although my friend Bette really does hate the idea, I do believe that weather truly is our favorite subject of conversation."

We sat quietly, watching the rain clouds move across the shining fields as the rain slowly lessened. Only the dripping from the elms beside the house broke the comfortable silence.

"Dick," I said, rising to leave, "you've lived most of your life away from here. Your perspective is a different one from Lake's. What is it that keeps good people like the Lindseys so out of step with the consensus of the country? Is it the local radio? The TV? The newspapers? What keeps them from knowing the score?"

He shook his head and frowned. "I disagree with your premise. You assume that they're unsophisticated because they refuse to join the national consensus. You think that they're prisoners of their local radios and their local papers." He stood and faced me. "You think that they don't really know what's going on. You're wrong—they get the news. From magazines, from letters, from their kids in the service, even from the television that comes into the state. No, Tracy. In some ways they're the most politically savvy people I've ever met. It's not that they don't know the score." His eyes were cool and candid. "It's that they don't like the score."

Once I had caught up with Charles McLaurin, I eased happily back into the warm company of an old and valuable friend. As always, he was my wise Baedecker to the ways and wiles of change in the Delta. And as always, my rental car gave him the wings to cover the terrain he needed to monitor.

Early in June we were heading back to Indianola after meeting with the executive committee of the MFDP. The Chevy purred quietly, moving north through the velvet darkness of the Delta. We rode for several minutes in silence, enjoying the cool of the air. Sharecropper shacks with tiny pinpoints of light seemed etched against the star-filled sky, looking like forlorn boats in the great expanse of the fields.

"We don't have farms like this up home," I said. "These just go on and on, for thousands of acres sometimes. Feels like we couldn't fit a baker's dozen of these in Connecticut! Earlier this week, Mac, I met Lake Lindsey again, touching base after being away for a year. And I met his friend Dick Milburn, who also has a large spread. You ever meet them?"

"Never had the pleasure," he chuckled.

"Well, they are genuinely worried about the radical changes they see coming with the Mississippi Freedom Labor Union and the new political power shifting with the Voting Rights Act. They're afraid that tax reforms will be passed by the Negroes that will break up the large landholdings. Do you think that's likely to really happen?" I stole a look at McLaurin. His face was turned toward the fields. The pale light from the dashboard defined the thick chest and shoulders, but the face was just a darker blur against the night sky. He continued to stare at the shrouded landscape before he answered.

"I think it probably will, eventually. Landowners like Lindsey and Perkins, with thousands of acres of land, really control all the wealth of these little communities. The towns are built around the plantations, and they depend completely on them. The owners have everything: the land, the tools, and the capital. Most Negroes own nothing but their labor. If they start to vote, certainly they're going to vote to tax the Man. It'll only be right if they do. The Man has always gotten his land for little or nothing, while the Negro pays high taxes on every dollar he makes." He paused and turned to stare at the road that raced ever away from the

Chevy's headlights. "And you know, you've been down here, he doesn't make many dollars here in the Delta." He shifted in his seat and faced me. "Yeah. I can see it happening. I guess historically it's happened that way before." With a slight smile and a faraway look, he said, "During Reconstruction."

Durrough

during the months I had been back home, an ambitious fund-raising effort was undertaken in the North to build a community center for the black community in Ruleville. Triggered by Linda Davis's family in Illinois and our efforts in Connecticut and Boston, the drive had been successful, and I was eager to discuss the project with Mayor Durrough when I returned in 1965.

Rising, he turned to face me where I stood just inside his office door. The sentinel face was unchanged by the year. The salt-and-pepper hair, a little longer, seemed grayer. His chin was down, creasing the jowl that matched the small paunch of his stomach. His eyes were careful as he regarded me over the horn-rimmed glasses.

"Sugarman," he said.

"How are you, Mayor?" We shook hands briefly, and he motioned me to a chair. Heavily, he eased into his own behind the desk.

"I'm pleased you remembered me," I said. "It's been almost a whole year."

With a fugitive half-smile, he pulled open his desk drawer. He lifted a sheaf of stapled newspaper clippings and waved them next to his ear. "Oh, I keep up with you." The voice was toneless. His eyes narrowed, and his mouth was tight. I squinted across the desk and recognized that the top clipping was from my hometown newspaper. It was a news story about our fund-raising efforts for a community center in the Sanctified Quarter of Ruleville. A satisfied smile spread as he watched me intently.

"Yeah. People send me things, and I manage to know something about you."

32. Three ladies from the Sanctified Quarter.
"This little light of mine, I'm gonna let it shine!"

"Well, that's fine. Then we don't have to talk about me," I said. "I don't know a thing about you. I've come down here to see what's been happening in Ruleville over the year."

His voice was chilly, and for the first time a smile creased his face. "A citizen up your way wrote this office that a damn Jew was coming down here with four thousand dollars for a community center for the niggers. That about right, Sugarman?"

I laughed. "He was wrong, Mayor. It's six thousand dollars. I've been doing a lot of talking up there in Connecticut about your Ruleville, so the folks up home have been working very hard." I studied the flushed face across the desk. "And so have the folks up in Boston, and the folks out in Illinois. It's six thousand dollars."

Durrough shifted in his seat, stooping to open a drawer. He took out a subdivision map of Ruleville and laid it flat on the desk. "You'll be interested in this," he said curtly. His finger pointed out the land that had been acquired for the center. "They want to build here."

"I know," I said. "I hope you're pleased about it. They need it over in the quarter. It should be good for the town."

He shrugged. "They can do anything they want. I'm not against it. But look here." One finger rested on the acquired land, and the other hand swept across the town expanse. "The land they got is a far spot from most of the Negro community. I think a center should be closer to the heart of the quarter." His stubby finger moved to the cotton field that lay along the highway. "This land is adjacent to the Negro high school. I think I could get the town to acquire it and swap land with the center people. Don't you agree it would be a better location?" He leaned back and waited for my reply.

"I can see your point, Mayor, but I don't have anything to do with it. That's the business of the Ruleville Community Center Trust. I think you ought to talk with some of the officers of the center . . . Mr. McDonald, Mr. Foster, Linda Davis, Charles McLaurin. After all, they raised nine hundred dollars for that land among the folks in the quarter. We outsiders are only interested in helping them get a building up."

He was plainly annoyed and started to fold up the map. "I talked to Foster. They don't want to swap," he said angrily. His eyes swung up and held mine. "So I thought I'd bring it to your attention."

I leaned toward the desk and put my finger on the acquired land. "I don't know, but I suspect their objection to swapping is one of security. At your location, they'll be vulnerable to any redneck who drives by and decides to heave a gasoline bottle. The site they've picked is on a dead-end road." I glanced at Durrough. "After all, Mayor, that's a real consideration. It's happened in Mississippi. The Indianola Community Center was burned to the ground last fall."

The flush on Durrough's face deepened. He scratched his chin and nodded slightly. "That's true, of course," he said, "but we've been able to hold that element down in this area. It's not a problem here." His voice rose. "We haven't let it become one, either!"

"Mayor," I said softly, "you had a cross burned on your lawn last fall for starting a small Negro job-training program. I read about it in the New York papers. I'm very sorry."

"That's so. And poison-pen letters, too." His eyes clouded, and he cleared his throat abruptly. "But that's a very small element, very small. I'd say that at least two-thirds of the town, white and colored, are prepared to go along with the movement now."

"What movement?" I asked cautiously.

"The movement in civil rights, the federal programs. Look here." His fingers moved along the roads in the Negro sections of Ruleville. Each had been marked with a red pencil. "The red-penciled roads indicate the federal housing project we're hoping to get started. Paving roads. Adding sewers and curbs." His pencil stabbed the Sanctified Quarter on the map, and his voice was querulous. "That quarter provided only about twenty-two hundred dollars in tax revenue. The road program for them will cost about sixty-five thousand. Without help from Washington, it would take thirty years to pay for it."

"If those folks had been educated properly and given some skills other than chopping cotton, you'd be getting a hell of a lot more than twenty-two hundred dollars, Mayor."

He tossed the pencil on the map and rocked back in his chair. The heavy brows met in a dark, disapproving line. "We inherited a lot of problems. We didn't invent them all." His voice was caustic. "You can make a good case that the Negro has been an albatross around the neck of the South, holding us back all these years."

"He didn't ask to come, Mayor," I said.

There was silence as he rose from the desk and raised the dusty window, seeking any vagrant breeze from the sun-filled street. Turning from the window he returned to his desk. His aggrieved voice broke the silence. "Just wait. If we get an urban renewal program into Ruleville, you all will be hollering that we're grabbing up the poor Negroes' property."

"Mayor, can I ask you a frank question?" His heavy brows rose as he settled back in his chair. He nodded. "Last summer you sat in that chair and told me you were convinced that the Negroes shot up their own houses in order to get publicity and money for the movement. And when

Williams Chapel was burned, you said the Negroes had done it. Now you've had a cross burned on your lawn because you started a small program of job-training for Negroes." I stared at him. "Do you still believe what you believed then?"

His eyes regarded me seriously. "Yes, I do. I didn't say last year that our Negroes shot up their houses. I said it was outside civil rights agitators. I still say so. And I still say there were people in the movement who set fire to Williams Chapel."

I couldn't conceal my irritation and astonishment at the willful obtuseness of the man. "Isn't it more logical to believe that the element who would burn a cross in your yard would fire a church? Does it make sense for a poor congregation to set fire to a church they can't even afford to repair?"

He smiled cynically, massaging the fleshy end of his nose. His eyes narrowed, and he chuckled. "Sure, I believe it. Fannie Lou Hamer used that church all over this country to raise money for the movement." His gaze moved to the steamy, noiseless street beyond the window. When he spoke again, his voice was so quiet that I had to strain to hear him. "I'll say this. I think a lot of us in this state wish we had done some things differently. Some of us wish we hadn't said what we said, or said it differently. I think a lot of us regret a lot of it." He shook his head, annoyed with himself, and straightened in his chair. "But the train is pulling out." His ponderous words filled the stuffy office. "You either got to get on it or get left." The big hands laced behind his neck, and he leaned back, studying the dusty ceiling. "It's hard to change everything . . . all at once." His voice took on a warmth that had not been there all morning. "I've got sons, and grandsons." His chair came abruptly up. "They have a different world. Another generation is going to see a lot of the hard core of the South burn out. I just got back from Atlanta, and I can see what's coming. Not quite here yet in the Delta, but it's coming. I'll tell you this." His voice growled, and the large head swung to challenge me. "There's always going to be white leadership! There has to be! Look at those Caribbean islands. They've been free a long time, and what's come out of them? Nothing! They're black and they're free . . . and they've produced nothing!" His voice was triumphant.

"I've been to those islands, Mayor. They're one-crop islands with people who are as poor and uneducated as the cotton choppers in Ruleville. Those islands are company towns, and the Negro doesn't own the company. But look at Africa. In a decade you're going to see great universities and industries, run and owned by blacks."

He shook his head hard. "Not without white leadership."

I stood to go, and he walked outside with me, locking the office as we went. We stood for a moment in the shadow of the tree that draped the tiny jail in shade. I sensed that the early hostility of the morning had quite melted away. "Mayor Durrough, in a couple of years half of this town that never voted before is going to be voting. Is it going to change things?"

He gazed across the road at the tiny fly-specked pool parlor. The window now boasted a freshly painted sign: RECREATION CENTER—PRIVATE CLUB. I had to smile. It was Ruleville's answer to passage of the Civil Rights Act opening public accommodations. The mayor shook his head slightly and turned to me. "If the Negroes put up a competent candidate, they might elect him," he said dryly.

"You know," I said, "in Tuskegee, Alabama, they had enough Negro votes to elect all Negroes to the boards if they wanted. Instead, they elected the best candidates, white and black. They'll vote for the people who will give them a fair shake." He remained silent, squinting in the glare. "You ought to be grateful to the movement, Mayor Durrough. It's giving the good young people a reason to stay and help solve the problems here. Kids like McLaurin, who are going to college and learning about government and sociology. They're giving you a hard time meanwhile." He looked sharply at me, and I grinned. "But they're going to make a big difference. They may even help save Mississippi!"

We shook hands at the corner. "I'm finishing office this term, and I'm done," he said. "It's not going to affect me one way or another. But I'll tell you one thing: in five years McLaurin will have his degree and make some money. And then he'll move out of the Negro neighborhood. Just wait and see."

"If you'd bet on it, Mayor, you've got a taker."

seventeen

Richard

i woke early on a steamy June morning, moving quietly so as not to rouse the Williamses. But there was no escaping the sharp ears and insatiable curiosity of Rennie Williams. As I tiptoed across the worn linoleum to the door, I could hear her voice: "Sharon, go tell Tracy he ain't had breakfast yet." Then her voice rose: "Where in the world you goin' so early anyway, Tracy?" She was pulling a cotton wrapper around her as the bedroom door swung open, and Sharon toddled across to embrace my leg.

"Good morning, Mrs. Williams," I said, laughing. "Will you please retrieve this child so I can get out to my car?"

"Sharon, honey, Tracy says he's leavin'. Don't know to where, 'cuz he ain't saying. So just let him go. Let him go." Her eyebrows arched, and she stood next to the door, arms akimbo. "So why you stealin' out like a robber?"

"Because I didn't want to wake you. And I wanted to get an early start. I'm going across the river to Arkansas. Today is my son's birthday, and I want to bring him a little present in Forrest City."

"Your son's in Forrest City? How come your son's in Forrest City and you ain't never told me before?"

"Because I haven't had a minute alone with you and Mr. Williams since I got here. We'll talk tonight when I get back."

"But you don't have any present," she persisted. "What are you going to give your boy on his birthday?"

"I'm picking up a fire extinguisher down at Hartman's Hardware," I said, and ducked out the door before Mrs. Williams could say another word. Richard's request for a fire extinguisher had been relayed the night before from Forrest City by a SNCC fieldworker en route to COFO headquarters

132

33. Mrs. Rennie Williams.
"We lives next to schoolteachers . . . scaird schoolteachers!"

down in Jackson. It was a troubling request, and I was eager to get going early, anxious now to get to my son on the other side of the river.

Soon after he had returned to Brown after working with the carpenter volunteers on the Selma march, he had decided he wanted to continue his involvement with the movement once school was over. "I want to do something, folks," he told us at spring break. "I saw the momentum in Selma. SNCC was in the forefront down in Alabama, and they're going to need all the available northern kids to help keep it moving." In a Boston paper he had seen that SNCC was looking for carpenters to go to Forrest City, Arkansas, where a Freedom House had been set ablaze by night riders, and he had called home from Brown. "They need college students who know how to swing a hammer. And I know how to swing a hammer." There had been a long silence as June and I stared at each other. "That's okay with you guys, right?"

When I found him at the site of the burned-out Freedom House, he embraced me and then stepped back, grinning. "Heck of a place for a birthday party, Pop! Wish Mom and Laurie were here." When I dug the fire extinguisher from the brown paper bag on the front seat he whooped, "Oh, yes!" and called three young men and a redheaded girl from the Freedom House. "Come meet my old man and see what he brought us!"

"What happened here, Rich?"

"Last month, when I was still at school, the Klan and the White Citizens Council people torched this Freedom House. So when we all got here two weeks ago, the place was uninhabitable. The roof was gone and so was most of the interior. So we've been hard at it, and the Klan keeps giving us a hard time."

"A hard time," I said. "What do you mean by 'a hard time'?"

His coworkers exchanged glances, shook hands with me, and returned to the work on the roof. "What do you mean by a hard time, Rich?"

"They play hardball down here, Pop. Every night, for two weeks, they've been shooting at the house. And at least six times we've had Molotov cocktails land on the repaired roof. And everybody from the police chief down knows what's happening and who's doing it." He examined my stricken face and chuckled. "Sound like Mississippi? But don't worry. We're not sleeping here. Mr. Clay gave this building to the movement to be used as a Freedom School. But until we get it in shape, we're sleeping at the Clay's Funeral Home just over there."

When he led me out of the blazing Arkansas sunlight into the semi-darkness of the basement of the funeral home, I could barely see. A strong aroma of formaldehyde made my eyes tear, and when I had blinked them away, I saw the four cadavers. Between them were the neatly covered cots of the civil rights workers. I swung my head to see Richard. He stood quietly by the door, watching me.

"Rich," I said, "you sleep here?"

He nodded. "Just till we finish the Freedom House." When he saw the expression on my face, he tapped my shoulder reassuringly and grinned. "You don't have to tell Mom." He held open the door, and I stepped quickly out into the sunshine, breathing deep in the damp Delta air. "That first week was really bizarre, Pop. I didn't know dead people make noises."

"Noises?"

"Oh, yeah. Cadavers make noises as ligaments and muscles go into rigor mortis." He laughed. "They *creak!* To tell you the truth, I was glad I was turning nineteen today. I wasn't sure at eighteen I could really handle it!"

When I backed out the rutty road from the Freedom House, Richard waved and then headed back to work with the others on the charred roof. I watched my tall nineteen-year-old in the rearview mirror until I reached the highway and he was lost from sight.

Linda

When I reunited with Linda Davis, I was struck by the gravity of her demeanor, the quiet watchfulness of the merry young woman I remembered from our Freedom School. "How was it, Linda? All that I really knew up home was that it sounded hard. For a while I was sending books to McLaurin at the Indianola jail, and then I knew he went back to college. But it was hard getting real news from down here. I thought about you, down here alone, wondering how you were managing to keep warm, let alone safe."

She tried to smile, but her gentle voice sounded hushed with sadness as she struggled to answer. "It was terrible, Tracy. I wasn't really ever alone. There was the staff in Indianola for company, but the staff was demoralized. We all watched it happening, helpless and miserable." Bitterness and dissension had grown like a rank weed in Indianola. Springing from the frustration in the unnatural heat of a besieged fort, it had all but destroyed the staff during the bleak months of winter. Personalities had become unbearably abrasive. There seemed to be no way of healing the thousand tiny wounds that bedeviled the young people. They had been inflicted during the days and nights of arrests that followed the picketing of the public library, the torching of the community center they so cherished, the beatings in Inverness and Moorhead, the bombings that had leveled the Negro homes in Indianola. The fury that had been fed by the faceless destroyers and the arrogant police rose like hateful bile. Having no natural release, it turned inward. It seized on petty alliances and suspected ambitions, alienating friends and robbing the vitality that had marked the promise of last summer's beginning. Linda's voice trembled.

34. Linda Davis with Freedom School students.
"You can paint the same brick with three colors if you want!"

"When word came in May that McLaurin was coming back from school to head up the project, some of us cried in relief."

Reflecting on that dreadful winter, Linda's eyes grew wide and troubled. "All hell had broken loose in Indianola," she said wonderingly. "There were a lot of arrests in Indianola, and a lot of burning. We had conducted statewide demonstrations to build support for passage of the Voting Rights Bill, and they were hugely successful events. We had hundreds of people circling the Indianola courthouse. Imagine. Hundreds of people in the very home of the White Citizens Council." A great smile broke out on Linda's face. "I never saw Charles McLaurin that happy. I think that after his jailings and his beatings, he felt that he had confronted death. And in an existential way, he had already died. So now anything beyond that was gravy. It was wonderful to see. Maybe it was religious,

I really don't know. But it gave him an incredible ability to operate in the face of fear." She paused. "All I can say is that I never got to that point," and burst out laughing. "I almost always felt safe when I was in the black community. I knew there were people there who would lay down their lives to protect me. But on the night the Freedom School in Indianola was bombed, it was just awful and very frightening. There were four separate fire attacks on the school, all orchestrated to hit about nine in the evening. There was nobody there, and the building was burned and gutted. At the same time the arsonists attacked the house where all of us civil rights workers were living. I literally saw the Molotov cocktail sail in the window, land in the front bedroom, and burst into flame. The house burned very quickly." She blinked hard, and the room was silent. She cleared her throat and quietly resumed speaking. "We all had to flee for our lives."

"Did you ever find out who did it, Linda?" I asked.

"Not really," she answered. "Some of the neighbors had seen all of the streetlights go out on the block in front of our house just before the bombing, so it certainly made us wonder who was involved and to what extent. The next day we went to the Freedom School to find our voter registration files because we didn't want the local authorities to have those names, and we all got arrested for 'failing to obey a police officer' who ordered us to leave. So after being burned and bombed, we were now being jailed." She laughed, still in disbelief of that winter when violence was just around the next corner, and justice was something much further away. Linda's eyes became misty as she resurrected those excruciating nights in the Delta. "To witness the courage of those folks in Indianola was so remarkable. Remembering how they kept going forward, even when there was no assurance that there was ever going to be a good result . . . to just keep on going. And they did it. And they did it again."

If the staff was shaken and exhausted, McLaurin was not. He returned from Mississippi Valley State bursting with energy and plans. There was no dramatic confrontation or showdown. Mac had once confessed to me that he considered leadership to be showmanship, and like a sensitive actor he had a sure instinct when to move and when to be still. Instead of ministering to the staff's bruised feelings, he set to work on programs of action that would demand all their youthful energies. "They're not going to have time to brood," he told me. "In a week this program's gonna be rolling, and there's going to be just too much to do." He had been right. The emotionally drained staff had turned gratefully to the work ahead.

I studied the weary young face of Linda Davis. "Lin," I said, "have you thought about going home? Christ knows, you've more than paid your dues. When they needed you here in Ruleville last winter, you hung in. But maybe it's time now to let go . . . to go home."

"I want to stay on here in Ruleville," she answered softly. "It's for me. It's my need. Having been here has given me the courage to say that. Definitely. I'm down here for myself." Her voice had a high, piping quality, hushed, a little breathless. "I don't want to get into a mystical kind of thing that we're doing. We're organizing along political lines, trying to give people political power, so I don't want anyone to think I've got my head in the clouds."

"You've become part of this community," I said. "At least Mrs. Williams and Mrs. Hamer believe that."

She was still, and there was a catch in her voice when she spoke again. "Just who is contributing to whom is the question. I feel guilty sometimes, and I wonder, 'Jesus! Am I really doing any work? Am I more of a hindrance than a help?' It makes me feel panicky sometimes. What am I doing to help people? Am I down here so much for my own sake that it's wrong? Maybe I'm not in a position to judge because when I talked to Mrs. Hamer about it, she seemed really to feel that there has been some contribution. If my being here with Mrs. Hamer, our talks together, our friendship, has helped her to keep going, then maybe that was my contribution. Maybe I've helped a few people like that, maybe the McDonalds." Linda stopped, and a small, warm laugh bubbled in the darkness. "I was just thinking how I've helped Mr. and Mrs. McDonald. I've worried them sick!" Her voice melted with the affection she felt for the aged couple.

"When I was arrested the second time up in Drew last spring, the whole community knew about it immediately because so many Ruleville people were up there with me. Poor Mr. McDonald. When he heard the news of the arrest he had a relapse with his bad heart. When my father came down to visit, he stayed with the McDonalds. When he left, he said to Mr. McDonald, 'You see after Linda and take care of her for me.' Mr. McDonald, of course, took this to the bottom of his heart. And when he heard I was in jail, he felt he had let my father down. Then some lady came into the quarter swearing she had seen my car somewhere in a ditch between Ruleville and Cleveland. So who gets into his truck and trudges off into the night searching for me? Mr. McDonald." Her voice trailed off. "Some helper."

"McLaurin thinks you're on the same wavelength with the community, and that you're operating the way you have to down here. Maybe you feel guilty because you're not functioning at all in the way you imagined you would when you were back at Oberlin."

"Oh, that's so true. It's funny. I go back north, and people say, 'What do you *do?*' and I don't know what to say! 'Well, there's this community, see . . . ,' She broke off, giggling. "It's awful trying to explain what I do to people who work from nine to five. I start to feel guilty that I don't put in a full eight-hour day, and then I figure, 'Hell, I don't get paid that much anyway!'" She hooted with laughter. "No one," she gasped, "would work for these wages! Ten dollars a week for a SNCC staff person . . . when we get paid. My parents used to supplement my pay, but I learned something about money. The middle-class value of having something in reserve doesn't exist down here."

"Maybe that's because there's no middle class down here," I said.

Linda chuckled. "Maybe. It's become kind of a game with me, seeing how fast I can get rid of money. Going broke and still living! You share when you have a little money, and when it's gone someone else shares."

"Have your political ideas changed, Linda?"

"I'm very naive politically, more now in some respects than when I came down. I'm less willing to compromise than I was before. It's given me such new ideas to consider. New ways of thinking, of listening, of letting other people talk, letting ideas come forth. I don't think our political system encourages that enough. But I get so frustrated at times. I get caught between the pragmatic and the idealistic, between Bob Moses and Guyot. All this political education and participation is fine, but we're not electing anybody, either. And then there's my dad, who I have great respect for as a man of principle. He's very politically oriented and really believes in the workability of our institutions. So I have all sorts of questions in my mind. What's more important? Having this kind of grassroots political organizing or electing one significant person to a political position who could maybe put a factory in this town? I don't have the answer. But at this point I'm not going to knock out any approach that can help bring change here."

"McLaurin wrote me from jail that you were in good hands in Ruleville last winter," I said. "Between the McDonalds and Cephus Smith, he knew you were going to make it through. I remember Joe McDonald and Mrs. McDonald very well. But who is Cephus Smith?"

Linda's face lit up when I asked about Cephus. "Cephus was always there for me. Always." Her eyes were warm in recollection as she described how the young Ruleville man had run interference for her, easing the suspicions of some of the Negro community who wondered at the motives that would keep a young white girl working in that freezing farmhouse during the bone-chilling winter months. "When the whites in Ruleville would cuss me out, it would be Cephus who was always there to reassure me. 'Just forget it,' he'd say. 'You'll hear it every day.' And that made it a lot easier for me."

Cephus

i found him with a few other teenagers in the yard of the mostly abandoned Freedom House. Without the remembered frantic and noisy confusions of the young people that had filled the yard with laughter in the previous summer, the old farmhouse once more appeared the weary relic we had rescued. When he caught my eye, I waved him over to my car.

"Good to see you again," he said, a shy smile easing the serious young face.

"Climb in, Cephus. Any friend of Linda Davis ought to be a friend of mine." I looked curiously at the young man. Try as I might, I could not really remember talking with him the summer before. He had merely been one of the pack of boys who moved on the periphery of the movement. Tentatively poised at the back of a mass meeting at Williams Chapel, they appeared always ready for flight. Or lounging, elaborately relaxed, at the end of the Freedom School porch. I never quite knew if they belonged to the classes that met on the lawn. But they were never quite out of earshot. They were boisterous as they played "rough tackle" on the parched dirt yard of the Sanctified Church next door, hard-muscled bodies thudding against each other without any protective equipment. Their shouts of exuberant laughter splashed the summer stillness. They had moved around and about the Freedom House all summer, shy of the teachers, nudging and grinning at each other as they edged ever closer to the discussions on the lawn.

The lean, broad-shouldered nineteen year old looked straight ahead. A foolish plaid hat with a skinny brim was tipped low over his forehead, not quite shielding the late afternoon sun from his eyes. His skin was a burnt sienna brown that glistened in the warm light.

35. Three teenage boys from Ruleville.

"They watch everything at the Freedom School and miss nothing."

36. The blessed shadow of the Sanctified Church.
"Shade from the Sanctified Church."

"It feels so different from last summer," I said. "Must feel even more different for you with all of the summer volunteers gone."

He nodded and turned in his seat to look me in the face and to answer. I strained to listen, for his voice was at once husky and shy. "Last summer was very different for me. I'd never known any white kids before last summer. It meant somethin' to be around white kids—to be able to say what I wanted to say." He continued to stare through the dusty windshield at the disordered yard of the Ruleville Community Center. "It meant somethin' not to be afraid to say it. I was sort of suspicious that they didn't mean what they were saying. It wasn't till I got to know Linda Davis that I got confident about the teachers." He smiled at the memory. "And then, in September, after all of the summer volunteers left, Linda stayed on to run the community center by herself. I was around and had nothin' else to do—I had graduated from high school—so I'd drop around and do what I could to help. I knew she was going to need somebody to help keep it goin'." His voice dropped, and he shifted on the seat, frowning at the orange disk of sun that was framed in the center of the windshield. "I felt that white people like Linda, who had left their homes to come down here to work with us, needed someone here to work with them. So I decided to make her happy, make her feel like she was home."

Through the long months of the Delta winter and spring, Smith had worked tirelessly with Linda and Mrs. Hamer on voter registration drives in Drew and Indianola. He wished to emulate Charles McLaurin both in his leadership skills and in his aspirations. "Mac is a good leader," he said firmly. "We're working together now in the Mississippi Freedom Democratic Party. We have to help change this state." New vistas of the possible were becoming apparent to Cephus. "I'm goin' to Tougaloo in the fall," he said with a touch of pride. "And then I'm goin' into politics. Sometimes I think I ought to stay here in Ruleville just to challenge the mayor." He grinned. "And sometimes I think I ought to challenge the governor!"

I laughed with him. "Run against the governor?"

He shook his head and chuckled. "No. I'll start from the bottom of things." The dry understatement made me peer closely at him. Here was one of the first crop, I thought, one of the directionless kids from the Freedom School last summer. Yet he had clearly taken root during that long, hot crucible of '64. How many others, I wondered, who seemed always to be running elsewhere, never listening, never meeting your eyes, never seeming to be engaged in the grand design of the movement, had really listened? Had really drawn conclusions? Might even now be putting out green shoots of curiosity and aspiration? How many, like Cephus Smith, might really have rooted in the rich, black soil of last summer's struggle?

"Tell me," I urged, "what advice would you give a volunteer who wanted to come work here in the Delta?"

He gazed at me for a long moment. "I'd tell him to be patient with the people." His voice was low, filled with tenderness. For the first time I realized how sensitive an organism lived inside the boyish figure in the absurd hat. His voice rumbled gently in the overheated car. "You have to be patient. When you talk with the people here about the movement, give them time to think it over. Because people are easy to hurt."

The sun had dropped below the horizon, leaving a gaudy smear of rose and pink. It softened and suffused the fields and the houses of the quarter. "You have to give them time," Cephus continued quietly. "When they say, 'Come back tomorra and I'll tell ya what I think about it,' wait until tomorra and go back and see them. There was a bad experience last spring, before the Summer Project got started. Some black students who were down here from Tuskegee to work on the voter drive with us spoke to some folks on the street, askin' them to go down to the courthouse and try to register to vote. When they didn't go, the guys from Tuskegee called them 'Uncle Toms.'" The young face winced at the memory. "Those folks were so hurt that they wouldn't even talk to me."

In the fading light, a tiny girl in a faded shift moved out to the stoop of Mrs. Johnson's little grocery on the corner. She pulled the wrapper from a bright-blue Popsicle and let it flutter to the ground as she settled on the top step. She stared, unmoving, at the frozen delight in her hand. Tentatively, she explored the ice with the tip of her tongue, and smiled. I found myself smiling with her. I cocked my head and looked at the serious young face beside me. "Do you feel optimistic about your future in Mississippi, Cephus?"

"No. No, I don't," he replied somberly.

"Oh? Well, do you think you'll see radical changes in your lifetime?" I persisted.

His serious face never changed. "I know I will. There will be changes, but I can't see how the changes will be."

I grinned at him. "I wish you luck, Cephus!"

He looked at me, surprised. "I have luck," he said.

Marguerite

a small addition was being constructed at the Negro high school. White carpenters shifted lumber as a ragged handful of Negro children, playing tag, scattered like sparrows across the tufted weeds of the playground. I slowed my car as I spotted an eighteen-year-old girl carrying a tiny infant in a flowered cotton wrapper. She stepped from the doorstep of a small, patched house that sat silhouetted against an immense cotton field beyond, and paused to watch my car. I smiled, remembering Marguerite from last summer, and recalling her unquenchable humor during the tight moments of the arrests in Drew.

She cocked her head and stared at the car. The slim, girlish figure moved closer, and then she recognized me. Her intelligent eyes crinkled, and she broke into warm laughter. "For heaven's sakes! I thought you were a bill collector! When did you get back?"

A clean and shiny sedan moved past us. It turned abruptly into the driveway of the comfortable white frame house that lay shaded by the maples in the schoolyard. I recognized the tall, slender Negro who swung from the car and mounted the steps to the porch. It was Principal Smith. Marguerite's eyes followed the figure until the screen door slammed. The tiny tip of her pink tongue moved along the full upper lip. She frowned, patting the tiny back of the infant that nestled against her shoulder. "Uncle Tom," she said. Her voice was flat and cold.

Marguerite's youth group that had formed last summer had tangled with the principal. Deputations had gone repeatedly to visit Smith's office, accompanied during the summer by Len Edwards. They had asked for an accounting of funds earned by the children during the cotton harvest

"These folks are so scared in Drew!
If only they would come to a meeting in
Ruleville!"

37. Three teenage canvassers from Ruleville.

"These folks are so scared in Drew! If only they would come to a meeting in Ruleville!"

when classes had been delivered in trucks to work on the plantations. No child had ever received a nickel, and all wages had been paid directly to the school. Marguerite said that they had argued against summer sessions for Negro children in the sweltering fields, an arrangement designed nicely to allow the Negro children to harvest the cotton for the white plantation owners in September and October.

"We also petitioned for library cards to the town public library, and insisted that Mr. Smith and the teachers go to Indianola and register to vote." Her eyes were bright with mischief and resolve. The petitions had been met with petulance and annoyance at first. The principal had been personally affronted by the students' demands. Word was passed that Smith had said that Marguerite "should beg the principal's forgiveness, on hands and knees if necessary, for embarrassing him so." The deputations continued, and the annoyance became hostility. Harried and disturbed by the "impertinent questions," the principal had called Mayor Durrough. Policemen had appeared at the school, and the deputations ceased.

A gulf had grown between the aroused and militant young people and the frightened school administration that was attempting to hold the line against change. Inevitably, it ended in a deep contempt by the students for the Negro arm of the establishment. An attempt on the part of the authorities to bridge the gulf abolished the summer sessions but brought no real reconciliation.

The students, who in their Freedom School classes had begun for the first time to value and delight in fine adult books, pressed their demands for access to the Ruleville Public Library. Finally, and reluctantly, their demand for library cards had been approved, but with a proviso. "All our cards had to be endorsed by a small list of Negroes drawn up by the mayor. And we said, 'No!'" Their cries for equality continued to embarrass the school authorities.

I sat motionless at the wheel after Marguerite had returned to her house, studying the principal's shiny sedan in my mirror. How terrible and sad a word, "Tom." She had spat it like a curse. When change would come to the Delta, I realized with a shock, it would not come from the educated, "acceptable" Negro. It would come from the disinherited and the uneducated adults whose lives had been stripped of all but desperation. And it would come from the kids, thirsting for knowledge that they now knew was there to be had . . . and for the power that they were just beginning to understand.

Liz

Liz Fusco had not gone home when the students departed at summer's end. She had left Ruleville and for five months had toured Mississippi, distributing educational materials to the widely scattered Freedom Schools. On my return to the Delta, when I found her at an organizing meeting of the Mississippi Freedom Labor Union in the poor, tiny town of Shaw, I was eager to learn why she was here rather than out with the Freedom School projects. One look at the usually vivacious teacher I remembered from the Freedom School made it clear that the months between had been a severe test for this introspective and questioning young woman.

"I was learning things, Tracy," she said soberly. "It took me all last winter and this spring to learn, painfully, that 'educational materials' is not the answer. Dealing with people is the answer." She hesitated, seeking the way to articulate properly the process of change she had observed. "All of us who came down here last summer as teachers came because we thought schooling was important. For us, schooling meant classes where you worked with kids, helping them to learn a little about who they were. Giving them some American history that they didn't get in the Mississippi schools. Even some Negro history. A few of the kids we found who were academically apt we even took back north at the end of the summer to get them into good schools. As teachers who had an abiding faith in education, we related best to those kids." She looked deeply troubled, and shook her head impatiently. "But in the process, we missed all those kids who were hostile to education, hostile to educated people like us, hostile to white people. We missed the angry kids. The revolutionary kids."

"I think you're being too tough on yourself, Liz. You can't really measure what those Freedom School classes meant to kids who had

38. Liz Fusco with Ruleville women.
"You know more than I do. Teach me about voting here!"

never known a sympathetic white, or a really well-trained and dedicated teacher. If you were really missing the boat in connecting with those kids, why didn't project leaders like McLaurin, who know what the movement needs, intervene?"

Her eyes narrowed. "I think they didn't because they felt intimidated by all of us teachers with all our degrees and educational know-how. So people like me continued to make a lot of mistakes. What's worst, of course, is that we lost contact with a lot of kids."

"I don't believe that Mac thought you lost contact with the kids. He told me, two weeks after the Freedom School started, that the Freedom School would only prove to be effective if the kids came to understand what the educational tools were for. But he didn't write off what was being accomplished by you and Linda and the others. I think he believed it was an evolving process."

"I was torn," she said, "between the teachers who were talking about 'remedial reading' and 'poor, deprived kids,' and Mac's notion that you educated kids by helping them deal with their problems in the community where they lived." She broke off with a weary shake of her head. "Well, this summer will be different. I intend to become a catalyst."

"What do you mean by 'catalyst,' Liz?"

I studied the young woman. The childish slightness, the jeans, the work shirt, and the bare feet were deceptive. There was a burning dedication about her. You could read it in the bobbing thrust of the sharp face, the staccato drum of the reedy voice, in the shadows that touched the bright, intelligent eyes.

"Like Linda Davis," she said, wetting her lips with her tongue. "She works as a catalyst in the community down in Indianola now. She not only works with kids; she trains people to work with kids. People need this training, and down here they need it from people like Linda who care deeply about freedom. Linda doesn't run the community center. She doesn't run anything. What she does is . . . be available. Available to sit down and talk with people about what it means to be a qualified voter, and how to get qualified. Available to raise questions, and then to be content to let the people deal with those questions."

After the meeting Liz met me at the door, and we walked together across the baking yard.

"A union organizing meeting! In Shaw of all places!" I nodded toward the unpainted, ramshackle houses that limped like aged cripples down both sides of the dirt road. "How did these people get to this point, Liz?"

She pursed her lips. "I don't know the 'how,' exactly. But I'm not surprised it started here. It was right here in Shaw that I started to see what Freedom Schools really were, and they had very little to do with the organized 'book learning' I had been involved with all last summer." She smiled wryly at the memory. "Here in Shaw I started to see that what the people called the 'neighborhood meeting,' or the Freedom Democratic Party precinct meeting, or any meeting where people began to really talk to each other, was Freedom School." She shoved her hands deep in the pockets of her jeans. A deep crease met the corner of her eyebrow, giving the young face a troubled air. "They weren't just school-agers, kids reading books. One of the teachers down here last summer said that you educate kids by organizing them. 'You listen to them,' he said. 'You hear what they want, and then you deal with their problems where they are.' So he organized them, and they came alive." She paused and looked at me, her lips beginning to smile. "And late in the summer those Shaw kids held the first school boycott in the Delta. The kids' boycott was not successful," she said, "but it was the beginning of a community movement that continued to grow. Adults and kids would sit together at Mississippi Freedom Democratic Party precinct meetings, and talk about their problems . . . about leadership . . . about what they wanted. People kept saying that what they had to do was to stay out of the fields and stick together. They began to implement the talk when forty of them signed a paper saying that when spring came, they weren't going to go to the fields for planting. People decided to plant gardens, live on fish. But most important, they decided that they weren't going back to the fields for three dollars a day. Not then. Not ever again." Liz's voice shook with emotion, and tears stood in unblinking eyes. "You'd see mothers with babies on their laps at the Freedom School, and they were reading *Freedom Road.*"

"What now?" I asked gently. "Are you hopeful, Liz?"

She turned her wide eyes on me. "Hopeful? Oh, sure! What's happening all over Mississippi, what the kids and their parents have learned in a year, makes me hopeful." She turned her head away, and her voice was delicate, hardly audible. "But I'm an organizer, Tracy. And I feel like I'm drifting. Things are already going down here. Shaw doesn't need me. Cleveland doesn't need me. Isaqueena County doesn't need me. Ruleville doesn't need me. None of these places need me." She seemed suddenly impatient at the note of despondency in her voice. She looked up the dusty street, empty now of the families that had crowded the little church hall. A tiny muscle moved in her cheek. "I've been in Mississippi a year—and I've changed," she said slowly. "Mississippi is changing. But I don't yet have the experience to evaluate the change."

The executive committee of the Mississippi Freedom Democratic Party in the county was to meet in the tiny town of Sunflower, and I stopped to pick up McLaurin at Amzie Moore's house. I had looked forward to the drive. Though he rarely initiated conversation, I found him completely lacking in reticence when asked a question. There was an amalgam of frankness and humor that was completely his own. Since I found myself insatiably curious about what was evolving in this violently tilting political landscape, Mac proved always to be a fine Baedecker.

The light was fading over the fields, and I relished the sweet stillness of dusk in the Delta. The air was cool and gentle after the sodden heat of the afternoon. I turned on my car lights, but they were hardly necessary. Like most highways in the Delta, Route 41 never wavered in its straight flight south.

"Last summer seems a thousand years ago, Mac. So much seems to have changed since last summer. I no longer get a stiff neck watching my rearview mirror for trouble. What changed it? COFO? SNCC? The Voting Rights Bill?"

"Probably all those," he said. "A lot of people paid a lot of dues so we can drive comfortably down to Sunflower tonight to a Mississippi Freedom Democratic Party meeting." He was quiet, watching the last light flicker to dark. "A thousand years ago, and a lot of dues."

"Is COFO dead, Mac?" I asked.

"Yes. It was born for a purpose in Mississippi, and the purpose has been served. SNCC, CORE, the NAACP, together they broke the boundaries, got things started. Now there's the MFDP." His voice became thoughtful. "I think in the same way SNCC will be through in Mississippi, too. And it isn't just because the original leaders are disappearing. It's because they've done their job well. Now the leaders are coming locally, from the towns and the cities. That's what SNCC was set up to do." He nodded his head vigorously. "And now these local leaders will act through the Mississippi Freedom Democratic Party."

"Is the MFDP for real, Mac?"

"It's for real." The voice was confident. "With the federal poverty program and the new Voting Rights Act, the MFDP can become a real political force down here. It can bring power to poor colored and white voters who have always been cheated by Mississippi. But it can only do it if it stays clear of the old middle-class Negro leadership. Those folks are out of touch with most of the people. The MFDP leaders they have now, like Mrs. Hamer and Lawrence Guyot, are good. And they're tough. Mrs. Hamer is important because she is like so many Negroes here. She's a day laborer, a sharecropper, up from the plantation. She speaks what they would say if they could. The country has always said that an educational background is the whole basis for success. Yet all of a sudden, here's Fannie Lou Hamer, from the backwoods, who is saying things that educated people ought to have said, but haven't said. She makes those people feel there must be others. With people like Mrs. Hamer, Tracy, the MFDP can shake up this state."

Farewell to the Lindseys

i t was not until my last morning in Ruleville that I found the time to return to the Lindsey home. I mounted the porch steps and knocked on the door. Ora May appeared immediately, and for the first time met my eyes and smiled. "Good morning, Mr. Sugarman," she said in a soft voice.

"Good morning, Ora. It's good to see you again. Is Mrs. Lindsey up yet? I'm leaving today, and I wanted to say good-bye."

She stepped aside, swinging the door open, and motioned me toward the living room. "Please come in," she said. "I'll tell Mrs. Lindsey that you're here." She paused a beat. "Did you enjoy your stay in Ruleville?"

"Very much, Ora. It was memorable."

"Well, that's good. Memorable." She grinned and hurried down the hall. Moments later Bette came through the door bearing Keirn.

"Good mornin', Tracy!" A white pique dressing gown with a huge shawl collar and enormous polka dots of black was buttoned high at the neck. She grinned and carefully placed the baby on the deep rug beside the couch. "Ora, honey," she called, "please bring some coffee. How do you take it, Tracy?"

"Black. I'm sorry if I dropped in too early."

"Oh, heavens, with Kevin around this isn't early!" She knelt beside the baby, resting her back against the couch.

"I'm leaving today," I said. "And I wanted to say good-bye."

She rescued Kevin who had toppled, gurgling happily, onto his side. The full pink cheeks made him look like a tiny toy replica of Lake. Bette kissed him and sat him erect. She tipped her head and regarded me solemnly. "Tracy, I hope you believe this. You've talked with me and you know how I am, I've got to say what's on my mind—or I bust!" She lit a

157

cigarette and shook out the match. Her eyes studied the tiny drift of smoke that rose from the ashtray. When she spoke again, her voice was subdued. "I'm a rebel . . . and glad to be . . . and I don't approve of a lot of what you're down here for. Some of it makes me boil. I guess it always will. But I respect anyone who believes strongly in something." She flushed, and took the tray of coffee from Ora. "I admire you for believin' so strongly."

I reached down and picked up Kevin. I rolled his tiny pull toy along the rounded tummy. He chortled, and Bette laughed aloud. "It doesn't take much to keep that boy happy," she said. "You better take him for his bottle, Ora." The maid extricated Kevin from my lap and carried him, crooning, into the kitchen.

Bette watched her go, and turned, giggling, to her coffee. "That Ora! How I do adore her. She's one of the finest people God ever made." She burst out laughing. "She's my partner in crime. When Lake and I returned from Mexico we toted two bottles of tequila. Do you know tequila? You put a dash of salt on your wrist and lick it between sips of the liquor." She grinned at the memory. "It's strong medicine. Well, last month Lake had to go up to Memphis overnight on business, and I was here, feeling bored and restless. Ora was about to go home around nine when I remembered the tequila. Oh, my, Tracy! I said, 'Ora, let's you and me have one drink together before you leave.'" Bette's eyes grew round and large. She nodded to the breakfast bar. "Do you know," she said in a hollow voice, "we sat right there, two damn-fool women, and we finished that whole bottle of tequila!" She threw back her head and hooted. "Tequila! My God," she gasped, "what a night! We were stoned!" She wiped the tears from her eyes and looked speculatively at me. "Do you know, I can talk with Ora about anything in the world. Anything at all." She paused. Very simply she said, "I'd die for that woman."

I nodded. "I believe you would, Bette." I finished my coffee and placed it carefully on the table. "There's somebody else in this town that you would love if you only knew her. You're very much alike in a lot of ways. She's direct . . . like you . . . and she can't pretend, either. She's got a heart as big as a barn. She'd like you if she knew you. But it's not likely to happen in Ruleville."

Bette's eyes were alight with curiosity. "Who?"

"Fannie Lou Hamer."

She nodded. "You're right. It's not likely to happen." She rose and refilled her empty cup from the carafe on the coffee table. "More coffee?" she asked.

"No, thanks, I'm driving."

She laughed and returned to the couch, perching on the edge of the cushion. For a long minute there was silence in the room, and Kevin's cooing could be heard from the kitchen. Bette's cup rattled in her saucer, and she cleared her throat nervously. "Would you answer me honestly if I asked you a very direct question, and not be offended?"

"I can't imagine being offended. And as for answering honestly, of course I would. Haven't I leveled with you and Lake?"

She bobbed her head. "I think you have." She tapped a cigarette from the pack on the table, and I leaned forward to light it. She settled back in the corner of the couch and seemed to be picking her words with care. She appeared anxious to say precisely what she meant, and her face was intent in its concentration. "If you were a communist, would you admit it to me?"

Her face was so serious that I had to restrain a smile. "No," I said.

"Why not?"

I considered. "Well, I guess because my first loyalty would be to my cause . . . not you. And my cause could best be served by my not telling you."

She studied my face intently. "Are you a communist?"

"No," I said, and burst out laughing. Teasingly I asked, "Now what do you know that you didn't know before? Look, Bette, there's no way you can tell if I'm a communist. You'll either believe me, or you won't. Period. But honest, cross my heart, Boy Scout's honor, I'm a New Deal Democrat from a Republican town. And in Syracuse, where I grew up, that was as radical as you could get."

Her eyes were troubled, and I regretted having teased her at all. As I watched her, I wondered if she believed me. Her eyes held mine. Her voice was very small when she spoke again. "Tell me, Tracy, what is a communist?"

There, I thought, is a woman without guile. I sensed the courage it had taken her to ask the question, daring my scorn or my laughter.

Neither response would have been a fair answer to this kind of honest searching. So for the next hour we talked political science. Her questions about communism were the logical ones that would come from a reader of the regional Mississippi press that characterized all challenge to the "southern way of life" as communist-inspired. Questions that in another context might have seemed unbelievably naive seemed here to be sincere and credible.

"Is Martin Luther King a communist?"

"Bette, a communist is an atheist. If you've heard King, you know he's just a small-town Alabama preacher who preaches love and nonviolence. He's not advocating class struggle or rearranging society along Marxian lines. He's advocating that people exercise their constitutional rights."

"Then why was he teaching at the Highlander School in Tennessee?" she retorted.

"King was at the Highlander School only briefly, and what do you know of the Highlander School?" I asked.

"They say it's a communist school," she said.

"I don't know who 'they' are, Bette. I do know that Highlander was sponsored by people like Eleanor Roosevelt, hardly a Marxist. The fact is that in that school they had racially integrated students and staff long before the law of the land said that it had to be so. Now you tell me something. What if there had been a school like that in Ruleville ten years ago. What would the folks have called it?"

"Communist."

I nodded. "And they would have been wrong."

She sat quietly, her face reflective. I watched Ora move across the kitchen, Kevin cuddled happily in the crook of her arm.

"Bette, do you know who Charles McLaurin is?" I asked.

The question roused her from her reverie. "No. Who is he?"

"He's a young man who means to make a name for himself in politics in the Delta. Maybe you'll get to know him one day. But he has a theory that Negroes in the Delta give birth to mostly girls. Unlike you, who gives birth to mostly boys! He's convinced that it's related to the emasculation of the Negro male, and that girls are preponderant because they harbor the strength of the race here. He's going to do a research paper on it when he goes back to college in the fall. I told him he's mad, that genes don't know about social mores . . . or care."

Bette's face was alive. "What an idea! I don't know whether it's so, but I do believe the Negro women are strong. And they're important, more important than we are to our families. But what an idea!" She rose from the couch as I stood to go. "It seems that in this place we never get to talk about interesting ideas like that." She appeared pensive as she walked with me to the door.

"Can I ask you a favor, Bette? The kids in the quarter want library cards, and they want them without a lot of foolish red tape that white kids don't have to go through. Will you talk to Mayor Durrough and help them get them?"

Her jaw firmed, and the pugnacious look returned to her eye. "Why do they want them? Just to push it in our face that they can integrate the library?"

"No," I said. "Because they really want to read the books. When we talked last time, Lake complained that the Negro boys on his place had ruined his valuable tractor because they didn't have the sense of the worth of things. He said they had no respect for private property or any understanding about responsibility. How can these people have a chance to develop these qualities if you don't let them learn to understand responsibility for public property?"

She lowered her chin, and a wry smile creased the sunburned skin around her eyes. "Now, dammit, if only people would put things that way . . . instead of pushing our face in it!"

Farewell to the Delta

i n my 1965 notes: *Tent cities of impoverished plantation castoffs are rising in the Delta. The "Magnolia State" is still shrinking from the hard questions and the honest answers. The exciting promise that the Movement brought here last year is fading.*

But when I sat with Fannie Lou Hamer, I was reminded of the unconquerable courage and faith that had sustained her. I wanted to believe, as she believed, that the moral struggle would finally overcome the cruel racism embodied in Mississippi. But how?

Her sweaty, broad face glowed in the late afternoon sun, and she smiled at my melancholy comments about my frustration at the creeping pace of change. "Tracy, my father used to read scripture from the Bible: 'Faith is the substance of things hoped for and the evidence of things not seen.'" Her eyes held mine as she raised a perspiring bottle of water and poured me a glass. "We Negroes had hoped, and we had faith to hope, though we didn't know what we hoped for. We had lived with the hope that if we kept 'standing up,' in the Christian manner, that things would change. But after we found out that Christian love alone wouldn't cure the sickness in Mississippi, then we knew we had other things to do."

The drowsy afternoon ebbed away in the somnolent pace of the Delta. The deep shade of the Hamers' pecan tree edged slowly across the lawn, nearly touching the shabby steps where we sat, deep in the comfortable reverie of old friends.

When Fannie Lou spoke again, her voice was lilting. "When the movement came here in 1964, to us it was the result of all our faith, all we had hoped for, all we had lived for!" She grinned reassuringly. "The evidence of things unseen, Tracy!" The deep voice quickened. "In 1964 the faith

Joseph Landfair
Indiana Age 17

39. A black boy.
"These kids have not yet learned to be afraid."

that we had hoped for started to be translated into action. People who had never before tried, although they had always been anxious to do something, began moving. Today even Negroes who live on the plantations slip out and come to civil rights meetings. 'We wanted to do this so long,' they say. When some of us blast out at the meetings, these women go back home, these men go back home. And in the next day or two the kids come! They say, 'My mother told us what you talked about last night.'" Her voice was exultant. "That's great! To see these kids, to see these people, to see how far they have come since 1964! To me it's one of the greatest things that ever happened in Mississippi. And it's a direct result of the Summer Project in 1964. Now we have action, and we're doing something that will not only free the black man in Mississippi but hopefully will free the white one as well. No man is an island to himself."

The memory of that low, melodious voice in the sultry stillness of that baking yard still sounds in my ear. "The sickness in Mississippi is not a Mississippi sickness," she said. "This is America's sickness." Her eyes searched mine as we said good-bye. "And America," she concluded sadly, "is on the critical list."

Part Three

The Roads from the Delta

twenty-four

Legacy

for millennia, the great Mississippi River has majestically surged south from its headwaters in the Far North, carrying its wealth from the very heartland of America. In its waters it has borne nutrients and mineral riches from Minnesota, Iowa, Illinois, Missouri, Indiana, Arkansas, and Tennessee. And when it has overrun its banks in the Mississippi Delta, as it has since before memory, it has deposited its riches in a vast floodplain, creating a soil as fruitful as that of the fecund Nile. Admiring agronomists have long said that "Mississippi is what America is." In the years that have passed since leaving Mississippi, I have come to believe that in a thousand ways Mississippi has indeed become "what America is." But what is undeniable and regrettable is that America has absorbed in its fabric a racism that it once deplored as "barbarous" when it was most blatantly displayed in feudal, apartheid Mississippi. The truth, of course, is that the cruel legacy of the "peculiar institution" of slavery was never the exclusive preserve of the South. Like the Mississippi River, racism, too, can overrun its banks, and spill across America. In our day, we have seen how it can taint our political discourse and soil the reputation of our leaders.

Nearly one thousand summer volunteers left Mississippi at the end of the "long, hot summer" of 1964, and reentered the frenetic political landscape of a rapidly changing America. What they had experienced during those intense months of confrontation, what they had achieved, or failed to achieve, I cannot fairly categorize or assume. As I had found during my years of service in the navy during World War II, drawing conclusions is best left to the historians. What I do know is true is that every kid who went to Mississippi, like every kid who ever went to fight in the

40. Summer volunteers in Ruleville in 1964 *(clockwise from top left):* Fred Miller, Ellie Siegel, Gretchen Schwartz, Dale Gronemeier, Linda Davis, and Jerry Tecklin.
"I'll never forget this summer."

military, fought only his *own* war. It was never "A Grand Clash of the Civil Rights Movement Versus the Establishment, Fought Across the Sweep of a Feudal Dixie." Not for the boy who came in sneakers, who was trying to conquer his fear, who was only eager to help and to survive. It was not a "grand contested landscape" for that girl from Oberlin, or that boy from

Howard, or that black kid who left the mean streets of Jackson to work in the Delta. Their war was often a battleground small in dimension, but immeasurably deep.

Sometimes that war was lit only by the fire of a burning church in Hattiesburg, or a torched Freedom House in Indianola. It was hard to see in all the smoke, or in the sad early dawn light in a prison cell in Meridian. Only sometimes could he or she even discern the real face of the enemy. That *school principal!* That *mayor!* My *Justice* Department? But what became undeniably clear was the discovery of a portrait of himself, or herself, that was somehow different, surer perhaps. Wiser, maybe. And the discovery of a startlingly alien landscape of their own native land. That was me! That was America! We *did* that? We *did* that!

When our son, Richard, returned from Arkansas, he wanted very much to make us all understand what he had learned. "What I think I know," he said, "is that the civil rights movement was successful. It proved that we were capable of helping grassroots people change the fabric of their lives. If the whole political structure of the South, which had been so repressive and unjust for hundreds of years, could be transformed in less than a decade, then it was worth all the lives and sacrifice it cost. I came home feeling and believing that anything is possible."

Like my son, the kids with whom I worked in the Delta had learned an enormous lesson. They had learned you can *win*. They brought that hard-earned confidence into the Peace Corps and out into the world; into the Vista Volunteers in the rusting, abandoned mining towns of Appalachia; into the sweltering inner cities of the North; and onto a myriad of campuses that were finally being roused by the news from the South and the communiqués from Vietnam. And that conviction that "you can *change* things, you really *can*," they carried into the movement against the war in Vietnam, and into the burgeoning women's movement. I watched them go, hoping I'd see them somewhere, sometime, down the road. They were special people.

My Road

Perhaps my road from the Delta was a little easier to navigate than the one traveled by the kids I had come to know so well. I was twenty years older than they, and I had been on an invasion before. My road was to dip and turn, twist around, and return again and again to this Mississippi they were leaving. I didn't have a map, but I was certain of my direction. But they were off to restart their lives after Mississippi without a compass, carrying only vivid memories of special moments, of humble people who were very brave, of big lessons learned in small places, of a struggle that had somehow enlarged them.

Unlike most of the summer volunteers who had come to the state in 1964, Mississippi has continued to be a "work in progress" in my life. The hundred drawings I had made there in 1964, which our family gave to Tougaloo College as a permanent archive of the movement, and the publication in 1966 of *Stranger at the Gates: A Summer in Mississippi* created bonds within the state that have grown only stronger over the years. In 1969, with Bill and Ellie Buckley, my wife, June, and I created Rediscovery Productions, Inc., a documentary film company dedicated to rediscovering the too often overlooked black contributors who had enriched American society. Our creative team of writers, camera operators, sound technicians, musicians, editors, and actors was an eclectic blend of blacks and whites, men and women who were hired only because of their talent.

During the years of research that spiraled forward from Freedom Summer as we began to envision and then create our Rediscovery films, I was able to reconnect with many of my original Mississippi friends—Rennie Williams, Charles McLaurin, Mrs. Hamer, Bette Lindsey—reunions that were often as provocative and emotional as they were memorable.

For several of our documentaries, we filmed segments on-site throughout the state. For me, it vastly enriched the racial canvas I had started to explore in the early sixties. I finally came to meet and know some of the remarkable African Americans such as L. C. Dorsey, June Johnson, Hollis Watkins, Charlie Cobb, John Lewis, Owen Brooks, and Leslie McLemore, names I had only heard about during those overheated days of the movement when my world was limited to the garrison of Ruleville, Drew, and Indianola. Like my earliest friends in the Delta, these were young blacks and whites who not only were shaped by their history, but with courage and sacrifice had created it.

Bette Lindsey

I n 1978, while doing research for our Rediscovery film *Never Turn Back: The Life of Fannie Lou Hamer,* I was able to renew a unique friendship with the white Lindsey family who had first invited me to their home in Ruleville in 1964. On a rainy September Sunday, June and I were greeted at the door by Bette Lindsey with the kind of affectionate embrace one would hope for from an old friend. Neither Lake nor the three children were at home, so the hours of the afternoon were shared with Bette alone. It was an opportunity I welcomed, for my memories of our three previous meetings were among the most vivid of my time in Mississippi. I had come to realize how special were those occasions we had shared, and I was eager to have my wife meet the woman who had initiated them.

Bette reveled in hearing about how we lived in New England, was full of curiosity about our children, and wanted to know about skiing and New York theater, all of which was exotic fare for her. On our part we were eager to hear about life in Ruleville and what was most meaningful for the wife of a plantation owner in the Delta, now that mechanization was changing the very face of Mississippi agriculture. Being gracious, she sought to answer our questions, though it was clear to me that she had another topic she really wanted to explore with me.

"Tracy," she began, and her eyes were shining, "something's happened in my life that I don't think you'll believe. I don't think that you could imagine it happening to me. I really don't."

I had to laugh at her intensity. "I don't know, Bette. I told June how you picked me up at the gas station, and that surprised the hell out of me. So go ahead."

"Now, June, you know he's telling a terrible fib. I never picked him up. Not really," she said with a mischievous smile. But when she turned to face me, her face became quite still and serious. "Tracy, I've become a born-again Christian."

I watched Bette in silence, not knowing really why that was something she wished to share with us. Religion, hers or mine, had never been a part of any of our discussions in the past. But now she was eager to have me understand that her revelation had changed her life.

"When I let Jesus into my heart, Tracy, it was like going home . . . opening a door." She hiked forward in her chair, closer to June and me. "It's been like a gift," she said simply.

"I think that's wonderful, Bette," I said. "But how has it changed your life?"

"When we talked back in the sixties, you know that my world was a very different place, Tracy." She smiled. "You and Lake and I had some pretty heated arguments about how we saw life down here in the Delta."

I nodded. "Yes, we certainly did."

"Well, since Jesus entered my life I've found ways to be a better Christian. I now go to Parchman Penitentiary and minister to the black women prisoners, about drug and alcohol abuse."

"How great!" said June. "That's really important work, Bette."

I reached forward and touched Bette's hand. "I'll be damned," I said. "You were absolutely right. I would never have imagined that!"

As the afternoon waned, I was feeling very guilty that I had never mentioned that I had written *Stranger at the Gates,* nor told the Lindseys that I had included in it my memories of our first meetings together. If they knew about the book, would it damage our friendship? I hated to risk that. But as we stood to leave, I summoned my courage. "Bette, did you know that I wrote a book about my summer down here in '64?"

Bette answered with a searching look and then a small smile. "Yes. *Stranger at the Gates.* And you changed our names from Lindsey to Cutler!"

I grinned with relief. "Yes, I did. I thought the least I could do after you both had been so honest with me was to try and protect you from your neighbors."

Bette did not comment further. She simply walked across the living room, took a book from the top shelf, and handed it to me. "Would you please sign my copy of *Stranger at the Gates?*"

June Johnson

When I first saw June Johnson in 1978, it was on the sun-dappled campus of Tougaloo College. Dressed in white, a very tall and striking woman with glowing dark skin, she commanded the scene merely by her presence. I was immediately aware of the total composure of the young woman. She was a person who was comfortable with her height, and stood confidently erect. The confrontational, unapologetic look in her eyes made me think, unaccountably, of a proud African warrior. She stood alone, watchfully waiting for our film crew to set up for her scheduled interview.

I had looked forward to meeting June Johnson because I knew that at age fourteen, she had been arrested with Fannie Lou Hamer, and the two had been brutally beaten in the Winona, Mississippi, jail. Her recollection of those events was to be an important element in our film biography *Never Turn Back: The Life of Fannie Lou Hamer.* I turned to Charles McLaurin, who had known her when she was growing up in Greenwood and had set up this meeting. "What a great-looking young woman," I said admiringly. "It's hard to visualize her being beaten up anywhere."

He nodded agreement. "She is strong," he said. "But anybody," he added dryly, "can get beat up in a police station." He cleared his throat and led me to meet June Johnson. "June is strong," he repeated, and then chuckled. "But you should have known her mama. Now *that* was one tough lady!"

Filming that interview for our documentary about Mrs. Hamer, a woman whom she so admired, established a trusting friendship that has prevailed over the years. "Was it Mrs. Hamer who got you involved in the civil rights movement, June?" I asked.

175

"No, Tracy, but Mrs. Hamer influenced me a lot by her example. I first heard her in 1963 in a Greenwood Baptist church. I happened to be passing by, and I heard this strong woman's voice singing. Something told me to stop, and I eased into the church and sat in the back. I was struck by her, just hearing what she had to say. She was such a Christian woman! She was a giant with the scriptures and the Bible. She knew how to paraphrase it. For her, an illiterate woman, to have such knowledge about the Bible, and wisdom about how things were in Mississippi, just touched me deeply. She was there with several others from the Voter Education Project, but she was the one I remember so clearly.

"It was really what I was seeing in my mother's home and in Greenwood that led me to get involved with the movement. Too often, I would see my mother come home very disturbed after working long, long hours. She would leave at five in the afternoon when I'd be coming home from school, and she'd get home at four or five the next morning as we were getting up to get ready for school. We were just passing each other. And she was making fifteen dollars a week." She frowned as her mind retraced those events, and her eyes were moist. "One night, she came home from work after walking over two miles in the rain. She was crying, and we asked her, 'Why are you home so early, Mama? It's only eight o'clock.' She was very upset, and pulled off all the wet clothes. 'I'm not going back,' she said. 'I'm not ever going back.' She had messed up on her job, she told us, put onions on this white man's hamburger by mistake. He had cursed her, and then he spat on her."

"What a terrible story for a girl to have to hear from her mother," I said sympathetically. "Did you, yourself, know any white folks while you were living at home, June?"

"I did because my mother did a lot of washing and ironing and cooking for them. I remember my mother taking in ironing on Sunday mornings, and I resented it. Because she got up and made biscuits for them before she cooked food for her own family. And in a closed society, like our black community in Greenwood, that was the way it always was. I watched my mother wash *their* drawers before she washed *our* clothes. I saw that she was 'Lulu Belle,' and they were 'Miss Joy' and 'Miss Anne.' Now that's not really *knowing* each other," she said bitterly.

"We had a routine that we lived by. You obeyed your family. You went to school. You went to the cotton field. You went to church because it was your outlet, and your community. And you catered to the white power structure because terrible things could happen anytime at all." She paused. "Terrible things, like the lynching of that boy, Emmett Till. My brothers were told: 'You're not even to *look* at a white girl.' I can still hear my mother: 'If anybody ever comes and asks you if you want to go to a white school, an integrated school, you tell them, 'NO.' You make sure that you remember what I tell you. *'You don't want to go to school with white kids. You're happy with the education that you're getting.'* My mother was a very powerful woman, but she had been programmed her whole life by the white power structure what to say. She'd learned it from their maid, or from their cook, but she sure as hell learned what her kids were supposed to say about integration," she said sadly. "'No.'"

"That's a tough box to break out of," I said. "How did you manage?"

June regarded me steadily, but her eyes held questions. "I don't know if my self-assurance came from my family, or from the movement. The truth is, I had always had to fight within my family for my identity. I was the sixth child of twelve, and the darkest of all my sisters. And that dark color was always something I had to address. My hair was kinkier than my other sisters', and I always felt that for that reason I got the hand-me-downs, the leftover shoes, the leftover coats." She swallowed, and then continued, her voice tinged with anger. "I was always made to feel second-class in my family. Color," she mused, "color made me have to struggle with my own mother and my own grandmother. My grandmother on my father's side was jet-black. But my grandmother on my mother's side had a whole lot of pride because she was a very light-skinned woman. She always talked about her upbringing, that her grandmother and grandfather were white and Choctaw Indian." June shook her head, and grinned for the first time. "She'd say, 'Everybody's making all this hoopla about color. Hell, my folks are white, too. They all slept with us!'" The humor leached from her voice. "I had to struggle with my family, Tracy. And I ran away a lot." She stopped, and a wonderful smile kindled June's dark, glowing face. "But at fourteen, I joined the civil rights movement, and that's what finally gave me a sense of freedom from all that!"

I stared at the beaming young woman. "But at what a price," I said. "You went to jail in Winona and were beaten!"

Her smile slowly disappeared, but her voice was calm as she recalled the jailing. "I wasn't struggling by myself then," she said simply. "I was with Mrs. Hamer and the other civil rights workers on the Trailways bus, and we had all decided to try to integrate the lunch counter when we reached Winona."

"When did you realize that you were in trouble?"

"Soon as we got to Winona," replied June. "It was clear that there was a planned activity because there were police cars all over the place, and policemen were sitting at the tables in the restaurant. Soon as we walked in, sat down at the counter, and asked, 'Can we be served?' the bus driver went directly to the police. The police immediately ordered us to get up, and started pushing us with their billy clubs, saying, 'Niggers, get out of here. Niggers don't eat on this side!' When we were outside, we decided to do what we had been trained to do at the training session we had just left. We would record the police names and tag numbers. That's what we were doing when the police came out and arrested us for 'tampering with state property.'"

"Was Mrs. Hamer with you, June?"

"She had left the restaurant and gotten back on the bus. When she saw us being arrested, she asked, 'Do you want me to go on to Greenwood and get some help?' And the police shouted out, 'Get that bitch, too!' They grabbed Mrs. Hamer and took all six of us to the jail in Winona. They started interrogating us about who we were, and told us what they had heard. 'You're the smart niggers from over in Greenwood who are coming to make trouble in Winona. Who's your leader? Are you the NAACP?' When we didn't answer, they said, 'We're going to make you wish you never got off that bus.'" The tall, proud woman stood silent, her eyes distant. "They put all the others in cells. 'But not you, bitch,' they said." She licked her lips, and continued in a strong voice. "And then they started to beat me. My eye was messed up, and I had a hole knocked in my head."

"Why you, June? Why did they single you out?"

"They said I didn't know how to respect a Mississippi white man and I had picked the wrong town to come to. I was fourteen years old. After they beat me, they threw me into a cell and started to beat the others. I could hear them. It was terrible. Then they took Mrs. Hamer to the far end of the cells." June shook her head, her eyes winking away tears. "You could hear the echo of their beatings, and you could hear Fannie Lou screaming. Finally, they dragged her back to her cell. She was in a terrible way.

"Around two in the morning, they woke us up and took us out of our cells, and we were tried in front of a white mob. It didn't take long. After it was over, they told me I was free to go because there was a dispute about my age. They wanted me to say I was twenty-one as opposed to four-teen, my real age. And the judge kept saying, 'We don't have any charges against you. You're free to go.' But what we had been taught in the training session was you don't ever isolate yourself, so I refused to go, and stayed with the others in jail. On the very day that Medgar Evers was assassi-nated, Lawrence Guyot came to the Winona jail to try and get us out. The police beat him so badly, we didn't recognize him. On our third night, they woke us at four in the morning and tried to make us sign their state-ment that *they* didn't do anything to us, that *we* did the beatings ourselves. On the next day, a couple of white FBI guys came to get us from the jail. But we were so hysterical at that point, we didn't trust anybody. We said, 'You have to prove that you really are FBI.' And that's when Andy Young came and told us it was all right to leave with those men."

Even with the distance of years, one shudders at the violence, denial, and humiliation that were the daily fare of so many black women in Missis-sippi. In 1980, I met with the great matriarch of the civil rights movement, the "mother of SNCC," Ella Baker. A highly educated, modern woman, she spoke fervently of the character of the nearly untutored farm woman, Fan-nie Lou Hamer, whose example had established an ideal for so many face-less and voiceless poor women. Mrs. Baker said, "When you go through that kind of brutality, even though you wanted to see things change, it could change your mind. It could stop you from moving ahead. But it seemingly never stopped her."

There were so many memorable women's voices I can still hear—bold voices, strong in their resolve, quietly triumphant voices. As L. C. Dorsey described her life, I started to perceive how deep in the soil, how strong at the roots, were the black women who had refused to be defeated in the Delta.

L. C. Dorsey

f annie Lou Hamer's death in 1977 left a tragic void in the grieving
community of the freedom struggle. She had been the fount of courage and hope that had nourished so many in the movement in Mississippi and far across the nation. Her passionate voice was now still, and
she was sorely missed. In 1978 we resolved at Rediscovery Productions to
produce a one-hour documentary, *Never Turn Back: The Life of Fannie Lou
Hamer,* to celebrate her remarkable accomplishments. We wanted to take
her urgent message of love, nonviolence, and black pride to the countless young Americans who would follow. Seeking to better understand
the audacious life that had led this modest black woman sharecropper
to become an icon of moral and political resistance, June Sugarman, the
director of research, and I, the script writer, began to explore the black life
of the Delta. It was a mission that took five years to complete. When we
found L. C. Dorsey, we uncovered yet one more tale of amazing survival
and victory by black women whose names may never be celebrated.

"I was born on a plantation in Washington County, raised on another
plantation in Leflore County, worked on plantations in Sunflower
County, and was a sharecropper on a plantation in Bolivar County when
I met and married Hilary Dorsey, the father of my children. Till I was in
my midtwenties, I had never been out of the Mississippi Delta." A sad
trace of a smile touched her lips. "Me and my husband operated some of
the farm equipment on the Dixon plantation, the mechanical cotton pick-
ers, the combines and such. That was our life, raising our kids, working
the plantation, until 1964, when Mr. Dixon informed us that he couldn't
afford any longer to have a sharecropping family on his place. He said
we had to leave." Dorsey grew silent, her dark eyes staring straight into

that past. She sipped her drink. "We had to move off the Dixon place," she said softly.

"Where in the world could you go?" I asked, appalled. "You had five little children!"

L. C. looked up. "And I was pregnant with the sixth. There was a landlord over in Shelby who had a condemned house on his property, nobody living in it. And he let us move in because we were homeless." She cocked her head, summoning up a picture of the place for us. With a wry smile, she counted off on her fingers. "We had four rooms. We had a kitchen. We had a sink. And we had running water."

"And no money," I said.

"And no money. So I did the only thing I knew how to do: go to the cotton fields. I caught trucks out to the fields at first light every morning until I got too big to go." She turned to me. "I can testify how hard it is on a woman's body to have five kids, another on the way, and go to the fields." She saw the wide-eyed look on my face, and broke into a caustic laughter. "Adversity," she said in a dry voice. "It builds character."

There are black voices that still echo in my ears from those seventies days in Mississippi. Some, like Fannie Lou Hamer's, or June Johnson's, or L. C. Dorsey's, spoke so profoundly of their lives that my vision of that whole culture was widened and deepened. And sometimes the voices were not from the Delta. When Charlie Cobb shared his stories, one could hear the faint echo of the urbane, sophisticated life of the East, of good schools and a privileged professional family. His father was an important preacher up north. But one sensed the steel beneath the quiet words. I perceived the hard center of a man who had chosen to come to this place, committed to tear up the roots of an apartheid that still echoed in his family memory, an injustice he still found to be obscene.

twenty-nine

Charlie Cobb

Charlie might have been the template for the SNCC leaders who had gone to Mississippi in the early 1960s. Unlike their rural and urban comrades from that state, they had been mostly kids from the world of academia and from the black middle class of the North. Our paths had first crossed at a civil rights reunion at Jackson State in 1994. I recall a wonderful, long, and passionate discussion of the verdict that had just been rendered in the O. J. Simpson murder trial that had kept many of us at the reunion debating long into the night. Cobb's comments had particularly impressed me by their clarity and a searching perspective that transcended race. Cobb's contributions to the early struggles were well known to me, but his work in Mississippi had never taken him to Ruleville while I was there.

When I met with him again in 2001, he was still stocky, vigorous, and keen-eyed. In a busy Washington setting, Charlie fit the picture of the sophisticated, world-traveling journalist he truly is. His hair and beard were close-cropped and neatly trimmed, a surprising preponderance of gray adding maturity to his youthful persona. He appeared urbane, seemingly at home with the world, and comfortable with himself. Married, the father of a twenty-seven-year-old son and a ten-year-old daughter, the Cobbs adopted and raised a teenage girl who now has a son of her own. "So we are now grandparents!" Charlie announced with a happy smile.

Whether writing about Afro-Brazilian culture in Brazil for the *National Geographic*, coauthoring a book about mathematics for inner-city children with Bob Moses, or covering a war in Zimbabwe, Cobb brings a searching intelligence and a scholarly and experiential memory to his observations.

"You were one of those early guys that came into the movement in Mississippi from outside the Deep South, Charlie. That must have been a tough decision for your folks up in Washington to make," I said. "Your dad was a minister."

Cobb smiled. "No. Not a tough decision. There was no hostility at home. I never detected the kind of fear in my folks that I saw among parents whose kids were involved in Mississippi. Nothing akin to that. Mississippi is where my parents and grandparents *came* from," he said proudly. "My grandfather founded a community in Mississippi, 'New Africa,' in 1888! He had migrated from Alabama as a newly freed slave after the Civil War. Mississippi then was 'going west,' the frontier. He went looking for land and opportunity. So my going to Mississippi was not a tough decision for my family. They have a very strong civil rights background.

"At the end of 1961, I left college. CORE had given me money to attend a civil rights workshop in Houston, Texas, so I decided to take advantage of that opportunity and tour the South. So I got a bus ticket from D.C., taking me through the South, winding up in Texas." He chuckled. "And I sat there at the *front* of the bus as we went through Carolina, Georgia, Alabama, Louisiana, and Mississippi. I was determined to sit there. When I got to Jackson, I knew there was a SNCC office there, and I remember walking up to the office. And the very first person I met was Lawrence Guyot." His eyes were warm at the memory. "I told him I was passing through on the way to a civil rights conference in Houston. And Guyot's response was, 'What's the point of going to a civil rights conference in Texas when you're standing right here in Mississippi?' It was a direct challenge," he said, "and I took it.

"SNCC was just planning to do work in the Delta. Guyot, Levon Brown, and Sam Block went up to start in Greenwood, and the Klan broke down their door. The three of them had to escape the mob out the back window by sliding down an outside aerial. Sam called us in Jackson, and we alerted the FBI." Cobb said flatly, "They said to let them know if anything happens."

"That was it? That's all they did?" My astonishment made Charlie smile.

"That was it. All of it. So Bob Moses and I went up to Greenwood. That was when I met Charles McLaurin. He and Moses were going to go open Ruleville, in Sunflower County. Unlike places like Drew, there was a network of Amzie Moore's people in Ruleville who would take them in. Sunflower County was important in a political sense. It was the home of the White Citizens Council, and it was the home base of Senator James Eastland. So when they left Greenwood, I wound up in the car with them." He raised his hands and looked very soberly at me before breaking into a great grin. "So I never got to the civil rights workshop in Texas!"

"I remember Amzie Moore so well," I said. "I wonder how many people have any idea of what he accomplished in getting Moses and SNCC started in the Delta. Not very many, I'll bet. And he was one of the bravest men I ever met, Charlie. When he came back from the service after serving with the air force in Burma, he had to fight all over again, just to get the vote in Mississippi and to be treated like a man. And he never quit. First with the NAACP and then with SNCC. A hell of a man."

Cobb nodded assent. "He was. You remember he had a restaurant and a gas station, got the franchise because he was an ex-G.I. He refused to put up WHITE and COLORED signs, and if you went in Amzie's restaurant you could use any bathroom and sit wherever space permitted." He turned, eager for me to understand how special that was. "His restaurant was right on Highway 41, on the main artery between Memphis and New Orleans. So Amzie thought that any night some mob was going to come in." His head swung back, his eyes remembering. "Amzie would sit in the window with a rifle, with floodlights on."

I smiled at the picture. Moore was in many ways a surrogate father to Charles McLaurin, and I recalled the night Mac had led me to Moore's house to sleep after a late organizing meeting in Mound Bayou. As I was about to retire, Moore came into my room and laid a revolver on the table beside my bed. "Put it under your pillow," he said kindly, "in case you need it." I thanked him, but refused the gun. "Nobody in the Summer Project is permitted to have a gun with them, Amzie." Embarrassed, I said, "As advertised, we're supposed to be 'nonviolent.'" "Okay," he said agreeably. "It's late. Get yourself some sleep." He picked up the gun and left the room.

41. Amzie Moore at first organizing meeting in Mound Bayou.
"Folks are still scared to come out. After tonight it will be easier."

"But that was in 1964, Charlie. Long after you first came to the Delta. There weren't a hell of a lot of SNCC fieldworkers down there then. Did you welcome the idea of people coming down from the North to help?"

"In the beginning there were arguments about whether or not to *do* a summer project in 1964," he reflected. "The discussions began to crystallize about a whole range of issues we hadn't talked about in the early years in Mississippi. A lot of those discussions have since been misrepresented as a *racial* argument." He shook his head emphatically. "It wasn't racial. It was mainly about how we civil rights workers, who had been working in Mississippi, could protect that work from 'outsiders,' people who we felt couldn't understand the work we had been doing twenty-four hours a day with the black community. We were reluctant to turn over any piece of that work to anybody from outside the state. And 'outsiders' could be black as well as white, ideologues who were not part of the culture."

I saw the concentration on Charlie's face, and detected his heartfelt need to clarify that piece of history. I was eager to understand.

"But the students who you saw at Oxford, Charlie, were hardly political ideologues, were they? If anything, they seemed to me to be innocent idealists, kids who just wanted to help."

He nodded. "It was hard for us to accept that then. Our fear of 'outsiders' was that with all their political connections, they would overwhelm the program. It would no longer be about what *we* were doing. It would be what this enormous group of people, who were politically connected in ways that we couldn't even fathom, would opt to do. We would have no more control over that."

"But wasn't Bob Moses pushing the SNCC staff to include the students?" I asked.

Cobb agreed. "Yes, he was. What was foremost in his mind was the need to address the violence that was unfolding in the state. He felt that neither SNCC nor the whole civil rights establishment had the capacity to blunt that violence. One of our people, Herbert Lee, had been killed by the racists, and Bob felt we were helpless to do anything to respond. So when Louis Allen, the man who witnessed the murder of Lee, was first harassed and then murdered, it was the turning point for Bob Moses. He began to push aggressively for the inclusion of the northern students." Charlie seemed to be looking back at some point in that troubled year, and his eyes were sad. "At that point our SNCC staff was exhausted from all the racial killings and beatings and burnings by whites that had been going on since '61. We didn't really want to deal with 'outsiders,' and especially *white* 'outsiders.'"

Charlie paused, and when he spoke again his voice was quiet and emotional. "Many of us who had been working there before that summer felt that by bringing in 'outsiders,' we were making a statement that the Mississippi blacks were not capable of changing things by themselves. That was a deeply offensive idea to me and to our Mississippi SNCC fieldworkers like McLaurin and Watkins and Guyot. Ironically, though, local Mississippi blacks who we had encouraged to take leadership, remarkable leaders like Mrs. Hamer, were all for the Summer Project." He laughed ruefully. "We organizers then had to deal with the fact that the people we had organized were in a different place than we were."

I was moved by the conviction in Charlie's reminiscence. "How do you feel today, Charlie," I asked, "knowing now that the presence of those students helped focus the attention of the country and really helped accomplish what you had been fighting for all that time?"

He smiled faintly. "I would probably still argue against the Summer Project," he admitted. "In retrospect, I think it was inevitable that the prohibitions on black access to accommodations and the vote would have eventually broken down." He shrugged. "If we knew enough, maybe we could have done it ourselves. We didn't have the resources in SNCC or, quite frankly, the experience. Remember," he said reflectively, "when Stokely Carmichael made his call for 'Black Power,' he was twenty-two years old! We were very young and without any experiential political skills. We might have developed them if we had organized in a different way." He looked at me and grinned. "*Might.* I can't deny that having those 'outsiders' radically changed the state. Mississippi was never the same after the Summer Project."

When I questioned Cobb about the white exodus from SNCC, he had a longer, cooler perspective on that time of racial transition. "SNCC had ducked the race question for a long time. Early on, in the early sixties in Atlanta, white people like Casey Hayden and Mary King had wanted to get out in the field, and the question for SNCC leadership was whether or not you could construct an island of integration in this vast racist sea. Long before 'Black Power,' SNCC was wrestling with the question, and finessing the answer. It was only with the '64 Summer Program that we had whites working with us in the Delta. We had never been able to work it out, and American society was working against our working it out. By the time the anger surfaced around the slogan of 'Black Power,' there was no good way to handle that."

"But what about you, Charlie? You had worked closely with whites like Bob Zellner and Casey Hayden and Mary King. How did you feel about their being invited out?"

Cobb had frowned, pondering an honest response. "In SNCC," he said, "particularly in the early leadership, we all had our exceptions. We maintained relationships with whites who had been with us from the beginning. Our inability in SNCC to grapple with the larger issue of race was attributable to our inability to decide before 1964 what form SNCC would take organizationally."

Charlie regarded me, quietly pondering the historical questions that had created the odd racial mosaic of SNCC. "There were real questions.

What does organizing *mean*? Once the Public Accommodations Act and the Voting Rights Act became the law of the land, what does organizing *mean*? When the Democratic Party of Mississippi is undercutting a Freedom Democratic Party by making overtures to the black establishment and to black communities, what does organizing *mean*? When there is a flood of federal jobs and federal money coming into the state, what does organizing *mean*? Those questions cut to the heart of what SNCC ought to be. If there is nothing there to organize protest around, what is the role for SNCC to play?" Charlie leaned forward, speaking slowly but with intensity. "Those questions were never dealt with in SNCC, and the racial issues, which had been set aside out of common commitment to the struggle for justice, began to surface."

There was silence, and when he spoke again there was a note of deep regret in his voice. "I don't see how they could have been resolved, and they weren't. By 1967, SNCC was history."

The demise of SNCC will always be a matter of sadness to me. The young blacks and whites who selflessly put themselves in harm's way to assist SNCC in its often quixotic struggles to achieve justice will always have a special residence in my heart. Among all the civil rights organizations that worked for racial justice, SNCC may have been "the mouse that roared." But none roared more resolutely. None nurtured so talented and creative a cadre of young leaders. None so won the hearts and trust of the poor and disenfranchised to whom they helped give voice. And none engaged so completely the enduring loyalty of the dedicated young of all races.

The agonizing lessons learned in the crucible of the Mississippi struggle have continued to resonate in every benighted crevice of American life, and in every infant nation seeking to find its way to democracy.

Charlie Cobb's observations were provocative. "When I covered the war in Zimbabwe, I saw more violence than I ever saw in Mississippi. But what I learned in Mississippi as an organizer was how to listen to people, how to figure out what the people were trying to do on their own terms." He laughed. "As a reporter, that's an invaluable skill! There are a lot of places in rural Zimbabwe, or in rural Eritrea, that resonate with the Mississippi Delta. Rural life doesn't vary that much from place to place." He smiled, his eyes searching out another continent. "Squatting down, talking with guerrillas in Eritrea, wasn't all that different from sitting down with the Steptoes in the backwoods of the Delta.

"I think the Mississippi tradition is an *organizing* tradition, as opposed to a *protest* tradition. And that organizing tradition predates the protest tradition in the black struggle in the United States. The protest tradition is relatively modern, perhaps fathered by A. Philip Randolph in the 1930s." Cobb's intelligent face mirrored his reportorial process, seeking out the threads that made sense. "When I go to a place like South Africa as a journalist, I'm interested first in how people are organizing. Then I look at how they are protesting."

Watching this still young but deeply experienced civil rights warrior bring all that he had learned to his contemporary tasks was compelling.

"I understand anger," he said quietly. "And I understand protest. I remember vividly the need to mount a sit-in, the urgency to set up a picket line. That is as true in Africa as it was in Mississippi. But what interests me *because* of my Mississippi experience is the organizing. People know, for the most part, what they want. What they don't like. And the politicians they don't trust. But what people *don't* have in oppressive situations like the Mississippi Delta, or Apartheid South Africa, is a way to articulate those feelings. A way to plan. A way to organize to change those things. They often have very good ideas about how to change things, but they often have other people speak for them."

I nodded agreement. "That was the significance of Mrs. Hamer. She could say what they needed to say."

"And that was the significance of SNCC, of the whole grassroots tradition of the movement. It was empowering people so that they could advocate for themselves." Charlie pushed back his chair, seemingly intent on crystallizing his perceptions and sharing them. "That," he said emphatically, "is what makes a civil rights movement radical. You can have people, you can have civil rights organizations, advocating till they're blue in the face. It's only when the people start speaking for themselves that you get significant change."

"But Medgar Evers was an advocate," I said, "and I always thought an effective advocate for change. I really believe that's why he was assassinated."

"Medgar was a native Mississippian," Cobb replied, "a good man who came out of the Korean War and wanted to create change. The problem was not with Medgar, in my judgment, but with his organization, the NAACP. It's an advocacy organization. I don't mean to disparage those advocacy organizations, nor dismiss the legal contributions they made for the struggle. But the NAACP did not believe you could change Mississippi. They thought you had to surround Mississippi, break down segregation and racism in the upper South. Then, they believed, you gradually would move in on the hard-core southern states like Alabama and Mississippi. Medgar got no support from the national NAACP, and that's what opened the door for SNCC and CORE to come in. In the 1950s Medgar was organizing youth chapters of the NAACP, and that's where a lot of SNCC leadership came from. Medgar, like Amzie Moore, was the forerunner of those who believed that advocacy by others was not enough, who believed passionately that local Mississippians could create change."

How remarkable, I thought, to have been there at the beginning and to have the satisfaction of watching his thesis start to unfold at home and in the farthest places on the globe.

Perhaps the radiant aspirations of the movement could never have been totally realized. "The beloved community" of racial justice remains an elusive grail, still to be seized by wiser and more loving hands in the future. Like so many in the movement who have stretched so far and worked so hard, Martha Honey assesses her society's gains with both disappointment and resolve.

Martha Honey

It was astonishing that nearly forty years had passed since that day I visited with Martha Honey at the Turnbow house in the Delta in 1964. Fresh from the orientation at Oxford, Ohio, I remember Martha as an eager, highly motivated pilgrim, wanting to find her way to help the Turnbows and their neighbors find real justice. Today she is a vigorous, confident, and handsome woman with grown kids of her own and deep knowledge of a world gained in over twenty years of travel beyond America with her journalist husband. Not surprisingly, she works today on behalf of the global environment.

"There have been a lot of changes since you left the States, Martha. The Mississippi you knew at the Turnbows is pretty much gone. What surprised you most when you returned?" Her bright eyes clouded. "What is really shocking, in terms of Mississippi, is that after all these years, political power has changed, but economic power has not. One result of the civil rights movement is that it gave opportunities to some African Americans. But often the best, the brightest, and the most energetic moved away from those wonderful communities we worked in. They went north to colleges, to the big cities, and the movement in the rural areas just disappeared. In some ways, those areas are now worse off because they don't have the capital or the human resources they once had. It's really sad.

"Coming back to the States after twenty years away, I was really appalled. I had sort of felt that we had really fixed this problem of racism. But one of the great learning experiences of my life is that you don't fix problems." She met my eyes. "Big issues like racism require constant vigilance, or they come back." She said it simply, but there was a vibrancy in her voice that I remembered from our very first meeting in the Delta.

42. Summer volunteer Martha Honey, Oberlin College, 1964, now an environmentalist.
"I would follow Mrs. Hamer anywhere."

"It means that once you're in the struggle, you're in it for life. If you drop out, you've never won."

The whole concept of time as it relates to an evolving Mississippi often seems incredible to me. Years race into history, and decades disappear. Has it really taken forty years to convict the murderer of Medgar Evers? Is it possible that more than forty years have passed, and the murderers of Emmett Till have not been brought to trial and that only now the killers of Andy Goodman, James Chaney, and Mickey Schwerner, murdered, martyred, and buried more than forty years ago, may be arrested and brought to justice? "Justice delayed is justice denied" in most of this democracy. In Mississippi racial justice has been so long denied that even the possibility of such trials creates headlines across the nation.

For this writer, who has witnessed the painful, sometimes brave, often frustrating evolution of this intriguing state for more than forty years, too many stories remain untold or unfinished. Even as my life as an artist and writer has moved across a patchwork of other landscapes in American life, the mystery of Mississippi has continued to challenge. The voices of Mississippi have continued to sound in my head. My "long, hot summer" has never found its autumn. As change came to the Mississippi I had known in the sixties, new arguments and strategies for creating a more inclusive society for the newly empowered black community were sounding. Men and women who had shared the struggles of the movement now often found themselves in contention with old comrades.

thirty-one

Owen Brooks

any conversation with Owen Brooks was overtly challenging. It was invariably a mixed, invigorating salad of opinions, shared experiences, and questions, all served with a robust humor and vigor. More than anyone else I met in my time in Mississippi, Brooks was the most challenging and provocative. When I would leave, there invariably were ideas to wrestle with, and new perspectives to explore. When I first met him in 1980, he told me of his beginnings in Mississippi.

"I had wanted to come south from Boston for a long time. I had the feeling that the liberation of black people had to emanate from that southern soil, and I wanted to be part of that. The Delta Ministry gave me the opportunity. And at age thirty-six, in 1965, I came to Mississippi. The Delta Ministry was putting together Head Start. I went to work with Amzie Moore and Fannie Lou Hamer, and I've continued to work in Mississippi ever since."

Very soon, I recognized that a very analytical, very self-critical, and very bold mind was at work. Blacks and whites, politicians and educators, leaders and followers—all were fair game for his searching criticism.

"We made organizational mistakes in the movement, and we made some bad choices. We could begin by saying we almost totally lost the struggle to educate our black children. Or we could begin by saying we didn't teach the following generation anything." He saw my look of skepticism and said firmly, "We didn't pass down to the children. We gave over to the establishment, almost completely, the education of our black children."

"But weren't you working to *integrate* the schools?" I was perplexed by his pessimistic assessment.

"We came out of the generation that valued education so much," he responded. "And we were told by the liberals and the moderates that black children would get a better education if they went to school with white children." He slapped the desk. "Oh, Lord! We tore the children from their mothers and transported them across town. We *did* that! And what did the white children do?" His look was challenging. "They left the schools. And what did they take with them? The resources. What they left behind was the appearance that we blacks were in control of education. The reality is that without resources, we just aren't there."

His sense of frustration and betrayal was palpable, and I waited in the silence for him to continue. He looked pained, and his voice was gentle. "The black parents had faith that their children would be adequately educated. We'd told them that for so long: 'If you get education, you get liberation.'" He pushed back his chair and looked at me. "Let's be honest about who is being educated in our country, and who is not being educated in our country. How 'educated' is a black child who can't spell, can't read? How 'liberated' is a black child who can't count? A computer is not going to help him. How can he use it?"

Leslie McLemore

Very different voices could be heard from many new black elected officials who had finally achieved a place where they felt they could finally effect change. When I met Dr. Leslie McLemore, a professor of political science at Jackson State University, he had just been elected to the city council in Jackson. I had sought him out at the suggestion of Fannie Lou Hamer. During four activist years at Rusk College from 1960 to 1964, McLemore had lent himself to the struggle that was engulfing the South. Founding the first NAACP chapter at Rusk, his campus activism had led him to friendships and political association with Medgar Evers, Amzie Moore, and Fannie Lou Hamer. Her life and mission had made an indelible impression on the young militant. He had worked closely with her from the very first days of the Mississippi Freedom Democratic Party. I knew that carrying Mrs. Hamer's legacy forward remained one of the pivotal goals in McLemore's educational and political life.

Still youthful, McLemore made a tall, striking figure with his silver hair and broad smile. He moved with the confidence of someone at home with the public, knowing who he was, where he had been, and what he was about. If his looks suggested an affable and successful politician, they were accurate. But what I found behind the warm facade and the sometimes booming voice was a passionate and tireless educator. More than a professional calling, education appeared to be his moral center.

"Living here in Mississippi is something I wanted to do, elected to do. Since the movement was the defining moment in my life, it changed my outlook on the world, on my role in it. And I bring that with me to the city council." He chuckled, smiling at his own utter seriousness. He eased back in his chair and sipped his neglected coffee. "I try to demonstrate that at the council, but sometimes it's tough when people don't under-stand where you are coming from, or where you are trying to go, particu-larly in terms of race. But I'm old-fashioned, or maybe just old enough to remember, that in Mississippi we tried for so many years to work it out as two separate bodies, two separate entities, and it didn't work. I believe in the spirit of the civil rights movement. It's going to take blacks and whites and people of color, working together, to create the circumstances where change is possible, where we can help provide for better housing, better jobs, and better education. Serving on the city council is an extension of my work in the civil rights movement, an extension of my teaching, an extension of my mentoring. What we black elected officials must do is use the council as a forum to help educate the community, and to use what access we have to help influence the direction of change."

Life is change, and change was transforming Mississippi. At the cen-tury's end, Mississippi had more black legislators than any state in the nation. What that would foretell was a history yet to be written.

thirty-three

In Memoriam

the time Fannie Lou Hamer and I had spent working together in Mississippi in 1964 and 1965 and on her trips north at our home in Connecticut was a rich gift to me and to our life as a family. June and Fannie Lou shared a special bond of affection and mutual respect, delighting in hours of conversation. Richard and my daughter, Laurie, came to treasure the times we broke bread with her and heard the marvelous stories of a life that would always be an inspiring example to them of what one remarkable spirit can accomplish. To me, she was the single bravest, most formidable person I met during my years with the Freedom Movement, and the most memorable.

In 1977, while working on one of our Rediscovery documentaries in our Connecticut editing room, I received a heartbroken call from Pap Hamer. His usual slow, deep, deliberate voice sounded muffled and shaken. "Mrs. Hamer is dying, Tracy. I think if you want to see her, you ought to come down real soon."

The hushed and sorrowful voice of Pap Hamer lingered in my mind as June and I hurried to Mound Bayou. The message was shocking but not really surprising. It had been months since we had last seen her, and we knew that she had been in declining health. The courageous spirit that had sustained so many of us was in the end no match for the cancer, diabetes, and failing heart that were laying siege to her. We prayed that we would reach our dear friend in time.

For two days we were at Mrs. Hamer's bedside, sharing happy memories when the fog of her palliatives would lift, holding her hand when she would drift to frightening places. On the day we had to leave, she was propped up in bed, seemingly at peace and looking calm. "Be careful driving up to Memphis," she said. The deep, resonant voice that once could fill a cathedral was soft and weak. Her large eyes turned to me, and a smile lit the large, expressive face. "I know you know the way, Tracy." We were both remembering how many times I had driven Fannie Lou Hamer to church, to register voters, to organizing meetings, to services in Harlem, to bail-fund lectures in Connecticut. Those conversations we shared I would never forget. They revealed a mind that was always seeking a deeper understanding of history and of the human condition. And most unforgettable were the abiding love and faith that sprang from her Christianity. I knew that I would probably never again meet a truer person of faith than Mrs. Hamer. She reached for June's hand. "And June, send my love to Dick and Laurie." They embraced, knowing it would be for the last time.

When we left the Delta, Mrs. Hamer's presence filled our silent car. We knew so well how extraordinary her life had been. This nearly untutored black woman, the seventh child of a sharecropper's family of twenty, had grown to become the voice and soul of the Freedom Movement. And now at sixty, much too young, that voice was about to be stilled. On March 20, 1977, only days after we were back in Connecticut, Charles McLaurin, who had been Fannie Lou Hamer's staunchest comrade, called from Indianola with the grievous news. "She's gone. Mrs. Hamer has gone."

In 1998, June, my wife and inspiring partner of fifty-five years, died of heart failure. She died peacefully and in my arms. Words cannot describe the enormity of the loss that I, our children, our grandchildren, and her extraordinary circle of loving friends encountered at her leaving. Her legacy lives in the gifts of love she gave so unstintingly to all of us. And it resides, too, in the integrity of the research and editing skill she brought to all the work we shared. June cared passionately about justice and fairness, and believed implicitly in the perfectibility of her fellow men and women, and the society we were creating. We miss her wisdom, her modesty, her wonderful sense of humor. To those who loved her, her loss is immeasurable, but her light still helps us to find our way.

June's passing was a seismic event in this artist's life. So many familiar landmarks in my usually tranquil landscape were suddenly unfamiliar, and the well-honed routines of shared work and pleasure seemed to be ruptured and beyond repair. Like many who have suffered grievous loss, I found comfort finally in a return to lifelong routines of work. For more than a year, my head and my heart were engaged in a project that began to assuage some of the sorrow and melancholy that I felt. The letters and drawings that I had sent her from Britain and the invasion beaches of Normandy became the materials with which I wrote my memorial to my wife, *My War: A Love Story in Letters and Drawings.*

As I was rediscovering the pleasure and excitement of writing, which I had not done since the publication of *Stranger at the Gates* in 1966, I retrieved a splendid friendship with Gloria Cole. Our families had been friends for more than thirty-five years. Now a divorcée, she was pursuing a varied and rich career in journalism. In that role she had reviewed several of our film documentaries and written a profile on my work in the war and in the civil rights movement. Her credentials as a considerate and loving friend had been established many years before June's untimely death. But to find that a wonderful friendship could grow and flower into a total, loving partnership in these autumn years was something neither of us could have anticipated. Love, we found to our delight, has its own season, its own clock, and its own calendar. And when we announced to our five children and ten grandchildren that we were inviting them to our wedding, it was eye-popping and wonderful. When we wed in 2000, it was a joyous occasion for both of us, an auspicious beginning of the next exciting chapter of our lives. I had found a beautiful, talented, and loving partner whose keen intelligence and fertile curiosity would bring new horizons into my life.

The year 2000 was a great personal watershed. Midwifed by Random House, *My War: A Love Story in Letters and Drawings* was born, a beautiful child that started a life of her own in a brand new century. And on the national book tour for *My War* that Gloria and I shared, I saw the contributions of sensitive insight that my new wife could bring to any creative work we might share.

thirty-four

Linda Davis

In November 2001, I had the chance to have Gloria meet the woman whom I got to know best among the summer volunteers. Linda Davis laughed with pleasure when she heard we were in Washington. "Come on over. There's so much to catch up on!"

"Let me bring in some coffee," Linda said. "It'll just take a minute. It's so good to have you both here!" She went into the kitchen, and we moved slowly through the well-lived-in family room. There was a relaxed feeling of comfort, the kind of a home where three young boys could stretch out without worrying about where they put their feet. I suddenly spotted my drawing on the wall. I took Gloria's arm and led her closer. "And on your left," I announced with pride, "you'll notice an original Sugarman of an original Linda Davis." It was the sketch I had made of Linda leading two of the girls from the Freedom School in a gambol across the sunbaked earth in Ruleville, Mississippi. "Circa 1964," I said, grinning at the memory. "She was nineteen and looked about fifteen. That morning she was leading the best and only modern dance class in the whole Mississippi Delta. The kids were panting, trying to keep up."

Linda had quietly reentered the room with the coffee and chuckled when she saw us examining the drawing. "Well," she said. "I was thirty-seven years younger."

Still slender and vivacious, Linda had apparently handled the years since the "long, hot summer" with grace. Some people just get older, I thought. And some, like Davis, just get more so of who they were. The seeming fragility of the slight young woman I had first met in 1964 was no longer there. It had been replaced by a ripening, a calm confidence that had been acquired during her tumultuous life as a political and legal

43. Linda Davis, now a superior court judge, leading the dance class at the Freedom School, 1964.

"You can do it. Yes, you can!"

activist. Now a superior court judge of the District of Columbia in Washington, the wife of Robert I. Richter, also an associate judge of the Superior Court, and the mother of three sons, she looks with quiet satisfaction at what the years have given her. Her gaze is steady and strong, the look of a confident and mature woman. But when she laughs her eyes are as wide, alive, and full of mirth as when she first arrived in the Delta, a sophomore from Oberlin College.

Gloria had been listening attentively, eager to hear more about the summer that had become so meaningful to both of us. "Didn't you need permission to go to Mississippi from your folks, Linda? You were only nineteen."

Linda nodded. "If you were under twenty-one, you had to. But my folks were progressive people, and there was a history of political activism in the family. So they had signed off on it in the spring. But when the news broke about the three civil rights workers going missing, they had second thoughts. They had a family meeting and deputized my dad, who was a corporate lawyer in Winnetka, to go to Oxford and talk me out of going. He arrived just after our incredible last session in Oxford when Bob Moses had so honestly spelled out the dangers that lay ahead. My dad pleaded with me to come back home, and I said, 'I can't do that.' And to his credit, he didn't insist. The whole family, once they got used to the idea of my being there, was terrifically supportive. Both of my sisters and my mother did tough volunteer work in the South, and my father was a great sponsor of the community center we started in Ruleville. The really hard thing for the family was when I decided to stay down in Ruleville at the end of the 1964 summer."

"Why did you decide to stay?" asked Gloria. "Almost all the volunteers in the Delta went home or back to campus."

"It was the fear we all had about what was going to happen when we all left," Linda replied, "wondering whether there was going to be retribution by the local white community against those whom we had encouraged to stand up during the course of the summer. I knew that when we all came down it changed the level of attention being paid to Mississippi by the country. And I knew that anytime we volunteers got arrested, there were people like my dad with political connections in Washington who could immediately contact the Department of Justice. When the local sheriffs started to realize that, the level of harassment and violence was cut down. That meant the black community was less powerless, and safer, too. That seemed a good reason to stay."

"It was a good reason," I agreed, "but it took enormous guts to stay on all that winter in Ruleville." I turned to Gloria. "To be practically alone, a white young woman living in the Sanctified Quarter, a sitting and visible target, took something very special. It's no wonder that the black community loved her as they did."

Linda reddened at the compliment, but quickly interjected: "Not everybody in the black community loved me. After you all left in the fall, I had an encounter with Mr. Smith, the principal of the black high school." Turning to Gloria, she said, "The school was just terrible and shocking. At the Freedom School that summer, we had been inundated with books from the North, wonderful books, but more than we could possibly use. I wanted to give the extra books to the high school, books they had never had, and Mr. Smith wouldn't take them." Her voice broke and she stared at us. *"Would not take them."* The scorn she felt embittered her voice. "He was afraid to take anything that was tainted by or associated with the Freedom House. *Afraid.* And I had a screaming match with him. No," she hooted, "Mr. Smith did not love me."

I remembered how upsetting it had been to discover that there could be fissures in the black community. No one at Oxford had prepared us for that reality. They were most apparent when the movement threatened the marginal influence of those blacks, like Mr. Smith, who had long been forced to do the bidding of the white power structure. People like Mrs. Hamer, or ministers who could offer their churches to the movement, were a threat to the quiescent pattern of behavior in the black community, and to the comfort of positions held by people like Principal Smith.

Linda said, "Being up there in Ruleville, feeling cut off from the others who were opening up Indianola, was lonely. And watching the beginning of divisions within the black community was hard. It was sobering to see that not everyone loved Mrs. Hamer, that some people who had profited from her actions were backbiting and jealous of her. I hadn't understood really that people could act like people do sometimes, that there could be factions. As the senior movement person there, I had to figure out how to respond in the most productive way. It was my first real stirring in politics, and it was very hard."

The world of the Delta in 1964 seemed to have eerily moved into Linda's bright Washington kitchen. We watched the slender woman move now to refill the cups, her eyes alight with memory and a smile playing on her lips. "It never seems all that far away, does it, Tracy?"

"But it was tough," I said, "trying like hell to empower people who had always been powerless. I remember talking with you back in '65 when I returned to Ruleville, and you were so troubled about that. You had stayed and spent the fall and winter, working with Mrs. Hamer to register voters. You were exhausted, and I think you shared that feeling of powerlessness, Linda."

She frowned, and her eyes seemed to seek a distant horizon. "Oh, yes. And how I hated it," she said vehemently. She turned to us. "I think that sense of powerlessness is what helped drive me to law school at Harvard after I left Mississippi, and eventually to the Justice Department." Her eyes kindled. "It was in '65 that I decided, in a very profound way, that I would never again be that powerless. And the Justice Department provided a wonderful forum where I could use that power to effect change."

Gloria looked quizzical. "You mean the power that can come when people can vote?"

"Certainly," replied Linda. "The power that comes *only* with the vote, Gloria. Much of my job in the Delta was trying to register black voters. I was working mostly with black women who had found the courage to go all the way down to the county seat in Indianola to try to register. Many of them had made that trip of thirty miles more than *twenty* times. And each and every time they had been refused by the white registrar of voters. *Twenty times!*" The anger in her voice was as ardent as it had been almost four decades before. "Imagine the feeling of rejection those women felt, the humiliation of being told, 'You're not *smart* enough to vote.'" The remembered pain and anguish she felt were mirrored in her face. "'You're not *good* enough to vote.'"

Those recollections still burned in my memory as well: the rigged questionnaires, the required "interpretations" of archaic Mississippi state laws, the brutal rejections by half-literate registrars of voters who were determined to keep black citizens voteless and powerless. For most of the summer volunteers, that cynical charade was a hideous perversion of the democratic process. But watching the black community refuse to be intimidated by all the powerful establishment forces that summer was at once humbling and inspiring. It was a lesson in courage that Linda and all the volunteers that summer learned, and never forgot. We had borne witness to people who lived every day in fear yet persevered.

"Their commitment gave me such courage later," Linda said in a subdued voice, "when I joined the Department of Justice. Our civil rights cases were not always the most popular with the FBI, and we had to battle sometimes to keep moving forward with prosecutions in the South. There were times that were very dark, very frustrating. But my experience with the movement in Mississippi, working for ends that couldn't always be guaranteed, gave me the strength to keep on pushing at Justice." Her voice brightened. "And it was great to be doing that work, to feel I had some power when I got back to the South." She took a deep breath, and her eyes were very steady. "It mattered a lot to me. A lot."

"What made you decide to work with the Justice Department, Linda? Certainly, the FBI seemed hardly our friend in 1964."

She nodded. "They weren't. But when I stayed on in the fall, the Justice Department was down in the Delta, involving voter registration lawsuits. County by Mississippi county, a very tedious way to proceed. But it was effective. And I got to see very good and dedicated Justice people, people like John Doar, whom I admired so much, doing their job. I remembered that after I got my law degree. I was happy to join Justice, and never regretted the years I worked there. It was often long and laborious effort. I worked on an investigation of a Klan cross burning and shooting with a fine FBI agent for three *years*. Three long years." She smiled happily, remembering. "And we ultimately got a conviction of nineteen of the twenty-one Klansmen. It was a wonderful, successful effort."

"Power?" Gloria asked with a smile.

"Power," said Linda.

"You paid a lot of dues, Linda," I said. "And you paid them for almost eighteen years at Justice. Now there are people who look back at that time and write that time off as "just a sixties thing, more smoke and mirrors than substance." How do you respond when you hear that?"

"They weren't there," she answered quietly. "You can look at the summer both in a personal way or in a more global fashion. Part of my job at Justice was working on hate crimes or police abuse cases in Mississippi. I did a lot of traveling. I'm sure everybody wishes that there were fewer cases of both, that there had been more progress and change. But I remember my first trip down there as part of the Justice Department in the early seventies, and how significant the change was. What a wonderful feeling it was not to have that terrible fear of the local government that we all felt in 1964. The incredible relief I felt to be able to ride on a Mississippi highway without being afraid that I was going to be physically harmed, run off the road, and left in a ditch. We both remember that that was the reality in '64 and '65, Tracy, and that has stopped. There simply isn't that fear now. Mississippi is like a lot of America today. And one of the reasons is because of the very tough work of the Justice Department.

"In the early days when I was there, my Civil Rights Division would bring cases all the time, but either the grand jury would not indict or, in the rare case when they would, the likelihood of a trial jury conviction was not very high. To this date, the State of Mississippi has never even indicted anyone for the murders of Goodman, Schwerner, and Chaney. Perhaps they will, now that they finally got a conviction on de la Beckwith, who assassinated Medgar Evers. But the Justice Department did bring the men who killed Goodman, Schwerner, and Chaney to trial on the only federal charges that were germane, the violation of the boys' civil rights. And they got a conviction out of a Mississippi jury. Those killers had to serve years of jail time. Now that is not a small miracle. That's a large miracle."

I regarded the composed young judge who sat opposite. Her eyes were alight with quiet pride. It had been a journey of thirty-seven years since that frightening announcement at the Oxford orientation: "Three of our guys are missing."

"Have you ever regretted that you chose the law as your career?" I asked.

"No," she said emphatically. "Not that there haven't been times of horrible pressure and bureaucratic battles. But the very year that I was helping prosecute the police defendants who had beaten Rodney King in Los Angeles, one of the hardest tours of duty I ever had, I received the very first John Doar Award from the Civil Rights Division. I'm very proud of that, because I remember what John Doar did. It was quite wonderful, and I felt somehow I had come full circle."

The Richters' youngest son, Billy, fresh from just passing his driving test, excitedly rushed through the room, pausing just long enough to get introduced. Linda's affectionate gaze followed him as he loped up the stairs to his phone, eager to pass the word about his license on to his friends. "Another lawyer?" I asked.

"I don't know," she answered. "If David, Charlie, or Billy really wanted to go into law for good reasons, as I think Bob and I did, that would be fine. But so many friends who are lawyers are not happy with their lives. They don't feel their lives in the law have had very much meaning. That seems very sad to me. I feel so fortunate. I've had a wonderful career in the law."

John Lewis

before going to Mississippi in 2001, Gloria and I met with John Lewis in his congressional office in Washington. Of all the leadership I had come to know in SNCC, this former chairman was the only one who could speak of love with a religious simplicity that did not permit embarrassment. Unlike many in the movement who regarded love and nonviolence merely as a sometimes useful tactic, Lewis had been taught from his earliest days to embrace love as a way of life. "I was taught that there was a divine spark in every human being," he said quietly, "and you didn't have the right to destroy or abuse that spark." That was not a voice often heard in the halls of the United States Congress, and it raised some skeptical eyebrows. But it was not derided by many because Lewis was a legitimate hero, nearly a martyr, of the civil rights movement. And he was a rare breed from Georgia.

John Lewis was a rising black political star of the New South. From the earliest days of the Freedom Rides in 1960 in Mississippi to the vicious attack by the police on the Selma March in Alabama, John has never deviated from the principle of nonviolence. Of all the people I came to know in the civil rights movement, none suffered more physical assaults and injury from those who would deny him his full rights as a citizen. Stubbornly and consistently, he has answered hate and violence with a calm dignity and forbearance.

"When someone spat at me," he said, "or started beating me, or arrested me, I didn't have an ill feeling toward that person. The struggle was not against *him*. It was against custom, tradition, the system, bad laws. So nonviolence was a natural way for me."

44. Calling Washington.

"Three of our boys are missing!"

"I confess I find it astonishing, John," I said. "I remember so clearly when the mounted police came charging into you and the marchers at the Pettus Bridge in Montgomery, and you were able to simply stand there. I could never have done that."

He sat quiet in his chair. "I had learned from my childhood that love is a more excellent way." His low, sonorous voice filled the room. The afternoon sun glinted on a tall wall of honors and tributes to the eight-term congressman from Atlanta. "A more excellent way," he said again. "And over the years as a congressman, I have found that violence tends to create more problems than it solves."

With his modesty and reticence, he had seemed an unlikely chairman of SNCC when I first saw him at the orientation in Oxford in 1964. But as I learned in the months to follow, real leaders came in all sizes, all colors, and all styles. Lewis, who has gained a reputation as a wily, sophisticated, and tough campaigner, besting even his old comrade Julian Bond in a Democratic primary, is successfully carving out a long and distinguished career in the House of Representatives. To many, he appears closer in spirit and style to Martin Luther King than to a political bruiser like Stokely Carmichael, who wrested the SNCC leadership from him. It was a painful loss for Lewis, but he has learned to be a survivor. There are some who believe him to be more calculating and determined than a casual spectator might expect, observing his quiet demeanor and knowing of his gentle, rural, Baptist background. But he is a fierce champion of the minority American, and a proud possessor of his Georgia seat in the U.S. House of Representatives.

"For many years," he observed, "within the movement itself, a group of young people wanted to build 'the beloved community,' a truly interracial democracy. I think in the summer of '64, in Mississippi, those young blacks and whites probably represented one of the finest hours in American history. Those people really did believe that somehow, and someway, that by literally holding on to those ideals, putting their bodies on the line, they could redeem the soul of America." His eyes grew distant, and then focused on the two of us across the desk. "They thought they could make America something different, and something better."

"And did they?" asked Gloria in a troubled voice. "There's still so much racism."

The congressman answered softly. "I think so, Gloria. When I look back on it, all these years later, I can see that although we couldn't immediately see the results of our work, the trees are bearing the fruits of our labor today. You go back to the Black Belt in Alabama, or southwest Georgia, or the Mississippi Delta, and it's a different world. Today you see blacks and whites working and sharing and building together. Well, we planted those seeds.

"I've seen unbelievable changes. Some young people I run into on campuses argue that 'nothing's changed.' And I say if you want to believe that, you can. But come, and walk in my shoes and I'll show you a different world than we had in the sixties. We have not created 'the beloved community,' and it's not the Promised Land. But we're on our way. I remember what Bobby Kennedy said: 'There must be a revolution, not in the streets, but in our hearts and our minds and our souls.'"

During that afternoon with John Lewis, I was stirred again by the simple idealism of the man. For more than sixteen years he has walked the corridors of political power as a black congressman from the Deep South. He has lectured widely and written significantly about the civil rights struggle that he made his own pilgrimage. Yet John Lewis, whom I first saw in Oxford nearly four decades ago, remains in his heart, mind, and soul a nonviolent revolutionary. It is easy now to listen to aging warriors like John Lewis as they reflect on those long-past battles, and easier still to applaud from our safe vantage point in history. What is so hard to remember, really remember, is what was so heroically paid for those victories of the spirit.

Nonviolence

t here's a whole story could be written about guns and Mississippi,"
said Charlie Cobb. "Nonviolence was never an issue when I came to
the Delta in 1961; it never came up. Maybe if you were doing sit-ins, where
you had to protect yourself, it would be something to talk about. But we
weren't doing sit-ins in the Delta. Violence in Mississippi was always mob
violence, and the way to protect yourself from a mob was not a question
of violence or nonviolence. It was a simple question: 'How can I survive
this?' It's not like a cowboy film where you're at one end of the street with
your righteous gun and the Klan is at the other end, and you're going to
face each other in a shootout.

"No." His voice was quieter, more intense than it had been. "You're
driving your car at night in the Delta, and all of a sudden a shot rings out.
And it hits you, like it did with Jimmy Travis, or it misses you." He swallowed hard, and plunged ahead. "Or you're in a church, and it gets blown
up. Or you're in a house in Ruleville with Mr. and Mrs. McDonald, as
McLaurin and I were, when faceless people fire shotguns into their living
room. These are not situations that get resolved around the philosophy of
nonviolence."

Charlie's face was taut as he relived that night. "The McDonalds had
to jump into the bathtub to escape the bullets, and Mac and I had to figure out how to not get killed." His expression softened, and a sardonic
smile crossed his face. "The next morning Mayor Durrough came with the
police and arrested me for the shooting. He said that I did it for publicity,
that I had set the whole thing up. His deputy, the man who killed Emmett
Till, the fourteen-year-old kid, for whistling at a white woman, hauled me
off to jail."

The subject of nonviolence, whether as a tactic in the struggle as seen by Charlie Cobb or as a moral North Star for other icons of the civil rights movement like John Lewis, has always been evocative. In a conversation with Martha Honey that followed our meeting with John Lewis, it seemed clear that one's position on nonviolence was the result of experience rather than of doctrine. When we chatted in Martha Honey's Maryland home, the comfortable living room was alive with sculptures, wall hangings, and native graphics. They were affectionate souvenirs of reportorial assignments shared with her husband, Tony Avrigan.

"Did your time in the movement ever make you question your early Quaker commitment to nonviolence, Martha?"

"In the context of the United States in 1964, given its social and political history, nonviolence absolutely made political sense," she said, ruminating. "Mississippi showed me a part of the United States I didn't know

45. Charles McLaurin with summer volunteers.
"Nonviolence is a weapon."

was there. The depth of hatred that was there." Martha's voice echoed the wonder she had felt on her tour of duty in the Delta. "I remember riding along in an interracial car and these carloads of whites going past us, sticking their arms out and screaming and yelling at us . . . " Her voice broke. "I had never seen hatred like that before . . . hurling hatred at people who were just wanting to exercise their constitutional rights. It was astounding. Mississippi in 1964 was like a foreign land. But my time in Mississippi made me want to go to Africa, to Central America, to see other foreign lands."

Her eyes drifted to the artifact-adorned wall of the living room, lingering briefly. "So Mississippi changed my life. I didn't just want to *see* those places. I wanted to sink my teeth into them. To live the experience." She smiled, nodding at her conclusion. "The rest of my life, and I'm fifty-five, has been trying to recapture that depth of feeling, that commitment and passion, the way I felt in Mississippi, where everything was so heightened."

She looked up sharply, and her voice was very firm. "I'm a product of enormous privilege, so I haven't really been tested the way I'd have to be to know if I'd always adhere to nonviolence. But what happened when Tony and I went off to Africa made me realize that other people in different circumstances can rightly make other decisions. But I still believe that in the United States' context, nonviolent direct action, assertive, not passive, can be absolutely the right tactic." The couple had lived for long periods away from the United States. Their reporting on the conflicts in Central America nearly cost Tony his life. After moving to Africa, they wrote of the struggles of the newly emerging states on that continent to break free of colonialism.

Still youthful and vibrant, Martha retains the calm, dedicated, and humorous qualities I recalled so well. Her grown children away at college, and her journalist husband off on an assignment dealing with the accelerating conflict in Afghanistan, we had the chance to get reacquainted after decades.

I had first known Martha when she was a high school student in my town of Westport, Connecticut. Shortly after I arrived in the Delta in 1964, I learned that she had gone to work as a volunteer in Holmes County as a Freedom School teacher, and drove over to visit with her. I was concerned that as an eighteen-year-old freshman from Oberlin she might be finding rugged Holmes County tough to handle. When I found her with the Turnbow family, relaxed and happy, I realized my concerns were unwarranted. Martha had decided to go south because the cause seemed that important, and now she was starting to do what she wanted to do. There was no sign of apprehension in her young eyes in 1964.

When I reminded her now of my early worries about her, she smiled appreciatively. "My interest in peace and human rights started very early, long before going to Holmes County that summer. It's just been part of my life since I was very young. I went to Quaker work camps, worked in Harlem on weekend projects, and went to Appalachia to a work site there." She paused, "Do you remember a group called 'Concern' in Westport, Tracy? Well, I was one of that bunch, one of those disaffected young people who didn't quite fit in with the stereotypes of what upper-class suburbia was all about."

I laughed. "Of course I remember. My daughter, Laurie, was part of 'Concern' a few years later!"

"I guess I'm not surprised. It was a great group. We picketed Woolworth's, though we didn't 'sit in.'" She chuckled, remembering. "'Concern' was sort of a mixture of emotional support, political action, and folk music . . . all on Friday nights and weekends! And when it was time to think about college, I picked Oberlin because I heard it was the first college to integrate and had been part of the Underground Railway! Oberlin was a pretty activist school, but I think I was the only student who decided to go to the orientation in Oxford."

"How did your folks take the news?"

"They were supportive, and they were nervous. Dad called me into his study, and that was always serious. 'We have to talk about this trip you're planning to Mississippi,' he said. Since his whole professional life had been spent in academia, I assured him that some of the organizers of the Summer Project came from Yale. So he called one of them to the house so he could make sure I would be well looked after. "And this young law student promised he would take care of me, and I would be all right." She burst out laughing. "Well, he had no way to promise that. And secondly, this young law student turned out to be Jonathen Bingham!" She hooted at the memory. "Jonathen Bingham! He ended up later helping a Black Panther to escape and had to go underground himself!" Her laughter now was unconstrained. "The antithesis of what my father thought a patrician Yale law school student was!"

Serious now, she settled back on the couch. "It was mixed emotions for my folks. Being a parent now, I can understand those feelings." I waited for her to continue. Quietly, she said, "To me it was just the right thing to do. I went without a lot of fears. The fears came later." She looked at Gloria and me, seeking to find the right words to describe what that hard summer had meant to her. "It was a marvelous summer for me." She hesitated, and grinned. "*Mostly* marvelous. I felt so privileged to be there, so humbled by meeting people who really had put their lives on the line, *on the line,* for just trying to get basic human rights! So moved by the experience, by the overwhelming generosity of the local black community. Mr. Turnbow and his wife and his daughter took us in, and we basically ate up their winter food. And they wouldn't take any money from us. We were hardly even aware of the depth of their need, or their thin margin for just getting by." There were tears in Martha's eyes. "For just getting by . . .

"Toward the end of the summer, Mr. Turnbow was chosen to go as one of the Mississippi Freedom Democratic Party delegates up to the Democratic National Convention in Atlantic City. And the other woman volunteer and I told Mrs. Turnbow, 'You must go with him.' And she said, 'I can't. I don't have anything to wear to Atlantic City.' So we bought her a dress, and Mrs. Turnbow went with Mr. Turnbow to the convention!" She looked enormously pleased at the memory. But then her face became reflective. "That was *all* they ever accepted from us."

I looked at the solemn, still young face, remembering the girl I saw at the Turnbows nearly four decades before. "How would you advise your child today about going into an apartheid situation, as you did then in Mississippi?"

Her gaze was steady. "From a very early age, our daughter has always been an activist. I guess I would have many of the emotions my parents had. But Mississippi was such an incredible learning experience for me that I long for my kids to have that same kind of experience. I want them to, and yet I'd worry about them. I would encourage anybody, even my kids, to have the life-changing experience that Mississippi gave me."

The pluck and resilience that so characterized Martha Honey were some of the astonishing discoveries I made first at Oxford, and then on a regular basis during that summer of '64. The young white women, mostly nurtured in protective middle-class homes, who chose to go to work in the movement, were tough. Many, like Martha Honey and Linda Davis, had ventured south to be teachers in Freedom Schools. But in quick order they became visible, courageous civil rights workers, daring the fury of the white establishment as they canvassed, picketed, and willingly shared the lives of the Negro families who had taken them in. It was striking how that process of racial immersion during those times of violence would often acutely alter their political perceptions. It might well be true that back home in the North concepts like "Black Power" were riling and upsetting many of the movement's liberal supporters, but very different perceptions existed within the movement itself.

"After Stokely Carmichael launched 'Black Power' as a uniting principle of the movement, some white civil rights workers were deeply offended, Martha. Some even left the movement. How did that affect you?"

"As you probably remember, a lot of us workers in the movement were critical of Martin Luther King. He just didn't seem militant enough. We approved of his nonviolence, but we had the feeling he was kind of 'selling out' by working so closely with the white establishment. So some of the ingredients for 'Black Power' were already apparent in SNCC. I had always had the feeling that I was in Mississippi serving a movement that was led by African Americans. In Holmes County, I was taking directions from the black community leaders. So I didn't feel really angry or hurt. I thought that that was the stage that things were at. But later we found that it was a more complicated matter. Part of it was learning that there had been outside infiltrators who had used 'Black Power' as a device to break up the movement, to split black and white unity. With hindsight, I think maybe I might not have been as positive and accepting, more wary that this was not a healthy path to be going down."

On the day that followed, we had the chance to explore that critical time of racial separation in SNCC with Linda Davis. No white whom I knew in the movement had volunteered as selflessly as she, or had so won and earned the love and respect of the black community in the Delta. "You had developed such a tight relationship with the community during this whole time, Linda. It was so mutually trusting," I said. "And then there was this rupture in the SNCC leadership which suddenly ended the racially integrated movement in Mississippi, and the white volunteers were no longer welcome. How did that affect you?"

Her face was reflective, and she slowly shook her head from side to side. "Oh, it was so sad, so disappointing. That all happened at the fall meeting in '64. And what a tense meeting that was. It was the time when Stokely Carmichael called for running the whites out of SNCC. There was a whole lot of discussion, a lot of argument that times had changed, that it was time for blacks to assert themselves. Stokely called for 'Black Power.' We whites should go organize in the white communities." She paused. "I don't think that any of us whites who were working down there ever worried about who was leading. I don't think that was the issue. I think the real issue was the black reaction to the racism that became so clear when the three workers were murdered. All of a sudden the country took notice of a brutal racism in Mississippi that had killed blacks for generations, and nobody had seemed to care. But when two of the murdered boys were whites from the North, the response was very strong and immediate. That was something that every black American recognized, and Stokely capitalized on it."

Linda's voice was hushed, and her eyes held mine. "SNCC's leadership decision to make it a black movement was perhaps a proper decision. But it ignored the truth that our white presence had helped generate attention and action, and opened up Mississippi. It was hard for me not to react in fury, even though I recognized that a pernicious racism lay beneath all of it."

"I think very many volunteers felt that way, Linda," I responded, but I was sobered by Linda's perceptions of the motivation of the racial anger, and annoyed at my own blindness in perceiving it. How difficult it is to think outside the racial box you were born in. No black friend in the movement, I realized, had been that candid with me about that gulf of sensitivity.

thirty-seven

Julian Bond

a s I eased our car alongside the curb, Gloria asked, "Isn't that Julian? I think I recognize him from seeing him on *The Today Show*." She paused. "Maybe not. That fellow looks too young." I turned off the ignition and stared out the rear window. The tall, slim man waiting at the corner spotted us and smiled. "That's Julian," I laughed. "And he's always looked too young!"

Nothing very much had changed in Julian Bond since we had last met eight years ago. He was speaking at Fairfield University to a rapt, young, and mostly white audience, holding the podium with a quiet authority and a ready smile that made him appear even younger. Here was a flesh-and-blood activist who had "walked the walk" and endured imprisonment for his efforts to gain the vote for disenfranchised blacks in Alabama, Georgia, and Mississippi. Here, standing before them, was an outspoken protester of American involvement in the war in Vietnam for which he had been pilloried by the Georgia legislature and denied his lawfully elected seat in the legislature. I watched the intent faces as this vibrant and engaged man breathed life into a history that for many in his audience was already mythic. Perhaps his close-cropped hair was a little more salt-and-pepper, his fine-featured face a bit more lined than I remembered. But he was still youthfully erect, and with the arresting presence I recalled from our very first meeting in 1964. As we moved to the terrace of the café, Gloria murmured to me, "I was right. He does look too young!"

From the time in 1964 when I joined the SNCC summer volunteers, our Connecticut home became a way station for many in the movement when they came north to raise funds or build support for the struggle in Mississippi. It was shortly after I had returned from the Delta in 1964

46. Canvassing voters in Drew.
"If you'll stand up, we'll stand with you!"

when we received a call from Shirley Belafonte at the SNCC office in New York City. Could we put up Julian Bond, who was on a fund-raising trip through New England? We were delighted to oblige, for we knew of Julian through his work as communications director for SNCC and as the editor of their publication, *Student Voice*. In one of the issues we had found that the editor was also a poet. The poem was passed around the family, and we eagerly looked forward to meeting its author.

I, too, hear America singing
But from where I stand I can only hear Little Richard
And Fats Domino.

But sometimes,
I hear Ray Charles
Drowning in his own tears
or Bird
Relaxing at Camarilla
or Horace Silver doodling,
Then I don't mind standing

a little longer.

The soft-spoken, slender young man with the short Afro who appeared at our door looked more like a poet than a revolutionary. Over the years that followed, we were to learn that Julian Bond was both.

Washington was basking in a warm September sunshine, and the three of us settled comfortably in a corner to talk. Gloria smiled as she regarded Bond. "I feel I know you from hearing you, and watching you, over the years. I'm really happy to meet you. Tracy told me about your getting involved in the movement when you were still in college. He said you went to Morehouse in 1957." She hesitated. "And that you didn't graduate until 1971. How come? What happened?"

Julian grinned and nodded. "He's right. It was SNCC that happened. I started working as communications director for SNCC in 1960, and it took more and more of my time. I started going back and forth to Mississippi and finally dropped out of college in 1961."

"How did your folks handle that?" I asked. "Particularly your father. He was dean of Atlanta University then."

Julian's face grew serious, and he was silent for a moment, studying the people passing in the street. "It wasn't easy for my parents seeing me drop out one semester short of graduation. My mother and father were the second generation of college graduates in their families, and they wanted the third generation to do the same thing. I do remember how shocked they were when I first got arrested at a sit-in during my freshman year." The recollection made him smile. Then, with obvious pride in his voice, he said, "I always felt my father and mother were very supportive of what I was doing." His eyes crinkled, seeing another time, and he chuckled. "My father even traveled to rural Mississippi with me, and made speeches there. That was not the kind of thing he'd usually do. He was used to speaking at academic conferences, not freedom rallies."

I studied this contemplative man who at sixty-one was still weighing the never-quite-balanced scales of parental expectations and child resolve, of obligation and personal desire. For more than forty years he has continued to forge an extraordinary public career of service that his academic parents could never have imagined for their young poetic son. From his college days as one of the founders of the Student Nonviolent Coordinating Committee to the chairmanship of the board of the National Association for the Advancement of Colored People, Bond has continued to be an activist in the movements for civil rights, economic justice, and peace. Yet the world of academia that for generations was the treasured turf of his family is still the chosen home for Julian. He is currently a distinguished scholar in residence at the American University in Washington, D.C., and a professor at the University of Virginia in the Department of History, and holds honorary degrees from twenty-one colleges across the United States. Looking now at this quiet, self-possessed, and scholarly man, it was hard to recall how demonized he had once been in those turbulent political events of the sixties.

Educated at a Quaker school in Pennsylvania, nonviolence had often been discussed in his classes. "But it always seemed to be a theory that didn't affect me," he recalled. "It was only when the civil rights movement began in 1960 and I became involved with the sit-in demonstrations that nonviolence became real to me."

I nodded in agreement. "Nonviolence only became real to me in Mississippi in 1964 when I witnessed unarmed civil rights workers, blacks and whites, facing down armed sheriffs." I had watched that dynamic turn the whole state of Mississippi around. It had been done by kids in sneakers, kids like Julian Bond.

Gloria had been intently listening to our recollections. Now she intervened. "But something changed, didn't it? Tracy told me that one of the songs that summer of '64 was 'Black and White Together, We Shall Overcome.' But by the end of '65 nobody was singing that anymore. All the talk was about 'Black Power,' and SNCC seemed to close itself off from white participation. What happened, Julian?"

"From the very early sixties, there had been a long debate about whether there should be any whites involved in SNCC," he responded. "In Georgia the SNCC leadership insisted that it be an integrated project. The argument was that the only way local blacks could lose their fear of white people was to see black and white kids working and living together. But in Mississippi, Bob Moses didn't want an integrated project. He wanted an all-Mississippi, all-black staff. He thought it was the only way the local blacks could make sense out of living in those wretched conditions. If they weren't going to be organizing to change their place, why live there? Later, of course, Moses became the greatest advocate for the integrated Summer Project in '64. He came to recognize how morally and strategically helpful that integration could be."

Julian leaned forward, eager to explain SNCC's tangled web of black and white history. "Moses was right," he said. "The deaths of Goodman, Schwerner, and Chaney focused so much attention on what the resistant white South would do to stop the civil rights movement that the whole country, for the first time, saw just how bad things were in Mississippi. That integrated lynching was the tipping point of the whole legacy of harassment, brutality, and arrests, the seminal moment of that whole summer. From then onward, things began to change. It broke the back of segregation in Mississippi."

Gloria frowned and pressed on. "So why did it have to become a black movement instead of an integrated one?"

Julian appeared thoughtful, wanting to be helpful in his answers. "After that 'long, hot summer,' the thinking of SNCC was that black people now could easily organize in the black communities. But no one was organizing white communities where so much of the real power resided. Since blacks couldn't organize in white communities, there was a strategic and political necessity for whites to leave and start that important organizing. At that time the argument seemed perfectly reasonable. It was only much later that I came to understand the enormous bitterness and hurt that many white workers felt by that decision."

"I think that some of us understood that there was a need for black self-realization at that time," I said. "It had been a long time coming, particularly for blacks in the South. Now blacks could start to express their pride and take power for themselves."

Julian nodded in agreement but looked morose. "I know that some of the white civil rights workers accepted the decision as strategic and correct. But it saddens me that others felt a rejection of their service and their sacrifice."

I agreed, "It is sad. But nevertheless, I've never met a summer volunteer who feels that his going to Mississippi was fruitless, or that his contribution was not of some value. What do you say, Julian, when people ask you what was really accomplished by the integrated movement in the South?"

He answered with an uncharacteristic vehemence. "Accomplished? We ended legal segregation. I'm old enough to remember when the law *required* racial separation. Now the law *forbids* it. In only five years, from 1960 to 1965, we *undid* an unjust segregation that had been in place for almost eighty years. We threw it out. Overturned it. That's what was accomplished." He stopped speaking, and his eyes scanned the busy Washington street beyond the terrace. When he spoke again, his voice was thoughtful and quiet. "It took a lot of sacrifice, a lot of struggle. And a lot of people died. But we did it."

His gaze returned to us at the table. "We're never going back to a segregated society, but we haven't gone forward enough to a society that's economically equitable, that's racially integrated. We can be very proud of what's been done up to now, but we have to realize there's a lot more struggle ahead."

"A hell of a lot, Julian," I agreed. "But what's so great for me is to see how far and wide the waves have gone out from the Mississippi Delta. The people we worked with left Mississippi, but they took what they learned with them."

Julian smiled. "They certainly did. Women from SNCC like Casey Hayden and Mary King were at the very beginning of the women's movement. Mario Savio and others went back to Berkeley and became the nucleus of the 'free speech movement' that grew into the successful movement against the war in Vietnam. You can see now that what they learned about their own power to effect change and how to organize helped them when they returned north."

"Julian," I said, "Mrs. Hamer always said, 'You just have to keep on keepin' on.' And I think a lot of us remember that."

A warm smile crossed Bond's face as he remembered Fannie Lou Hamer. "And she was right. She was always right."

As we stood up ready to leave, Julian paused at the table. "Seeing you again has been great," he said. "Somehow the friends I made in the movement are even closer to me than my high school or college classmates. The movement has been like a fraternity, like a big family. You know," he added quietly, "my years in the movement were the best years in my life."

It was time finally to leave Washington, to go home, sort out our thinking, and make plans for Mississippi. Now I wanted to talk with Charles McLaurin, my oldest mentor in the movement, and I wanted Gloria to meet him. Our plans to fly to Mississippi early in September were delayed by the catastrophe of the terrorist attack on the Twin Towers. This cruel invasion of terrorism into the American psyche suddenly seemed to make our impending research in Mississippi more relevant than I had even considered. I'd seen terrorism before. I'd seen it in Mississippi.

Part Four

Mississippi, October 2001

Mississippi Redux

t he terminal felt awfully quiet for a Friday morning," said Gloria, as she stowed her portfolio in the overhead rack. "Didn't you think so?"

"Yeah," I agreed. "But I guess we shouldn't have been surprised." It was only weeks since the terrorists had leveled the Twin Towers. I glanced fore and aft. "The plane is only half-full. Like the terminal."

As we settled into our seats for the flight to Mississippi, my wife's eyes seemed thoughtful as she stared out her window. "Tentative," she said softly. Turning to me now with a satisfied smile, she said, "Tentative. The terminal looked tentative." She laughed when she saw my look of surprise.

"What do you mean?"

"You know. Not quite ready for 'prime time.' Not quite ready to open for business. *Tentative.*" She nodded, comfortable now with her thoughts, and turned once more to the window as the plane began its slow journey to the runway.

I had to grin at my journalist wife. The comfort she found in words! *"Tentative."* I tried the word. "It's the right word, Gloria. Everything since 9/11 has felt tentative." Whether to fly at all had been a calculated decision, not easily arrived at. But Gloria knew I was reluctant to cancel the long-planned return to Mississippi, and she had gamely booked the flight.

I squeezed her hand as the airplane gunned its engines, lurched briefly, and then began the long, long race down the runway. Engines roaring, it lifted, finally, high into the New York sky. As the wing tilted, revealing the whole sweep of the New York harbor, I reached across her seat. "There! Look, just to the left . . . where that pall of dust is. . . . That's where they were."

As we departed the plane in Jackson, we paused at the bottom of the steps, squinting in the brilliant afternoon sun, and breathing deep of the warm, moist air that blanketed the tarmac. "Welcome to the Magnolia State, Gloria honey," I drawled. "That's Mississippi air. And from now on, we walk slower."

Heading north from Jackson, the gently rolling rises of green began to flatten, and once we passed Yazoo City, they fell away completely. Through our windshield we could now see the distant horizon that told us we were entering the Mississippi Delta. Soon the seemingly endless rows of the cotton fields were cartwheeling past our windows.

"It's pretty," murmured Gloria. "Much prettier than I had imagined. I expected something browner, desolate, drier. Look!" she happily exclaimed. "It's even got lakes!" The sun was glancing off the surface of water, making grace notes in the repetitive green pattern of the cotton rows.

I laughed. "Well, little lakes. They're really ponds, Gloria, catfish farms. We'll be seeing them scattered all over the Delta in the next few days. Big business now for the farmers down here. They were just being started when I was first down here in the sixties."

Gloria looked pensive as she turned from the window. "Funny how different things can be than you imagined." She hesitated. "From all I had read I thought the Delta would be . . . scarier."

I looked at her questioning eyes, and smiled at her for reassurance. "It was scarier back in the sixties. The first time I came to the Delta, driving this two-lane highway to meet up with Charles McLaurin in Ruleville, I was scared to death. Spent most of my time watching my rearview mirror and sweating. But that's a good long time ago, Gloria. Times change."

She nodded, chuckling. "They sure do. Back in '64 you flew out of tranquil New York and found terrorism in Mississippi. And this morning, we left terrorism in New York and found . . . this." The last burnished rays of the sun were touching the fields. It looked like *The Angelus* as we pulled into Indianola.

The reunion with Charles and Virginia McLaurin seemed a seamless extension of a long, mutually treasured friendship. Not everything changes, I thought. The years of separation since our last meeting seemed simply to evaporate. Gloria's eyes were alight, savoring the shared reminiscences, experiencing for the first time the special qualities of my old friend. He had grown thicker through the waist, I noted, but was still muscular and agile. His hair that was once an Afro helmet of black was now a pepper-and-salt mixture. But there was a comfortable presence now, a greater openness that had come with the maturity and self-confidence he had gained in his years in public service with the City of Indianola. The dark glasses that once jealously protected him from unwanted scrutiny were not visible.

"Hey, Mac," I teased, "where are the shades? How do I know it's you?"

McLaurin laughed, easing back in his chair. "Don't need them at night. I'll wear them tomorrow morning when we drive up to Ruleville for the opening of Mrs. Hamer's park. Just so you'll know me!"

The four of us lingered long after dinner was done, all of us reluctant to end the conversation. Late in the evening, Gloria turned to McLaurin. "I'm really looking forward to the celebration tomorrow, Mac. I've read so much about Fannie Lou Hamer. Some say she was the 'soul of the movement' in Mississippi."

"She was," murmured Virginia.

McLaurin smiled. "Yeah. She was. Mrs. Hamer would never say that. But she was."

Gloria's hand covered mine as she continued. "Tracy has told me that it was you who found her up in the hills after they had shot up her house, and that it was you who brought her into the movement. He said there was nobody she trusted more than McLaurin. It sounds like such a wonderful friendship, Mac, a special one with a very special woman. I wish I'd known her!" She paused a moment, her eyes searching the face of McLaurin. "You knew her for such a long time, Mac. What made her so special to you?"

He pondered her question, then answered in a very quiet voice. "She saw a spiritual reality I didn't see." When Gloria looked questioning, he continued. "Mrs. Hamer became a real inspiration to me because she made me see values beyond the political, beyond the social. *Spiritual* values. She would always remind me, 'Mac, we ain't finished here on earth. There's a "forever," Mac.' He sipped his drink and then placed it carefully down on the table. "Mrs. Hamer questioned whether or not I was as involved, spiritually, as I should have been. More than once she'd remind me, 'If God is with you, Mac, then the devil can't stand against you.'" McLaurin's eyes moved about the table. "That was something I've had to learn over the years."

thirty-nine

Return to Ruleville

i t was Gloria who first spotted the sign from the backseat. "Ruleville. The Home of Fannie Lou Hamer," she said excitedly. "Isn't that nice!"

I had to smile. "It is. Wouldn't Mrs. Hamer be proud? But where's the Billups Gas Station, Mac? Used to be right over there on the left."

McLaurin turned in the passenger seat and looked at me. "Long gone. Lotta things you remember about Ruleville are long gone."

Gloria touched my shoulder. "I want to see where you lived. Can you still find it?"

"Turn here," said Mac. "I'll direct you. There's been some changes."

I felt disoriented. As we moved down the road, we passed the spot where Perry and Fannie Lou Hamer had lived. The old, dilapidated house had vanished. All that remained was the great pecan tree that had given all of us blessed shade. "It's all so different, Gloria. The road's paved now . . . there are streetlights . . . the sewage ditches are gone . . . and most of the houses I remember have been replaced."

"Federal housing," said McLaurin with satisfaction. "One of the good things that came to the Delta once we got the vote in '65." He shifted in his seat. "You remember Jack Harper down in Indianola? Used to think Jack was just one of the good old boys who didn't want anything to change in Sunflower County. But once the Voting Rights Act was passed, either Jack changed or what I had always thought changed." He laughed. "In the years since then, Harper and I have gotten on real well."

"I do remember Harper," I said. "He was chancery clerk and recorder of public documents. We always saw him at the county courthouse when you were still trying to get folks registered. I interviewed him when we were making the documentary film about Mrs. Hamer in 1980. He told me, 'Mrs. Hamer was initially perceived as an agitator. But as time went on, as change came about, she became known more as a leader of black people.' I had to smile at the recollection. On the very sidewalk where nearly every attempt to get blacks enrolled on the voting lists had been frustrated, the chancery clerk was now declaring: 'Mrs. Hamer's perception of the usefulness of the Voting Rights Act for the black people in Mississippi was correct.'"

McLaurin nodded. "A smart guy. Law school graduate from Ole Miss. Well, Jack always seemed to keep all his political options open. Mrs. Hamer knew that, and she worked with him when he was still chancery clerk down in Indianola to push for the federal housing subsidies for Sunflower County. HUD came through, and in the early seventies the neighborhoods you remember started to change." He stopped abruptly, and chuckled. "But not everything. There's Mr. and Mrs. Williams's house. Pull over."

The small, low house, covered with an imitation mustard-colored brick, looked just as I remembered it. "See that corrugated iron roof, Gloria? How I hated that iron roof. Every summer it made the inside into an oven." The little house appeared deserted now, and lonely. The houseplants in the empty tin cans that Mrs. Williams always kept on the ancient, listing wooden table outside the door were not to be seen. And the zinnias that had always made the place cheerful were gone. Weeds had obliterated the tiny lawn Mr. Williams had kept trimmed and overwhelmed the small coveted vegetable garden in the back where, on a hot summer afternoon, the elderly man had taught me how to chop weeds properly.

"What happened to Mr. and Mrs. Williams, Mac? It looks like nobody has lived here for a very long time."

"Mr. Williams passed a good while back," he replied in a low voice. "And I don't really know about Rennie. She left for California to be near Sharon, her granddaughter. Hey, you must remember Sharon. She was living here then, two years old. A beautiful little girl. Rennie was always talkin' about Sharon. And after Sharon went off to college in California, Rennie left Ruleville." Mac cocked his head and smiled. "I liked Rennie. You didn't mess with Rennie Williams." He nodded appreciatively. "They were good folks."

47. The house of James and Rennie Williams.
"My home at the Williams house."

"Show us more, Mac. Anything changed across the highway, other than the Billups hangout?"

"Some things," he said with a private smile. "The office where Mayor Durrough used to give us hell. It's been improved, it's bigger, and the color's been changed." He chortled. "The new mayor is black, and her name is Shirley Edwards!"

"Terrific! A black woman instead of that racist bully!" I caught Gloria's eye in the rearview mirror. "How about that for little old Ruleville, Gloria? A black woman mayor! I'll never forget when Durrough came into the quarter, arm in arm with an FBI agent, to investigate after the Klan tried to burn down the Williams Chapel. And right in front of all those poor folks, grieving that *anyone* would try to burn down their church, he pointed at them and said loudly: '*They* did it!'"

Mac just nodded. "That was Mayor Durrough. Well, he's long gone, too."

I eased away from the Williams house, crossed Highway 41, and drove slowly through the white section of Ruleville. The neighborhoods that back in '64 had been so forbidding, and had seemed so remarkably luxurious after the poverty of the housing in the quarter, were still green and inviting. The plantings were fuller, the trees even more stately than I remembered. The business center of the farm town, though, was still heartbreakingly poor. The town square where the police used to exercise their police dogs when we would venture into town appeared nearly empty of movement, the old movie house boarded up, the little ragged hotel no longer open for any business. The surprise for me came as we circled the center of town and headed back toward the highway. Some of the old, comfortable houses with shaded lawns and colorful gardens were now the residences of black Ruleville families. Black families—mothers, fathers, kids—could be seen on some of the porches, relaxing like their white neighbors, hiding only from the oppressive heat of the Delta.

"I never thought I'd see that, Mac," I said, shaking my head in wonder. "Never."

Mac was enjoying my surprise, leaning from the window and waving to old friends as we went past. "Long gone," he murmured. Ruleville had indeed changed. Like in the rest of the Delta, most of the Ruleville whites who for generations lived so comfortably in the shadow of the plantations had now abandoned the little towns. Mechanization had decimated the tens of thousands of black farmhands who had sustained the cotton economy, and the passage of the Voting Rights Act in 1965 had dramatically altered the political scales. Life, as I had observed it back in the sixties, had been transformed. Along with thousands of blacks who had pulled up stakes and moved to the promise of the cities, most of the whites who once filled these shady verandas were "long gone."

I crossed back into the quarter, and we headed for the dedication of Mrs. Hamer's park. A large truck was blocking the road as we approached the site of the dedication. Four sweating men were wrestling a large object from the bed of the truck, and tilting it carefully into the waiting hands of four others who were on the edge of the park. As they righted the awkward cargo on the ground, the truck backed slowly away, making room at last for our line of cars to pass. As the workmen removed the wrapping, we could discern that the great package was the large quite ornate sign that, in the future, would mark the entrance.

McLaurin stared at the lettering. "The Fannie Lou Hamer Memorial Park," he said softly, his eyes damp. "Hey, it's about time." A large smile lit his usually contemplative face.

Dusty cars and pickup trucks were ranged along the curb at the edge of the field, and we were more than fifty yards beyond the celebration when I found a spot to park. Looking back, I could see the small canvas that made up the dedication. A clean white tent marked the place for the listeners who desired shade, and perhaps fifty church folding chairs had been set up for those who wished to be closest to the speakers and were not intimidated by the sun. A small wooden platform with a microphone, public address speakers, and a few folding chairs stood alone in anticipation of the events about to begin. Gospel music flooded from the speakers, giving the occasion the feel of a church supper. The music flooded across the empty cotton fields and reverberated against a nondescript structure that the folks in Ruleville called the "Facility Building." The building's main function was to serve as a small unequipped gym or as an auditorium for the children. A single skittles table was all that the facility offered. Today, it appeared to be empty, for the kids were out behind the building, having races and playing baseball on the scrubby sandlot. Their shrill yells and laughter were the only sounds that competed with the gospel music. Below it all was the warm hum of neighborly greetings as the people began to assemble.

I looked skeptically at the still thin crowd, but Mac appeared elated. "Folks'll come," he said confidently. "Cephus told me folks are coming. And Cephus is 'my man'! They'll be here." We started to follow him to the tent area when he abruptly stopped. When we came abreast of him, he pointed across the field. "Mrs. Hamer," he said quietly. "And Pap, right next to her." The two handsome gray granite headstones stood alone in the cotton field. I stepped closer to see them better.

No epitaph marked Perry Hamer's headstone. In death, as in life, Pap remained the quiet, proud, and unassuming partner to the woman he loved. If Fannie Lou Hamer was the personification of the indomitable black Delta woman, Perry Hamer was movingly emblematic of the endlessly patient and unconquerable Delta Negro male.

Pap had opened his home to the civil rights movement from the first day of our arrival in Ruleville. In short order it became the nerve center of all our activity, and there was a constant flurry of clacking typewriters and phones ringing as Dale Gronemeier and Dennis Flannigan pumped out communiqués to the North and appeals for bail funds. The Hamer kitchen was a hive of odd-hour eating, and their porch was the hangout for newspaper correspondents and summer volunteers. For Pap Hamer, a Delta tractor driver, the transformations of his home and the destruction of his privacy were but two more phenomena in the disorder of his living.

From the day his wife had gone to apply to register, Pap's life had become a crazy quilt of violence, exhilaration, loneliness, and often despair. Fannie Lou's refusal to withdraw her name from the registrar's rolls had torn to pieces the even fabric of their life working together on the plantation. Their boss had spelled it out plain. "I'm not gonna have you registerin' to vote, Fannie Lou. You go down tomorra and tell 'em to take your name off that list!" And she had answered with a passion that had surprised them both. "But you don't understand. I'm not registerin' for *you*. I'm registerin' for me!" And after seventeen years as timekeeper on the plantation, she had been fired.

Two weeks later, Pap's thirty years at the plantation cotton gin were over as well. He accepted the changes with the quiet, appraising calm that he wore like a protective garment. For a Mississippi Negro, life at best was a mean and burdensome path. If you were a man like Pap, you walked that path with a gentle stubbornness, knowing that the path usually moved uphill. I knew from our long talks on his stoop that few things in "Mr. Charlie's" world deceived him. His hard-won knowledge rested behind his watchful eyes, and he walked his stony path without breaking his stride. No one knew better than he what it was to live the marginal life of the Mississippi Negro. One step from utter poverty, a half-step from the wrath of the white community, he had learned long ago to mask his hurt and to bridle his anger. When the job he had held for so long was snatched from him, he was dependent on occasional part-time jobs to keep the family together. Like most Negro men in the Delta, he lived with the knowledge that he was incapable of providing properly for his family. "I drink," he told me one twilight evening when Mrs. Hamer was away up north, raising bail money. He said it simply, without apology. "When I work, I don't drink. But when I'm not working, I like to drink." Whenever I would return to Ruleville, I always packed a pint of Jack Daniels that I could share with my old friend.

As I turned from Pap's grave, a memory returned that I had cherished but long forgotten. I was sitting with Pap when Mayor Durrough had driven up to the Hamer house and parked. Perry had risen from the stoop and stood silently. Tall and heavy-set, he was a handsome mahogany figure in his clean overalls. Durrough's glance flicked past him to the porch where Dennis Flannigan was typing. His nostrils dilated, and a small vein had throbbed between his bushy eyebrows. He continued to watch Dennis, but his words were dripping with contempt and were directed to Perry Hamer. "How do you feel having white men sleepin' in your house?"

Pap remained where he stood. His dark, soft voice sounded clearly through the yard. "I feel like a man." His eyes were calm, and his voice was level. "Because they treat me like a man."

Unlike Perry Hamer's, Fannie Lou Hamer's stone bore an inscription. "I'm sick and tired of being sick and tired." I stared at the stone and found myself unaccountably angry. No! It's not enough, I thought. What does that mean to somebody who never knew this woman? What can it mean? *Resignation? Petulance? Whining!* Fannie Lou Hamer? No, damn it. Not near enough. *"Keep on keepin' on"*—that would have been better. She'd always say that: "I'm sick and tired of being sick and tired. *But I keep on keepin' on.*"

Gloria and Mac had resumed their walk, but I found myself lingering unhappily at the grave site. What is it about graves that troubles me so? Maybe it's because they say "gone," because they drain the life out of flesh-and-blood people, transforming their vibrant memory into "history." "Here lies Fannie Lou Hamer . . . " History? For McLaurin, for me, for so many, many others, Mrs. Hamer was alive, ineradicably alive! Even at her funeral in the Williams Chapel in 1977, her death was seen in terms of a precious, living legacy. Old friends from the plantations, from the halls of Congress, from the American Mission to the United Nations, from every cadre of the civil rights movement, all had come to honor the woman from Ruleville. In the stifling heat of the packed Williams Chapel, Fannie Lou Hamer was vibrantly alive in the words of love and pride.

In tears, a white Mississippian, Hodding Carter, said, "Mrs. Hamer did a lot of freeing in her lifetime. And I think that history will say that among those who were freed more totally and earlier by her were white Mississippians who were finally freed if they had the will to be free. From themselves. From their history. From their racism. And I know that there is no way for us, who have been freed, to adequately thank those who freed us, except to try to continue the work that Fannie Lou Hamer began."

Vernon Jordan summoned the spirit of Mrs. Hamer by quoting Oliver Wendell Holmes. "'Life is action and passion. It is required of men and women to share the action and passion of their times at the risk of being judged not to have lived.' By that standard," Jordan said, "Mrs. Fannie Lou Hamer truly lived. And she lives today through her legacy of service, sacrifice, commitment, and love."

Twenty-five years had now passed since that emotion-laden memorial. Looking across at the gathering of Ruleville families, I felt a great sadness. Most of them never knew Mrs. Hamer, could never know her now. For all but a few of the elders, the passionate, often difficult, controversial, inspired woman was now only a historic landmark, the person who put Ruleville, Mississippi, on the map.

I gazed up and past the silent headstones, tracing with my eye the long, naked rows of cotton as they stretched farther and farther, ending at the low silhouette of the stand of trees in white Ruleville. I remember making a drawing from this place during that long-ago summer of '64. I felt I was barely perceiving another world—distant, forbidding, and alien from my protected haven on this side of Highway 41. I had scribbled on the sketch "A view of white Ruleville from black Ruleville."

A tall, stocky man with a kindly face and hair slowly going to gray stepped away from McLaurin and Gloria. He cocked his head, and then nodded. A great smile crossed his face as he approached and extended his hand. "Cephus Smith, Tracy. Been a long time. A *long* time."

I took his hand in both of mine. "We gotta stop meeting this way, Cephus," I teased. "Every thirty-seven years! It might get habit-forming!" Like a photo slowly emerging from the developer, the Cephus I had last talked with in Mrs. Hamer's front yard in 1965 began to emerge. The amber memory came flooding back, and the melancholy that I had felt at the grave disappeared in the sense of pleasure I had in meeting Cephus Smith again. "A *nice* habit," I said emphatically, and we both laughed.

What goes around comes around, I thought. Watching McLaurin and Cephus during that dedication, there was a mutual sense of affection and a shared sense of pride that transformed the mundane ceremony into an act of faith and purpose. The father who had once led now happily placed himself at the bidding of the son. It became clear as the day progressed that the promise of a new park and perhaps the addition of a museum dedicated to Mrs. Hamer had rekindled an exciting activism in McLaurin. Weeks before, he had come up from Indianola to offer his counsel and help to Cephus, knowing that it would take imaginative leadership in Ruleville to bring the project to life. Today was proof that Cephus had creatively enlisted officials in Ruleville and Sunflower County, securing the land and beginning to build support among the citizens of the town.

McLaurin was now a stalwart at the Public Works Department in Indianola, a position of public trust he had held with satisfaction for more than a decade. But the old warrior who once bragged that he knew every corner, every back road in Ruleville, who had been the closest political friend of Fannie Lou Hamer, joyfully seized the chance to "keep on keepin' on."

The program of the dedication had the meandering tempo of the black Delta that I had quite forgotten. It was a concept of time that had so thrown me when I first came to Ruleville that I had begged Mrs. Williams to explain it to me. "When a mass meeting is supposed to start at the chapel at seven, how come nobody shows up until seven thirty, or eight, or eight thirty? Happens every time!"

She gave me an indulgent smile, the kind she gave Sharon, her granddaughter. "Folks get back from the fields after working 'cain't to cain't,' Tracy, and they gotta feed their families and maybe get a little rest."

"What's 'cain't to cain't'?"

She shook her head, and laughed outright at my confusion. "Cain't see in the morning when you go to the fields 'cuz it's still too dark to cain't see at night when you stop your choppin' in the fields 'cuz it's too dark to see. Them are long days, Tracy. And sometimes the meetin's at the chapel just have to start a little later."

From time out of mind, the measured tread of the seasons, not clocks, had paced this region of planters and cultivators and harvesters. And in a constrained black society where one predictable, unchangeable endless day of labor had been followed by another, and another, measured time had little meaning. The need to parse and cut and dice time as we did in the North was because change had to be anticipated and planned for. That was not an important concept when you were black in Mississippi farm country, and change had long been the exclusive prerogative of white folks. But during that leisurely day of singing, recitations, and speeches by local politicians, it was abundantly clear that Ruleville had moved well past the place I remembered.

We were introduced by Cephus Smith to a tall, relaxed, and engaging black man who was now the town's police chief, and to a slender, attractive black woman holding a baby who was the mayor. In her thoughtful and intelligent remarks from the podium, she made it clear that every resource of the town would be put to achieving the goal of making the Hamer memorial come to life. How I wished that Mayor Durrough could have been there to share the moment.

When I surveyed the crowd, however, it was also strikingly evident that some things were still implacably the same. Black Ruleville now had the voting power to elect "one of their own" to the offices of government, but white Ruleville remained aloof from these tides of change. The only white faces in the crowd were those of one journalist, a Sunflower County official, and Gloria and me. Where, I wondered, were Bette Lindsey and Lake Lindsey?

When I inquired how I might reach them, no one seemed to know for sure. One elderly woman said she hadn't seen any Lindsey in or around Ruleville in years. "Heard they might have moved." She turned to her companion. "You remember the Lindsey place, Laura? Ora was with them for years. You know where they gone?"

The woman said, "Not really. But last I heard, somebody said they might have moved down to Brandon." She peered over her glasses. "You know the Lindseys?" she asked.

"Long time ago," I said. "I'd like to see them again. You said Brandon?"

The New Light Gospel singers were just concluding their final song of praise and thanksgiving at the end of the dedication program when I spotted Cephus Smith standing alone at the rear of the crowd. As people began to drift back to their cars or started walking the sunbaked roads to their homes, Gloria and I made our way through the departing crowd, eager to finally have the chance to speak with Cephus. We found him stacking folding chairs in the silent and shady cavern of the Facilities Building.

"What's a successful contractor like you doing, hauling and lifting? Mac tells me you've built a real business in the eight years you're back from California. There ought to be younger backs out there to pick up the load, and stronger," I teased, but there was no response. I looked questioningly at Gloria and then pushed ahead, no longer bantering. "You must feel great about the turnout, Cephus. About the whole dedication."

He moved in silence to the stack of chairs in the corner, and carefully set down the chair he was carrying. When he turned to speak, I was alarmed to see that tears were staining his cheeks, and his shoulders were shaking in a struggle to control his emotions.

"Are you all right, Cephus? Is there something we can do?"

He shook his head no, and in a moment more had composed himself. "I'm okay," he said huskily. He drew three chairs together and nodded for us to sit down. He looked at us with no trace of embarrassment but, rather, with a look of wonder. "It was something that happened a few minutes ago, and it just made me weep." He said it simply, wiping away the tears from his cheek with the back of his large workman's hand. "Two men . . . had to be about forty-five I'd guess . . . just come up to me out there and told me: 'You taught us how to read, Mr. Smith. Back in '64, at the Freedom School, right over yonder.'" He paused, his eyes bright now with the memory. "'At the Freedom School.' I did not realize that at the time. I remember I'd read the kids comic books, get books from the shelves for them. And I would sit with Linda and them, and we'd all read together. And today these two grown men came back and tell me, 'You taught us how to read'!" He looked at us with unfeigned joy. "That *means* something." His eyes searched ours. With a sense of discovery, he said firmly: "That's the meaning of all we did back then, and I didn't really realize what that meaning was in 1964."

Gloria leaned forward. "But what did you gain from that summer, Cephus?"

His eyes were thoughtful as he sought his answer. "Sixty-four, when the Freedom Riders came down here, and they was black and white together, it showed me for the first time that all whites were not bad. That lesson helped me through a lot of years and a lot of places after I left Mississippi and went off in the military. I've been in other countries where I saw people discriminated against who *didn't* have a dark-colored skin."

The crowds who had thronged on the lawn had wandered toward home, and the platform had been lifted to a truck bed. When the truck ground away, the large echoing room was silent. Cephus stretched comfortably, apparently happy in tweaking out his recollections for us.

"When I left Mississippi in 1965, I never intended to spend so much time away. But jobs were not available here in the Delta, at least not for me. I was known to have been part of the movement. So I went to California looking for work, for a life that I knew would make my parents feel comfortable because I would be in an area that was not as restrictive as Mississippi." He grinned, nodding. "My folks knew about my attitude, and having survived my time in the army, they wanted me out of harm's way.

"Funny what you remember. The day that Martin Luther King was assassinated was just as I was crossing into California. Should I go back and get involved with people like the Black Panthers and H. Rap Brown?"

"And what did you decide? I think everybody was totally bewildered," I said. "I know we were."

"I thought there was a different way than the Panthers or Rap Brown," he replied slowly. "I thought there was more going on, more choices. I decided whatever I do, wherever I go, I'd do it the right way." Cephus looked intently at me. "And right will prevail." He said it firmly, without embarrassment. It was an echo of Mrs. Hamer. "That's what the movement taught me."

He eased back on his chair. "The summer you were here, Tracy, the movement taught me that you have to make sure that you treat a man like he treats you, that you value a human life." He turned to face Gloria. "What did *I* gain that summer? That people *can* care. It was the lesson I learned. It's the reason that today I don't have any hate in my heart."

I cherished those moments with Cephus, so resonant of the naked and honest emotions that had made the summers in Ruleville so special in my life. Gloria could begin to sense the emotional intimacy that had forged the friendships born in the movement. It was a moment in time when the word *love* had a special sweetness, an inclusivity that spoke of community, of trust, of sharing, of faith. The "long, hot summer," as almost any summer volunteer could tell you, was not most memorable for the hate one had had to confront but for the love we so unexpectedly found.

Cephus said, "I'm sorry you weren't here for the reunion last year. Everybody grown now. Back in '64, a lot of those kids were just glad to get away from home! Now they all come back, and some with families of their own." His eyes crinkled, and he nodded appreciatively at the memory. "You know, Tracy, you can just reach down and still feel the bond. When one of them greeted me with a hug, his son said, 'Dad! Stop all that hugging crap!'" He laughed, and we laughed with him. The three of us had kids, and Gloria and I had grandkids. Each of us could well remember being told by the children, "Don't embarrass us!" Cephus grinned. "I understand that kid. But you know? You hate for that feeling to end."

After the long, emotional day at the dedication of Mrs. Hamer's park, McLaurin and I lingered in an Indianola bar after our wives had gone to bed. We were both enjoying the shared recollections of a vanished time that on that day seemed very close to both of us. And for me, time with Mac always revealed new insights, new answers to old questions.

"Level with me, Mac," I said, pouring us both a bourbon. "It's something I've wanted to ask you for a very long time." I studied my old friend's face. "Were you really as cool and confident at those confrontations in Drew as you looked? I sure as hell wasn't."

He sipped his drink and nodded vigorously. "Yes. I was then. That was a whole year after my first trip down to Indianola, when I learned to hide my fear." He held my eyes and grinned. "A whole year." When he spoke again, his voice was soft. "I used to be so scared when I first came to work for SNCC in the Delta. I'll never forget the first day I got three old ladies to agree to go to the courthouse in Indianola. These ladies were from fifty to eighty, and I was wishin' that there were some younger people goin' who could give *me* courage! It felt so strange. You ask people to go to the courthouse, and you tell them that they should, and that there's nothin' to be afraid of." He paused, and his eyes moved across the tables of the grill. "And you're so afraid yourself."

He hunched forward, eager now to continue his reminiscence. "I was shakin' before we ever left Ruleville, and when we passed that Billups Gas Station where those white guys were known to beat up Negroes, I got down in that car seat as low as I could get! As we drove, the old ladies were talkin' to each other, but I wasn't sayin' a thing. I acted as if I was interested in watchin' the folks workin' in the fields along the highway. But, really, I just didn't want those old ladies to hear the tremblin' in my voice!

"When we finally got to the outskirts of Indianola, I felt I had to say something if I was going to overcome enough fear at least to tell the Man in the registrar's office what we wanted. So I started to talk to my old ladies a little, and then a little bit more, and finally the shakiness in my voice started to pass. When we finally reached the courthouse, I just didn't want to get out of the car. But those old ladies . . . soon as we stopped . . . were out of the car and movin' up the steps! I sat there, tryin' to figure out why it was that all those years people had been sayin' that the folks in the Delta were afraid to register, afraid to vote. And here I was . . . younger, stronger . . . a registered voter who had no trouble registering down in Jackson . . . and I was hangin' back while those old ladies were walkin' right up to the Man and tellin' him what they wanted! I finally followed them up the stairs, just waitin' for someone to grab me!" He paused, remembering, and when he spoke again his voice was warm with affection. "I'll never forget those old ladies. Never. That's when I started to become a man."

We sat late, reminiscing about the long journey from our first meeting in Connecticut in 1963. "Been some changes, Mac," I said lightly. "It's been nice watching you grow up!"

Charles lifted his glass and touched mine. "By the time you all came to Ruleville, I had been arrested four times in four different towns!" He grinned widely. "By then it was my mouth that was gettin' me in trouble. When a policeman or a sheriff or a plantation owner would say, 'Don't do something,' there I'd be tryin' to explain why we should! By sayin' something . . . by being 'uppity' . . . I was able to overcome my fear even in the presence of large numbers of policemen. From 1963 I had started to move around the state, learning how to get around the danger spots anywhere in Mississippi, and especially learning all I could about Sunflower County. So by 1964 I felt I knew all that I should know, and that I could take care of the people I was going to be bringing back with me from Oxford, Ohio.

"At first, I hadn't wanted that responsibility, and I told Bob Moses that some of those student volunteers wouldn't last three hours, that a lot of them were going to get hurt. But Moses talked me around, and I decided to work with the Summer Project when they said I could have my own group in Sunflower County." He paused, and his eyes softened. The voice was full of pride. "By then I felt like I owned Sunflower County, that it was mine. And not one person in my project was hurt all the time I was in charge. Not one person." McLaurin looked relaxed and happy, tapping his glass gently on the edge of the scarred table to the beat of the music that never stopped.

"You look content, Mac. You have kids now. Do you want them to stay in Mississippi?"

He raised his eyes in surprise. "Yes." He said it quickly, instinctively. "Yes, I do. In spite of all the places I've gone, I always end up back here. I don't think I could spend more than two weeks away from Mississippi. I always get homesick. I've wanted my kids to be born here and raised here. And *educated* here," he added emphatically.

"But well educated," I interjected.

He nodded. "Well educated. Educational standards are higher now, and they are able to go to those schools with no trouble now." He smiled.

"People like me who started to push integration back then can see our kids actually walk through the doors we opened!"

For many of us who came to the South to work in the civil rights movement, Mississippi was essentially defined by its poisonous racism. As outsiders we found it difficult to look past the arrogant and violent image, and confounding to find that there could be, and were, human qualities in the life of Mississippi that endeared the place not only to the whites we mistrusted but also to many of the blacks we came to know and cherish.

Charles McLaurin was the SNCC leader whom I came to know best. With great admiration I had watched him demonstrate an intelligent and sensitive leadership in situations of immense peril as he confronted apartheid. What I came finally to understand was that Charles, despite his encounters with bigotry, remained first and last a proud Mississippian. Born in Jackson, raised on its mean streets, come to manhood in the crucible of the Delta, educated at its black colleges, McLaurin finds Mississippi to be his natural habitat. It is the place he has chosen to raise his family, the community in which he wants to make his way. To his marrow, he believes he has paid with blood and pain to make the state better, and he savors the profound changes he has helped create.

I have often wondered whether SNCC leaders like Julian Bond, Bob Moses, and John Lewis, who had chosen to come to this state as a moral commitment to make it more just, could ever share the emotional ties to the place that people like McLaurin, Guyot, and Hollis Watkins felt. Mississippi was the place both groups had bled in. But perhaps you had to be born and raised here to see it for what it could be. Unaccountably, as I was drifting off, I remembered Bette and Lake Lindsey. Why weren't they at the Hamer Park? I had to remember to tell Gloria about Brandon in the morning.

Our trip the following day was a total frustration. The Lindseys were not to be found in Brandon. Even inquiries at the police station were met with, "Sorry. We have nothing to tell you." Discouraged, we concluded that our hopes for a rich discussion about today's Mississippi with whites I knew who would be candid and honest were not to be rewarded. Yet we were both reluctant to abandon the quest. On our return to Indianola, I approached Charles McLaurin.

"Mac, where can I find Sheriff Caldwell and Jack Harper? I'd like to talk to both of them."

He frowned. "No way you can do that with the sheriff. Bill died last year. You remember what it was like back then, when we'd have to go to the courthouse? What a hard time we'd get from the police? But not from the sheriff. He always played it straight with us. In the last few years after he retired, he and I talked a lot together. He even showed me your picture of the courthouse that you sent him." He smiled. "'Sugarman sent that to me,' he told me. Said he was proud of that. No, he's gone now, Tracy. I was sorry when he passed. We appreciated each other."

"I'm really sorry to hear that. I'd sent him my drawing because I liked him. Is Jack Harper still around?"

McLaurin smiled. "Well, that old fox has retired to his plantation on the edge of town. Call him. He'd probably like to talk to you."

Jack Harper

In response to my telephone call, Harper invited me to come to his house. Following a long, private driveway that wound beneath fine old shade trees, I reached his substantial brick home. It was generous, handsome, and confidently unpretentious, an inviting oasis in more than a hundred acres of sun-drenched farmland. When he greeted me at the door, his face was a trace older and his voice a little softer and thinner, but the watchful blue eyes were as I remembered them. We shook hands, and he led me into the richly comfortable living room. Courteous as always, Jack was a charming and relaxed host, eager to put me at my ease. As we settled to talk, the old calculation in his smile that I always remembered was replaced by a genuine look of unguarded good humor. Retired now, and obviously enjoying these years, he seemed eager to speak of the past, and share his perspective with one who was roughly his contemporary.

"You make retirement look great, Jack," I said. "Is there ever any reason to miss the courthouse?"

His blue eyes regarded me solemnly. "Do you realize I went to work there in 1956, Tracy? Served as chancery clerk, recorder of public documents, and treasurer of Sunflower County for forty-four years. A long time. And you have to remember I had an election every four years." He paused, and a grin broke across his face. "Miss it? No. No reason I can think of."

"You obviously enjoyed it," I said, "and they must have enjoyed having you if you made it through eleven elections!"

"The people were good to me, and I tried to be good to them," he said. "I came here after I graduated from Ole Miss Law School, not that I knew any more than anybody else." The old look of calculation returned, and he grinned. "But I could find out."

252

"You were there during some extraordinary changes, Jack. The whole South was in the eye of the storm. What did you think would happen when you heard the civil rights movement was coming to Sunflower County?"

His eyes were serious now, and he answered with deliberation. "There had been so much that had gone on before, it was reasonable to expect that heated arguments and differences of opinion would arise."

"*Heated arguments? Differences of opinion?* That was all you were concerned about?" It was impossible to mask my disbelief.

Harper paused and cleared his throat. "I knew that there was friction here in the state, and I knew that the movement coming here could set off a spark." His voice was quiet, and his eyes held mine. "I had reason to believe that violence might take place."

"Well, the violence was all about letting black Mississippians getting the vote, wasn't it, Jack?"

Harper nodded. "There were some folks down here that wanted to hide behind the Mississippi State Constitution, and stay there until they got pulled into court. It was a political thing, a way of making it appear that blacks were second-class citizens." He raised his chin and said very firmly, "But people like me knew the value of civil rights, Tracy. And knew what the Civil War was all about. Some of us knew it was time for a shift

48. Summer volunteer in Indianola.
"You guys can help change history."

in politics. When the federal government acted by pulling those obstructionists into court, I gave them credit for doing it."

I looked at Jack Harper, wondering what would have happened to him and to his long political career in the Delta if he had enunciated such beliefs back in the sixties. Would he have survived long enough to eventually be in the position to work with Fannie Lou Hamer to bring federal housing programs to the Delta? If there had been guile and manipulation in Harper's political calculations, he was not the first, or certainly the last, such elected official. And if he was critical now of the obstructionists who had made life hell for those struggling for freedom and equality, his affection for his constituents still prevailed.

"I've always counted on my people here in the Mississippi Delta," he said with pride. "I really wasn't fearful about anything. I knew all the people here, white and black. They got the message about political change, and I think they properly reacted to it."

forty-one

Losing the Children

i heard Owen Brooks's distinctive voice even before we stepped into the busy cafeteria. His is a storyteller's voice. It challenges you to listen, and when I spotted the leonine head at a far table, I was not surprised to see he had an audience. The timbre of his voice was as I remembered it from the eighties, but the wild black Afro was gone now. In its place is a luxurious growth of trimmed salt-and-pepper hair that frames Brooks's expressive face. When he spotted our tardy arrival, he raised his head and grinned, waving his busy fork toward two empty seats at his table. "Get some food," he commanded, and leaned forward to continue his story.

When we rejoined the table with his coworkers from the Jackson Summer Youth Program, Owen was reminiscing, fueled by the attentive young faces and his own pleasure in narrative. "I grew up in the strug-gle," he was saying. "My sister and I joined the NAACP Youth Council in Boston in 1944, inspired by Mary McCloud Bethune and Paul Robeson." He looked appraisingly at the young people. "Those were good people." He turned toward our end of the table and nodded. "Good people," he repeated.

The group rose to return to their offices, and Owen led us down the corridor to a conference room. "We can talk in here." The tall man smiled and extended his hand to Gloria. "Tracy told me on the phone about you. Looks like he was right. Welcome to Mississippi!"

This was my first meeting in nearly twenty years with Owen, and I was eager to hear his assessment of the tumultuous years that had passed. Each of our few meetings had been memorable for me. I was happy that Gloria now had a chance to meet someone who, at age seventy-three, brought so much memory and passion to the table.

"When you and I talked back in '84, Owen, I was asking you about Mrs. Hamer's legacy, and wondering what she would think about the political changes that were finally happening."

Owen nodded. "And I said she would be deeply disappointed that there hadn't been a real political party created yet that would be interested in people's lives, not just electoral politics." He tilted back in his chair, his gaze focused far beyond our room. "She would have been disappointed in 1984," he said softly, "and what's sadder is she would still be disappointed in 2002."

"I don't understand, Owen," said Gloria. "Back in the sixties there wasn't a single black elected official in the whole state. Now there are more than eight hundred elected black officials, and one of them is a congressman!"

"Mrs. Hamer thought electing blacks would change things. She even ran for Congress herself," I said. "Was she just being naive?"

"No," he said sharply. "She just had the vision a lot of us had then. A lot of us. And change did come. I would have to be a fool to think I would want to go back to 1963. I am not a fool." Owen looked at each of us in turn, then leaned forward on the table. "What do eight hundred black officials translate to so far as *power* is concerned? Who are those black men and women modeling themselves after? And what are they doing to lift the understanding of their constituency?" Brooks's voice was bitter, and his disappointment was obvious in the look of fatigue he wore. "When they elected black mayors in Newark and Gary, they were going to transform the lives of all the poor people in those cities." He stared at us. "It didn't happen," he said slowly, each word lying like a challenge on the table, "because the white folks stayed right there, and the *economic* power did not get handed over. That is the reality."

"So electing black officials means nothing?" asked Gloria. "Changes nothing?"

"Politicians do the bidding of those that have the power, Gloria, whether their faces are white or black. If you know that these legislators and mayors are black," replied Owen morosely, "you are heartened, and then you drive across town and you see that power has *not* been handed over, that the reality of life for the dispossessed, or the hungry, or the poor, has *not* improved. And that's when you start to understand the larger reality . . . that the per capita income of the state of Mississippi is still the lowest in the whole of the United States. Economic power," he said dryly, "does *not* get handed over."

Owen's ardent wish to remake society in a more just and responsive way seems sometimes to reflect a deep cynicism. He is outspokenly critical of hypocrisy, and his righteous anger is directed at blacks as well as whites. But time spent with Brooks reveals a profound love for those oppressed, and an unquenchable belief that man can reshape his own world given the chance.

I studied my old friend, wondering whether his long engagement in the search for a more equitable society would ever, could ever, create the loving community he envisioned.

"Tell me, Owen," I said, "about your own evaluation of the remarkable decades you've lived through here in Mississippi. What has it added up to for you?"

He tilted his head, and his eyes narrowed. A small smile eased his usually intent face. "Now there's a question," he murmured. "There were real *experiences*. I count myself as a feeling person, a person with values surely, and a person with commitments, and I lived through that time." Brooks paused, reflecting. "I got a lot out of that time, in terms of maturity and growth. In learning to understand the nature of the struggle, in being able to evaluate mistakes and errors." He frowned. "My errors and others' errors. Because we made a *bunch*." His voice was throaty and emotional.

"We lost dozens of people, and we lost wars, Tracy. And we lost some of our children forever. Two of my daughters . . . I lost them during those times. It's easy for me in retrospect to pass it off, to say I got caught up in the times, neglected to do for them because I was doing for others . . . " His voice broke. "You only go this way one time." Owen's voice was full of regret. "My oldest daughter is just turning fifty, and the other day she said, 'You're just beginning to get interested in the lives of your children.' Oh, wow!"

"I have kids, Owen. They can sometimes be quite unfair, and hurtful."

"Her sister said a similar thing," he said ruefully. "No, those are personal mistakes, mistakes I made."

Owen's impatience with his own mistakes was more than matched by his disapproval of the political evolution of the movement. In particular, he believes that by not maintaining a political agenda different from that of the establishment political parties, the civil rights movement made a huge error. To his core, he maintains that structural, meaningful change will not, indeed cannot, be effected by the "establishment." That conviction has made him distance himself from those veterans of the movement who have chosen to work for progress from within the electoral process. The absorption of the Mississippi Freedom Democratic Party into the greater Democratic Party he observes as co-option, and he wears the angry scars as proof of a betrayal.

"But what about John Lewis?" I protested. "He's in his eighth term in Congress . . . from Georgia! Julian Bond continues to teach at two southern universities, and is chairman of the board of the NAACP. Those guys are working for change."

Brooks calmly assessed what I had said, and carefully chose his response. "We personalize things in our lives, make personal choices about how to go forward." His eyes bore into mine. "John Lewis made a choice. You might call it a vocational choice. He made a choice in terms of how he saw the big picture. I don't see the big picture the same way. John's choice was dictated by his politics and by his religion. If you knew him, you weren't surprised by the choice he made. At best," he added dryly, "he is a very liberal Democrat. Of course, there's some ego also involved."

"Wasn't Malcolm's life, Martin's life, even Fannie Lou's life involved somewhat with ego?" I was annoyed by his apparent dismissal of Lewis.

Owen nodded assent. "Exactly. Everybody's life. There's always ego involved. We struggle with our egos, and sometimes they get the best of us, particularly with the choices we ultimately make. In my opinion, that particularly, though not exclusively, applies to both Julian and John. It's interesting that they both wound up in the same political stream, vying with each other for prominence and position in the Democratic Party."

"That caused a lot of hurt, a lot of enmity between two valuable people, Owen, two old friends who had paid a lot of dues in the movement."

Owen nodded. "But we all sometimes hold on to our enmities. We shouldn't."

"But it's human," protested Gloria.

Owen regarded her solemnly. "Yes, but we shouldn't pass it off and just say, 'It's human.' Holding on to the enmity identifies a weakness within us, because intolerance is a weakness."

I had to suppress a smile because I knew how disapproving Brooks was of the courses taken by Lewis and Bond. But when he spoke again, I could hear echoes of the ardent young minister he had once been.

"We do not have the right to judge. I've reflected on that over the years. As members of the army we like to think we're in, we're called to be more tolerant."

"Maybe, Owen, learning to be more tolerant comes with education, learning that people can choose different paths when they try to effect change."

"No," he said emphatically. "Change starts with *values*. If a kid goes to school with wrong values, that education is not going to do for him what needs to be done. We have dominant values in this society, and we folks don't control them. Corporations control them, and whites control the corporations. As a result, we folks have lost our rap, our bebop, our jazz, and our swing. And the corporations and the people who run them are making millions for themselves."

"But there are hustling companies who sell those cheapened values who are black as well as white," I argued.

"Of course there are. That's the nature of the society we live in. The big picture is that we don't control those market values." He was despondent, his eyes unfocused. When he spoke again, his chin lifted and his voice took on a new vibrancy. "We have to figure ways to recapture the minds of our young people in America, and that transcends race. How do we get them back?"

Once again the suppressed preacher was finding his voice. "We can only relate to the kids on a certain level. We can't see the good kids who have values, because ugliness always rises to the surface and is more visible. It's only because those kids come to me as director of the Summer

Youth Program to get them a job that I get to see them. To give them the benefit of my experience. To counsel them. To help guide them."

Owen sighed, easing back in his chair. The crusty critic seemed contemplative, more a professorial grandfather than a revolutionary. A smile flickered on his lips. "I love this job! My wife laughs at me. 'You and your children!' And she's right. I do love those kids." He chuckled and nodded agreement. "And sometimes I have to be checked, somebody has to put the brakes on me and say, 'You got to be careful. You can't be too hard on these youngsters. You talk one kind of language, and it might not be so salable for those kids.'" Owen opened his hands and grinned. "So I got to be careful."

He was adamant in his refusal to assess blame on the young people whom he believed were more the victims than the perpetrators of immoral behavior. But for Owen, there were always questions to be asked. If there was a failure in moral consciousness among the youth, what created it? His years in the struggle had developed a dogged determination to dig deep, learn what you could learn from the failure, but go on. For Brooks, compassion was not something you rationed. It was an essential part of being human. But there was work to be done, a future to be shaped. And the future was about the young.

Gloria asked him if he detected more apathy in the young people he worked with now than in the early years of the movement.

"There's a slightly different kind of apathy among the kids today, and history is involved with this," he said reflectively. "If black kids come to me from the street, and they have no sense of history because they have never been taught their own history, it's irrational to think that they wouldn't be apathetic." He turned in his chair and looked at me appraisingly. "You and I understand black kids of three generations back having fear and enmity," he said, "because history was closer to them. The worst manifestations of racism were closer to them. So we can understand why those young people didn't like or trust 'the other.' But now it's a different time, and you have to ask yourself, 'Where do these kids today get this mistrust, this hatred? What did they miss?'"

Owen's eyes were deeply troubled, and he sighed. "This is every day in the black community, Tracy. And it's every day in the classrooms I teach.

It's right there. You go amongst these young children, and you ask them, 'Why are you so intolerant?' And you see why. In all the black communities in the Delta, it's very difficult to teach tolerance of others, because everybody looks the same." He smiled at my look of surprise. "No Latinos here. No Chinese. No nothing but blacks. And these kids in the Mississippi Delta are just as hostile and intolerant of 'the other' as some kids in the heart of Roxbury or Harlem."

"But what is the hatred from, Owen?" Gloria's voice was plaintive. "Where does it come from? These kids aren't ducking night riders and putting out redneck fires."

Brooks eased back in his chair and looked kindly at Gloria. "These kids don't come into the world knowing about hatred. They see their mothers and their fathers, who are maybe two generations away from the racially inclusive civil rights movement, who have an innate dislike and distrust of 'the other.' They are the kids' models. There's no teaching going on, no rationality involved at all. So these kids learn, first thing, 'It's okay to hate.' And in our society, we make it 'okay to hate.' So," he said with disgust, "hate prospers."

Gloria persisted. "But isn't it reasonable to hate hateful things, like racism?"

Owen smiled. "Unfortunately, Gloria, *with* reason hate prospers, and *without* reason hate prospers. What it feeds on are the individual kinds of divisions among people now."

"It was a simpler equation when we met, Owen," I said. "It was the good guys . . . us . . . and the bad guys . . . the people who were making life miserable for us."

Brooks nodded. "This was a smaller world thirty-five years ago, when I came to Mississippi. The enemy was right there. And we could justify hate and division and killing with the Bible, and the Koran, and the Torah. We did that. When did we learn that if you hate enough, you're going to kill somebody?" He paused, and when he continued his voice was thick. "And when did we learn that if you killed the *right* somebody, you get forgiven?" He pushed back from the table, and his hands squeezed the arms of his chair. He stared at some point far distant. "Oh, Lord! So many contradictions for the children to deal with. Capital punishment . . . the

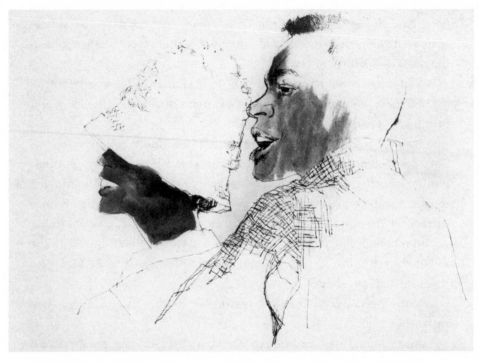

49. Indianola teenagers.

"These kids don't come into the world knowing about hatred."

death penalty . . . " His voice faltered, and his gaze once again focused on his two visitors. "We could just go on forever with our contradictions," he said softly. "And the Lord looks down from somewhere and says, 'What in the world is *this?*'"

We stood up and were moving slowly toward the door when Gloria paused and turned, searching Owen's expressive face. "What about you, Owen?" she asked softly. "Can you still be hopeful?"

"I wouldn't still be here if I didn't have faith in humanity," he said simply, "if I didn't think good could prevail. I couldn't have stayed in Mississippi. All of us change over time. There were times in my life I couldn't understand what I was doing to myself by holding malice. There is no black person in America that does not have a little malice in his heart. And that's bad, even though that malice has some foundation in history. But irrational malice is totally bad and can't be justified. It's born of ignorance."

If Owen's voice was poignant, it was not uniquely so. In nearly every meeting with the veterans of the movement, we sensed a common, throbbing pulse of concern for the generation that followed. Having been shaped by their own life-altering decisions to enter the racial revolution when they were young, they wished fervently to find that their youthful commitment was being emulated by their children. When they failed to perceive it, they sought to explore the societal changes that had intervened to set their children adrift, and to leave them troubled and frustrated. When they succeeded, they quietly rejoiced that the precious torch had been passed on. But all of them came to recognize that the world their kids had inherited was nearly unrecognizable from the one they had known.

The Story to Tell

June Johnson was an engaged participant in the spiritual and political development of her son. Her level of expectation consistently remained high, a challenge to the young man, but the daily dynamic of the street culture for his generation has made June impatient and angry. "I don't think his generation has a real perception of what's actually happening in their lives," she said. "They don't trust anybody."

"But your son knows what you went through in Mississippi, June," I said. "He must be proud of that, and he must trust you."

She nodded slightly. "I've heard him. He says to his friends, 'My mother knows about the movement, about taking a stand. She was *in* it.' He says it proudly. But their heroes are the rappers, and people like Louis Farrakhan, because they think everyone else has sold them down the river. For them, it's every man for himself." She hesitated, a frown furrowing the broad forehead. "When I talk to them about finding a sense of direction, they say to me, 'Look how you turned out. The whites are all rich, and look at what you have. You don't have anything.' That's their attitude."

I was moved by the deep disappointment in her voice. But how could those young people know what a long, arduous journey this woman had made from the apartheid confinement of Greenwood in the sixties? How could they possibly measure her success? Here was a black woman who had hung on, determined to graduate from high school in Mississippi, who had gone on to a junior college in Alabama, worked in legal services in the Delta, and triumphantly earned her master's degree at Jackson State University. "For my son's friends," she said sadly, "it's not about 'the struggle.' It's about the dollars."

"In some ways, June," I suggested, "maybe you had better anchors back in the sixties than they have today. You had the movement. You had heroes like Amzie Moore and heroines like Fannie Lou Hamer. You had your church. And you had your enemies who were very visible."

She raised her eyes to mine. "These kids have *no* faith in the church. They have *no* time to give back to charitable organizations. They are taking *no* frontline positions on anything." She paused in her critical litany, moistening her dry lips with the tip of her tongue. "And when you ask them to work at the election polls, they say, 'Don't ask us to put out for those lying politicians.'" Her voice was bitter.

I said, "I hope that's not the last word on that generation, June."

Her eyes were hard. "I hope not. But it's going to take something very dramatic to change those attitudes. Because of the drug culture they've grown up in, they've watched a lot of their friends die, fighting over *things*, materialistic *things*, not over ideas."

As we rose to say good-bye, she touched my arm. "The saddest part about it, Tracy, is when I ask them, 'What story would you like someone to tell about your life, your work on this earth, and what you did for mankind?' And my son said to me, 'I finished high school. I'm not in prison. If I'm not in jail, I've made a great accomplishment.'" Her eyes held mine, and her voice held no inflection. "He said, 'I get up and go to work every day.'"

Young Power

the malaise among young blacks that June Johnson observed had disturbing echoes in our conversation with L. C. Dorsey. As a professor who had long been teaching black students at Jackson State University, we welcomed her candid and penetrating insights. L.C.'s astonishing success in the maturing and education of her own five children seemed to be a triumphant validation of the aspirations of the sixties movement. When we spoke of her children, her eyes shone with pride, and there was a buoyant note in her voice. "I'm very satisfied with the lives they are pursuing."

Gloria nodded. "You should be satisfied. It was such a long, hard climb for you and the kids. And you made it! How did you manage to motivate them, L. C.? So many of their peers seem to be aimless and adrift."

"Whether you're a parent or a teacher, you've got to be 'plugged in' to where the kids are," she said. "As a single parent I was very close with my children from the get-go, and it made a difference."

"And as a teacher?" I asked.

The usually ebullient woman stared back, her eyes unusually despairing. "As a teacher, I am very depressed about kids today," she answered softly.

"Why?" I asked, disturbed by the resignation in her voice. "You've always known kids so well. Are they different now?"

She nodded slowly. "They are *so* different, Tracy. It's painful for me to be in class with them. I don't teach anymore. I'm now a mentor. It's so sad to realize that they don't equate earning a college degree with unlocking doors to eternal questions that we were meant to answer, or with the mysteries of how things have evolved." She slumped in her chair, her eyes searching for clarity. "They don't even want to *hear* those things. That is the saddest part. What they want is the piece of paper at graduation that means 'I can go get a job, sit in an office, and tell people what to do.'"

Gloria listened intently, frowning at the sad litany. "I feel for you, L. C. It seems particularly strange to hear that here in Mississippi. Where are these kids in relation to the civil rights struggle . . . to politics in general?"

L. C. shook her head. "I had a group of graduate students, Gloria, teaching a class in politics. I asked them about their elected representatives, and they had no clue about who they were or how long they would hold office. No clue. Most of them weren't even registered to vote. If they voted at all, it was only in the national elections. They didn't understand that the actions that most affected their lives were at the county level." Her voice was irritable. Curtly, she declared, "Anybody conscientious enough could come in the country and organize . . . communism, socialism, whatever. *Anything!*" Her bright eyes snapped in anger. "Anything! Because there is no commitment on their part to government of *any* kind!"

"These are black kids in Mississippi, where the vote was so damn hard to get. It doesn't seem to be a matter of race or gender," I said. "What in hell is it, L. C.?" I watched as the anger slowly left Dorsey's face.

"I think it's historical," she replied. "In the sixties we probably had the ability to make more of a difference than these young folks have. The issues were easier to understand. When I see the many people now who turn out to protest against global marketing, proliferation of weapons, desecration of the rain forests, I'm often confused myself. It's hard sometimes to get a handle on why they're so upset. It's not like fighting Jim Crow. We knew why. I do get angry, but I'm hesitant to write off the young people. Their interest is apparently more internally focused. 'How will this injustice impact on me?' as opposed to 'How will this injustice impact on the people in this county, in this state, in this world?'"

"We all feel manipulated sometimes," I said, "by corporations, by the media, by government. We're all struggling with these issues, L. C. It's not just the young."

"Bob Moses's theory," she said, "is that if you put the kids out to do community service, they can emerge from the college cocoon and start to see how things really are. Then they will start to ask questions about why these things are happening, and how do we fix it? Bob believes that their personal experiences can lead them to the answers."

"Bob always believed that the answers could be found in the community," I said. "Do you agree with Moses?"

L. C. nodded. "I do. What I've observed over the years is that whatever affects people is what they'll move on. Young people have to learn about their own potential power."

"Like you students in the sixties," I teased.

She grinned. "Right on! And when they exercise that power, the authorities will have to respond. What I worry about are people that just let the truck run right over them, and say, 'Okay,' and keep on giving up and giving up." The smile left her animated face, and her eyes were distressed as they held mine. "I worry about those people. I worry that when they finally won't give up anymore, can't give up anymore, they will come out and shoot everybody."

Standing on Shoulders

i was eager to see Leslie McLemore again. Mississippi was never a simple historical, psychological, or political equation for me, and my old friend had helped for decades to reset my compass whenever I visited his chosen turf. Traveling now with Gloria, reexploring this memory-laden place, I felt the need of Dr. Leslie McLemore's insightful perspective. Les had first come into my view when I was researching our film about Fannie Lou Hamer, more than a decade after that summer of '64. Now it would be a chance for my wife to perceive the civil rights struggle in Mississippi through the eyes of a wise and observant veteran of the movement.

Although his wife, Betty, an accomplished Jackson lawyer, was out of town, he brought Leslie Jr., a bright and gangling adolescent, to join us for dinner. The three McLemores present a handsome family portrait to the Jackson public. I was not surprised to learn that Leslie, the head of the Political Science Department at Jackson State, had also become president of the Jackson City Council.

"Is it satisfying, Les?" I asked. "City government can be a limited arena in which to operate."

He cocked an eyebrow, then smiled appreciatively. "On most days I'm not sorry I ran for the council," he said diplomatically, then laughed. "But I do have my days when I say, 'Why the hell did I do this?' Sure, it can be limited and frustrating. But I have carved out certain special areas to tend to down there. And, at bottom, I do believe you need some people to help bring some sanity to the political process. But I'm very aware always that when I'm at the city council I'm standing on the shoulders of all those people who made it possible." Leslie paused, looking appraisingly at his son. He seemed eager to have him feel included in our conversation. "In another era," he continued, "my grandfather, Les Jr.'s great-grandfather, up in Walls, Mississippi, would have been a councilman or a mayor. He taught me so much. I take the wisdom of my grandfather and I take the friendships of the people I've known who believe in fairness and justice and equality, the folks who voted for me, and I bring that with me to the city council."

I glanced at Les Jr. "But I don't know where today's kids are. Speaking with L. C. Dorsey and June Johnson I got the feeling that those words seem very irrelevant, romantic, unreal to the kids they know. The words don't seem to fit their world. Owen Brooks thinks that there is so much racial isolation, particularly in the inner cities, that the kids can't even get to know each other."

Leslie put down his cup carefully before responding. "I don't really disagree with Owen. He works closely with a lot of those kids. But I think many of the students I see here at Jackson State have two minds about race. In an all-black setting there is some resistance to an integrated approach to problems. A lot of them have not been in settings where they've had the opportunity to have a dialogue with white students, or with anybody in the white community. As we learned in the movement, once that dialogue takes place they are much more open to that kind of an integrated relationship. I think we have to use those lessons from the movement."

"Owen Brooks said that racial isolation feeds on itself, that the reality they see becomes the only reality they can believe in. It breeds mistrust of anything they don't see. You're both on the same page," I said.

He nodded agreement. "The reality that I try to teach in my classes," said Leslie, "is that whether we're talking about the civil rights movement or Black Power, we didn't come this far by ourselves. We came with the help of others. When black students learn about a white southern kid like Bob Zellner, who was repeatedly beaten by whites more than his black fellow workers in SNCC 'because he should've known better,' when white students learn about the courage of a Fannie Lou Hamer, then the students have gained a new insight they didn't have before. If they have a heart, they have to say, 'Oh, yeah.' There are so many heroes and she-roes who have never received proper credit for their gifts to us all! The challenge is to tell those untold stories, to make my son's generation and those to follow understand that we are a better state, a better society, because black people and white people worked and sacrificed together to change it."

Leslie's enthusiasm and conviction rekindled memories of an earlier and more tender time, when sometimes belief alone was the only fuel that could sustain the struggle. So much of the fervor remembered of those shared and committed times in Oxford, Ruleville, Drew, and Indianola, now decades in the past, seemed often to have melted away. Yet that time remains incandescent in McLemore's life, still lighting the path he continues to climb after more than forty years.

"We have to build on that history." The voice that resonated in the room was of a man more consumed with plans for the future than regrets for the past. I stole a look at Les Jr., whose eyes were fixed on his father. "That's what we're doing at the Hamer Institute that I started with the Fannie Lou Hamer lecture series twenty years ago. Now we have honors and awards programs named for many of the giants in the civil rights movement. We use their biographies to show how their life struggles redefined democracy, not only for African Americans, but for all Americans."

Leslie smiled. "Check this out, son, and remember it. Our movement made waves, and they've gone far from Mississippi. Now you can hear 'We Shall Overcome' sung all across the world as brothers and sisters struggle for democracy in Africa and eastern Europe. And they're using the same tactics and strategies which we used here in the South to achieve our freedom!"

"It's a wonderful legacy, Les," said Gloria, "and a proud one. So what now? What comes next?"

"We want to memorialize those struggles and victories. And we want to reform our educational curriculum. We have to change our history books so people can see themselves in American history. We want to create an inclusive narrative that truly reflects who we are. When those things come to be, we can change our civic culture so that young people like my kid here can appreciate what it means to be a first-class citizen, and an active participant in a genuine democracy."

Over the long and leisurely dinner, Leslie's seventeen-year-old son was an avid listener as we explored a history that was yesterday for us but already a legendary time for him. How privileged he was, I thought, to have the closest person in his life so embedded in that history. For most kids, even in Mississippi, the "bad old days" of the epic struggles of the movement were "yesterday's newspaper," the dry dust for a term paper, or a class quiz by some eager-beaver teacher in social studies. But we could see that behind the bright, sometimes amused, but always attentive eyes of the boy was a deep bond of affection for his father that would not permit him to be a stranger to that history. The lanky Leslie Jr. could probably challenge Leslie Sr. in one-on-one at the basketball hoop out back of their handsome and comfortable home. But if he beat him, it would be because he had gained a step on his father, not because his father let him win. The mutual pride in each other was so clearly evident at that table.

"Les, you've been teaching young people since you came to Jackson State in 1971. In no time at all, now, your son is going to be going off to college. Will his class be very different than the first ones you taught here?" My question made him pause as he pondered the answer. His eyes flicked briefly to his son, and he frowned before answering.

"I think the students today are as bright as the students I taught earlier," he said slowly, "but they don't have the consciousness, the sense of community that the earlier students had. In part, that's because of the success of the civil rights movement." He looked at his son. "Students like Les don't have to fight the battles we had to fight thirty years ago. The racism is much more subtle now. There are many more opportunities now." His head swung back to face us. "That's a gain, but as a result of our success a lot of the kids seem to feel 'we've got it made.' They feel a different challenge. They look at society from a different angle. 'How do I make a fast buck? How do I get into the mainstream *immediately?*'" He shook his head impatiently.

Leaning forward, elbows on the table, Leslie's son cocked his head, listening intently. I had the feeling that this was a theme that was still being thrashed out and was not about to be concluded at this sitting. I smiled at the boy. "Getting into the mainstream *at all* seemed to be something almost unimaginable when your father was your age, Les. You have to be patient with people like your old man." He grinned but remained silent, seemingly studying the dessert menu.

McLemore smiled faintly, touching his son's shoulder. "It's a real task to get students like Les, sons and daughters of folks who were associated with the struggles of the movement, to establish a perspective on what's happening in the world. Many of the students we see at Jackson State are the grandchildren of people who were born in Mississippi but whose children grew up in Chicago or St. Louis or Detroit, kids who are returning for their education. So the syndrome isn't just a Mississippi phenomenon. Many of these young people have been provided with such a comfortable life that they can't easily connect with the painful experiences of their folks' generation. Some of their parents have refused even to talk about that painful experience with them."

"It's not unlike some children of survivors of the Holocaust I've known," I said. "Their parents were trying to spare them, but in the end they often were deprived of something unique and valuable."

Leslie nodded, frowning. "And so are a lot of our kids. They are not familiar with the civil rights movement. They don't even recognize the names of the great martyrs of the movement here in Mississippi! So part of what I and a group of colleagues have been doing for five years now is teaching teachers and students about the roles that the civil rights movement and the labor movement played in developing citizenship and democracy. Our aim is to show these youngsters coming up, kids like Les, how to use the opportunities that they have now to participate in the decision-making process." He looked affectionately at his son. "After all, pretty quick it's going to be their world."

"Taking part in the decision making means using political power, Les. In the past few years you've been electing more black mayors in the towns, more black legislators from around the state. Even a black congressman for the first time. Has it given the black community a powerful voice?"

"Some impact, but very limited," he mused. "As an educator, I'd give the black impact a C. The political system has a way of co-opting people, regardless of color, and once you sign on as a legislator you find yourself guided by the framework in which you must operate. When it comes to issues that are strictly African American, emotional issues, the black legislators hang together. And they have enough clout to gum up the system in the legislature. Recently, for the first time in memory, the leadership of both the legislature's and the senate's Conference Committees were both black. So when it comes to having to strike a compromise over close issues, even nonracial issues, they have enough numbers to do that, and they've done that on a number of occasions.

"But the key to real political change is first getting our people to see the importance of education, and then providing greater access to it on all levels." There was an edge of frustration in his usually affable conversation. "Too often, as a people, we break the good cycle we've started. We get two or three young people to go to college, and a little down the line we find two or three other youngsters dropping out . . . not continuing the cycle. I look at my own family, the numbers of bright cousins up in Walls and Memphis, who didn't go off to college as I did. And I think that of their several children, equally bright, only one or two have ended up going to college. If we want to get responsible leadership in the state of Mississippi, we must figure out a way to keep the cycle going."

Leslie frowned, his intent face looking resolute and determined. "According to the last census, the trend clearly indicates that we are having more African Americans moving into the state than are leaving. It's a healthy indication that we are going to stay here, that the racial climate has improved. But we Mississippi blacks have never realized our tremendous potential for wielding power, for creating public policy, because we have been educationally limited." His eyes brightened, and there was a new vibrancy in his voice when he resumed. "What I envision, if not in my time, hopefully in my son's time, is finding a way to formally educate *all* my brothers and sisters in Mississippi. It is the only way we are going to achieve the political clout we need."

Long Time Passing

there is a special place in the heart for those with whom you shared danger, hope, apprehension, and even exultation when, together, you found joy in unexpected victories. For me that part of my heart will always be filled with the memory of those young men and women I first met at Oxford, Ohio, and accompanied to Mississippi in 1964. They were not the heroic pioneers like Bob Moses, Jim Foreman, Hollis Watkins, Bob Zellner, Lawrence Guyot, or Charles McLaurin, who carved the way into an apartheid Mississippi, leaving a path for the rest of us. They were just kids who believed so deeply in the American promise of freedom that they were willing to follow that path wherever it led. If history was to later judge their journey as uniquely heroic in our evolution as a nation, those summer volunteers would dismiss the idea as nonsense. The real heroes, they would remind you, were the blacks in Mississippi who stood up, demanding their freedom. Those were the folks who were there before they came that summer, and were there after the volunteers had gone away.

I have often wondered where those kids in sneakers went when they waved good-bye at the Trailways depot, and I watched the bus grow smaller, disappearing finally in the August dust of the Delta. Of our little garrison in Ruleville, I have been able to reunite with several and hope that others will surface. Their stories cast a special light on who they have become, and where the country has gone in the years since their leaving.

50. Organizing meeting.

"This is your town, and these are your folks. We'll give you all the help we can."

forty-six

Dale Gronemeier

When I spoke with Dale Gronemeier in the spring of 2002, he was busy on a pro bono civil liberties case in his Pasadena law office. Years had passed, yet the conversation instantaneously moved us both back in time, and we might have been still chatting on the front stoop of Rennie Williams's house. We laughed again, recalling our first frenetic trip into Mississippi.

"I think you had a stiff neck by the time we got to Rennie Williams's house," he said. "I never saw anyone drive that far while looking in the rearview mirror!" Recollecting those first days at the Williams's house brought a noticeable warmth to his voice. "Thinking about that time now, Tracy, I realize how remarkable Jim and Rennie Williams were. Remembering how they exposed themselves to all of Ruleville by taking us in! They were powerless people, yet they could choose to do that!" He paused. "People like Jim, Rennie, Mrs. Hamer made Mississippi the most significant event in my life. That Freedom Summer impacted in a whole variety of ways. It enriched my own life, even though I had had a long history of activism before, and it certainly strengthened my commitment to social justice." He laughed. "It even led me to the decision to marry Temetra, the girl I had been going with!"

I guffawed. "Come on, Gronemeier, are you attributing your getting hitched with Temetra to your commitment for social justice? I don't think so!" We both laughed. Long conversations in the Williamses' bedroom with Dale had first introduced the lovely black and Native American Temetra to me. From his description, love, and not social justice, had motivated the union "You're just like all the lawyers, Dale. They take too damn long to make simple decisions," I said. "How long have you been married?"

51. Dale Gronemeier, Ruleville communications director, 1964, now a pro bono attorney.
"Working here in Mississippi doesn't have the political contradictions of the North."

"More than thirty-five years," he answered with a chuckle. "A pretty good decision."

Knowing he was aware of my long-lived marriage, I teased him. "It's a good start, Gronemeier."

"It's hard to imagine any circumstance in this country now that would replicate the experience we shared in Mississippi in 1964," Dale ruminated. "You'd have to have conditions of very naked oppression, and wherever we are, Tracy, we've gone beyond that.

"You might find parallels today in the struggles of other emerging countries. But then we were threatening Mississippi's apartheid society, and were living in the belly of the beast."

There was silence for a moment, and then Dale continued, sounding reflective. "I felt good about what we did in 1964, and I felt after that summer it was time to move on to other things. I don't feel guilt about leaving because I went on to fight other battles. But I wish now that I had been around to help Linda Davis in the ordeal she and the others endured in Indianola after we all had left."

"I share your regret. I never knew till much later what hell they went through. Where did you go after you left the Delta?"

"I worked for three years, organizing in the Abolish House Un-American Activities Committee. Then I worked at Berkeley organizing the union, and took the teachers out on strike. I was the vice president of the union and was leading the picket line with the president of the union when I got arrested. Berkeley was the only place I ever got arrested!"

"You dodged the bullet in Drew," I said.

"I did. Because in Mississippi my job as the communications person in Ruleville was to not get arrested because I had to coordinate with people. It was different in California. After the arrests I was fired for organizing my department, and we shut down the campus. Ten thousand of us marched on the California Regents!"

"When did you find time to become a lawyer?"

"Not till after Temetra and I got jobs at the University of North Illinois. I was active in the teachers' union, organizing against the war in Vietnam. Tem was active with the black students movement." He paused, chuckling. "And we both got fired for our political activism! That was the time that I decided to go to law school at the University of Illinois. In 1981 I started my law practice in Pasadena and have been doing a variety of legal things, most of them politically progressive. I was active in local politics for a while, but now I do a great deal of civil liberties litigation and pro bono work for causes I believe in."

"And you don't get arrested anymore?"

"And I don't get arrested anymore."

Len Edwards

thirty-eight years after Congressman Don Edwards had joined his son at that Ruleville meeting in the Williams Chapel, I asked Len, now a superior court judge in California, if it was his father's political activism that had induced him to come to Mississippi.

"I joined the movement because it was the right thing to do," said Len firmly. "I was raised in a family that said, 'If you can make something better, you ought to do it.' It was more a matter of attitude and opportunity than the specialness of the event." He paused. "But the Mississippi summer of 1964 was the most important participation or intervention in my life to that point. It meant a great deal to me, and I knew I was doing the right thing by going."

"But you had never before put yourself in 'harm's way,' had you?"

"No. I had just been a student. First at Wesleyan in Connecticut, and later a law student at the University of Chicago. There was a great deal of danger attached to going to the Delta. But being young and unattached, I didn't think twice about it. And I had great parental support, too."

I well recall Len Edwards. Throughout the long summer, his confident presence was always a welcome part of the confrontations and struggles. Whether picketing in Greenville, demonstrating in Cleveland, confronting the sheriff in Indianola, or trudging the dusty roads of Drew trying to enroll frightened black sharecroppers, Len's alert intelligence and deep conviction added great strength to the Ruleville program. We all discovered a political and moral maturity in the slim law student from California that far transcended his years.

"I feel strongly that there was a special legacy that came out of that summer, Len, that we were all changed by it, by getting to know people like Mrs. Hamer."

52. Len Edwards, telling his father, Congressman Don Edwards, about the torching of the Ruleville church.

"After the church was burned, the FBI arrived arm in arm with the mayor!"

"You may be right," he replied. "I have always said that Mrs. Hamer was the most inspirational person, the greatest person I ever met. The nice surprise for me, Tracy, and I should have guessed it, is that when I went to a civil rights reunion recently in the Delta, nearly everyone who came back has led a life dedicated to social issues."

"Well, you certainly have. Going to Malaysia in the Peace Corps for two years, being a public defender, your work on the bench on abuse of children, and serving as president of the National Council of Juvenile and Family Court Judges. That's a full plate."

"The picture of my life is that I become involved in issues," he said quietly, "and the opportunities I find to improve the situation for underdogs, for people who are not being treated the way they should be treated. For people who are not being given the opportunity to partake of the American

53. Picket line in Greenville.
"Black and white together, we shall overcome."

dream. I remember so vividly the segregation we found down in Mississippi, and how painful that was to me. The big stuff like Jim Crow public accommodations you could take at face value. It was the little details that hurt me the most. When you saw that black people had to go to separate bathrooms, drink from separate water fountains, couldn't have their kids go into Little League, things like that, *every* hour, *every* day . . . " His voice trailed off. "Those things surprised and hurt me every time. But I don't see those things anymore. Here in California and in much of the South, segregation and discrimination like we saw it would be newsworthy events because people are against it."

"You seem to have been able to make the law court your pulpit, Len," I observed.

"Well, since Mississippi, I've had opportunities to work in juvenile justice with issues of abuse, neglect, and domestic violence. In each of these issues something has popped up in front of my eyes and said, this is wrong. People are not being fairly treated. And, as a judge, I was in an ideal place to make a difference." He paused a beat. "There's great prestige which goes with being a judge, Tracy. But, traditionally, judges don't get off the bench to do things."

"And you?" I asked.

"I'm very different from that. I've written a lot about how judges have an obligation to do certain things within a community. I'm an organizer from the bench."

I chuckled. "Maybe you learned more about organizing for the powerless in places like Drew, Mississippi, than you realized, Len!"

"Maybe," he assented, with a smile. "We've had a lot of very successful projects and organizations that I've helped build. And they all have to do with improving the lot of underdogs. The strong and the tough have always beaten up the weak and the meek." He paused, and when he spoke again there was resolution in his voice. "We've got to set up a society that doesn't let that happen."

I have to smile when I recall how, forty years ago, just the sight of Len Edwards strolling with a black girl in the Sanctified Quarter was seen by some whites in Ruleville as an outrageous and inflammatory occurrence. How could they have known that of all the volunteers in Ruleville that summer, none was more straight-arrow, morally upright, and rigorously virtuous than the congressman's son?

Fortieth Reunion, 2004

W hen I moved into the noisy reunion in Indianola in the summer of 2004, it was a homecoming unlike any I had ever been part of. Tears, embraces, and shouts of delighted recognition gave the room a palpable feeling of celebration. Unlike college and fraternity and military service reunions I had been part of, this was family. These were the kids you had loved forty years ago. Forty years!

Jim Dann was talking with animation in a corner with John Harris, who had been his tightest friend on picket lines and in the Drew jail. When Dann spotted me at the door he waved, and they both made their way through the tangle, spilling drinks as they came.

"Tracy! Man, it's so good to see you!" Jim nudged Harris. "Jesus, John, this guy was 'the old man' in Ruleville forty years ago!"

"And he's still 'the old man'!" said Harris with an embrace.

In the course of the next hours, the faces of old comrades morphed repeatedly into the remembered images of the kids from '64, singing freedom songs at the Williams Chapel, drenched in sweat in the shade of Mrs. Hamer's pecan tree, dirty and exhausted as they emerged from the Sunflower County work farm, laying flat on the lawn and laughing as they reveled in the blessed relief of a Delta rainstorm.

There was Linda Davis, almost untouched by the passage of years, with three tall, handsome sons, her husband, and a sister in tow. It took only a moment to see her again as she had pirouetted across the hard turf of the Freedom House, a gaggle of giggling teenage girls dancing in her wake.

And there was Chris Hexter, in from St. Louis, no longer the sylph I had drawn when he was tackling the high school kids at the Freedom

54. Confrontation with white students from Delta State, July 1964.
"We're here to help Mississippi blacks get the rights you've denied them for one hundred years!"

School, but unmistakably Chris as he laughed aloud at a story remembered by Alan Cooper.

Rabbi Alan Levine, whom I had seen last on the night in Indianola when Slim, the rogue cop, had shoved his .45 into the rabbi's stomach and threatened "to kill somebody." *Forty-five years ago!* He had returned with his smiling, wide-eyed wife, Suzie, for this reunion after more than thirty years working in Israel. I had known him only briefly, yet we shared a vivid memory that was now part of our history.

"This is the man, Suzie, who saved my life," he said.

"No, Suzie, I didn't. But I'm glad that he thinks I did!"

It was a cocktail of emotions, bubbling across the hours. Mike Yarrow, in from Seattle, grayer and taller, it seemed, but grinning nonstop as he ran into Dennis Flannigan, just arrived from Tacoma. And Otis Brown from Connecticut, arm in arm with Bright Winn from California, who was with him the night the Klan burned down the Freedom School in Indianola. And scattered throughout that evening and the next day were the children, wives, and husbands who were eagerly trying to connect the names, the faces, and the stories they had heard from these civil rights veterans who were now forty years older. The talk never ceased, nor the affectionate comradeship that was so quickly and effortlessly rekindled. And I was able for the first time to ferret out the details for a fuller portrait of the kids I had only sketched during that "long, hot summer."

Jim Dann

i find Jim Dann in a lot of my sketches from the summer. It's not surprising. Built like a welterweight, tough and fearless as any of the workers that summer, he was in the middle of every confrontation and every police bust. Nothing seemed to cow him, and his righteous wrath could be turned on a sheriff, a policeman, or a hostile redneck. Were it not for his high intelligence and his essential self-discipline, Dann could easily have abandoned the movement's code of nonviolence. The fact that he did not was because he instinctively knew it would be a losing tactic. But the injustice he saw all about him kept his anger at a furious pitch. When we got together in 2004 in Indianola, I first had the chance to find out where the passion I had observed in the Delta had come from.

"For me, it started when I was an engineering student at Carnegie Tech, and had gone with my girlfriend on a vacation in Cuba. You could still travel there then. I was very naive, and I remember thinking that the revolution there was just 'another South American revolution.' I figured that Cuba would be a nice place for a holiday with my girl. But that changed dramatically for me when I came back, and suddenly saw all the U.S. antagonism being directed against Cuba. It made me angry. Because I had *been* there, and had a tremendous sympathy for what the Cubans were trying to do. For the first time, I thought that there was something very wrong about American foreign policy.

"At almost the same time as I came back from Cuba, the freedom movement was beginning, and I began to look closely at what was happening to people of color in the American South. I was working at an engineering job on military planes. But after the Cuban missile crisis, I felt that there was too much contradiction for me, working at Boeing on a military

287

55. Volunteer Jim Dann with Negroes trying to vote.
"We'll be with you when you go up those stairs at the courthouse."

job." His chin rose, and he smiled. "So I quit and went to graduate school at UCLA, and switched from engineering to history."

"That was a hell of a change. Swords into plowshares!"

Dann laughed at the memory. "When you're young, and I was still very young, everything seems so black-and-white. Physics was bad, and history was good!"

"But what got you down here?"

"I was strongly influenced by a SNCC volunteer who came to speak to us on campus. He had spent a year in Mississippi. And when the call came out for volunteers for the Summer Project, I knew that was what I had to do. I never had second thoughts. And when I went to the orientation at Oxford, I was in awe of the SNCC volunteers." He looked at me and grinned. "You were there, and you know. It was a stunning week."

I nodded. "It was. But it was also scary as hell. You never had second thoughts?"

"I think we were all scared about what would happen. But the answer is no. I didn't really ever consider not going. I headed right for Ruleville, where I heard that Fannie Lou Hamer lived. And when the kids started to arrive from Oxford, I thought they were wonderful people."

"I remember that you came from a very mixed religious background," I said. "Your dad was a German Jew who was kicked out of the University at Hamburg when the Nazis took over, and he married your mother when he fled to Italy."

He nodded. "In 1939 they caught the last boat to America. And I and my brother and sister were born here. The family was not terribly religious. They were not practicing Jews, and when I was ten years old, they decided I could assimilate better if I converted to being a Protestant." He spread his hands and grinned. "So I grew up as a Methodist."

"And then you met Fannie Lou Hamer, who took her religion pretty seriously," I said. "How did she strike a mixed cat like you?"

"Oh, well, Mrs. Hamer." He shook his head, and his eyes were warm in memory. "At the time I came down to the Delta, I was not a believer at all, Tracy. But if every Christian behaved like Mrs. Hamer, even I could become a believer! She combined such compassion, wisdom, and courage.

And she had the greatest leadership qualities. People would follow her anywhere. I would have followed her anywhere."

"What surprised you most after you got down to the Delta?"

He frowned, and his voice was very quiet when he spoke. "The *utter* devastation. And the poverty was something that I never ceased to be amazed by. Compared with towns like Sunflower and Indianola, the folks who took us in in Ruleville were comparatively prosperous. Most at least had houses and scrub boards and bathrooms with running water. But that wasn't the case in other parts of the Delta. Even after I was there a year I found the poverty unbelievable."

"You and I were used to black leadership in Ruleville with Charles McLaurin and Mrs. Hamer, Jim. Did the idea of 'Black Power,' black leadership, ever trouble you at all?"

Dann pondered only a moment. "In all honesty, no. I felt there was some good argument for 'Black Power.' I didn't think it was my place to be involved in the argument of whether or not it was desirable to have only black leadership in the movement. Bob Moses was very sympathetic and open to both ends of the argument, but he felt the only way to succeed was by bringing in the white students. I accepted his reasoning. But I confess that I found that Jim Foreman, Moses, Guyot, and McLaurin, who wanted to welcome or work with the white students, were far superior to the SNCC leaders who wanted to follow the 'Black Power' movement. I do feel that those other leaders were narrower people, and were not capable of leading a multiracial group."

"I'm interested in your analysis," I said, "because you're a history teacher. I wonder if you agree with Alan Levine's perspective that he gave me last night. He's been gone for thirty years, working in Israel. He said that the remarkable thing he had observed about the multiracial working partnership in Mississippi in '64 was that the whites, who had come down there to work, had no problem, by and large, with the blacks taking the leadership roles they insisted upon. And that no accommodation deals were ever made. What surprised and pleased him was that there was no quid pro quo beforehand. He thought that was a unique American occurrence."

Dann replied, "Perhaps from a racial point of view it was somewhat unique, but historically there were many aspects of the labor-organizing

efforts in the South in the thirties when similar arrangements were accepted."
The history teacher now grinned, pushing his point. "And before them,
there were the abolitionists! Everything in history is a little bit different."

"And a little bit the same!"

He laughed with me. "And a little bit the same."

"As a high school teacher, Jim, how do you evaluate the Freedom
Schools we created in Mississippi?"

"I think the Freedom School kind of education that was so democratic,
rather than authoritarian, was much more effective than the traditional
system. And we had very committed teachers like Linda Davis and Liz
Fusco, who were working for practically nothing. Certainly the kids were
totally engaged! Whether or not that Freedom School model could better
prepare a student for life in the higher-education system, or even in the
life of the corporate world, is another question. Maybe it would only prepare students for a more progressive society, not the one we have today.
The Freedom Schools were really a wonderful educational thing. But they
were reflective of a very different society."

He hesitated, seemingly eager to continue the thought. I smiled at Jim.
"And?"

He grinned. "And after twenty years in the public education system,
I've learned that the problems are not *in* the educational system. The system just reflects the values of our society. It doesn't create those values."

"And you think the public is getting what they want?"

"Sadly, yes. But I think the kids today are being undersold, and being
underchallenged. I think that we kids of the sixties are now being over-
sold. People remember the fervor and the activism of those who stood up
and demanded change. But the vast majority of those sixties kids were
apolitical about the civil rights movement, and many were antagonistic to
those of us who were active in the antiwar movement. Sixties activism has
been very exaggerated in memory. But I think that the issues like racial
justice, and the Vietnam War, were much more clear-cut than today's
issues the kids are considering, like the environment and globalization.
But I keep on being hopeful about these kids."

I regarded the deeply thoughtful man across the table, remembering
the ardent youngster who was always at the head of the confrontation line

in Drew and Indianola in '64. "Would you encourage your kids today to go into a situation like the Freedom Summer?"

Dann studied my face before answering. "*Encourage* is a hard thing to say, because kids have to want to go. I wasn't encouraged to go. My father even went to a fund-raiser for SNCC and said to Bob Moses, 'Are you done with my son, Jim Dann, yet? Send him home!'" He laughed out loud. "Not exactly encouraging!" I joined him in the laughter, knowing that even old embarrassments are hard to forget.

He settled back in his chair. "Let me tell you about my daughter. Last year she joined a Fellowship of Reconciliation group and went to Palestine. She spent weeks in Lebanon, Palestine, and Israel. And as a father, I was worried sick about her, and was so happy when she came back. But I was extremely proud of her."

"So 'the apple don't fall far from the tree.'"

He smiled. "Not far."

"It's a tough world out there, Jim. Are you optimistic about our chances to make it better?"

"I don't think you can be an activist and be a pessimist about anything. I still seem to get into things all the time. I thought I just wanted things to be quiet, to slowly fade away. But all of a sudden I'm getting active in the teachers' union, something I never intended to do. But I find myself being optimistic." He grinned, ruefully shaking his head. "You have to be optimistic if you're going to struggle for a better contract, or you're trying to replace a board of education. Hell, Tracy, you have to be optimistic if you're going to win the battle."

"Keepin' on?"

He was frowning as he rose to go. "We really don't have any choice, do we? America is taking on the world, Tracy, and it's being arrogant. I think we're in trouble, real trouble." His face cleared, and I recognized the spirited youngster who took on all comers. "But the fact that people can still protest, that people can still speak out, that people can still do things that can effect change, the fact that we're not a cowed society, that we can, if we choose, replace the present government . . . " Dann paused, his eyes alight. "I still have a lot of hope that our people are better than our leaders."

John Harris

a reportorial artist has to be a sponge, capturing the truth of his subject through fugitive clues of body language, carriage, tilt of the head,
a set of the jaw. Those images are preserved in your head, waiting to be
transferred to your hand. They provide the alphabet you must use, the way
you create the particular visual image you want to save on paper or canvas. I had drawn John Harris, and have him ensnared in my sketchbook.
So even forty years after I had said good-bye to him in Ruleville, I still
retained a sharp image of the slender young man. He would be standing,
relaxed but wary, with his head tilted slightly back, quietly surveying the
territory, making his judgments, testing the emotional weather. His handsome face would be in repose, a small smile playing on his lips. His hands
would be jammed into the back pockets of his jeans. It pleased me that that
image, so long in my head, was here in the room in the live John Harris.

Somewhat lined, still youthfully slender and erect, John appeared to
me to be a little fragile. When I probed for the reason from his old friend,
Jim Dann, I was told that John had insisted on a short leave from his regi-
men of dialysis in order to attend this reunion. As usual, personal information about this innately modest man had to be learned from someone
else. But the sense of serenity I had always felt in Harris's presence was
unchanged with the years. It is characteristic of a man who, step by step,
has purposefully moved in the direction he had long ago chosen to travel.
And as I was to learn the next day, his personal compass for his journey
from the apartheid world of Birmingham to recognition of personal worth
and possibility had consistently pointed in the direction of achieving self-
understanding. It had been a difficult but steady journey for that young
Negro. But on the way to freedom, he had to stop in Mississippi.

"I grew up in the Baptist church in Birmingham," John recounted at my probing. "My father was an uneducated man, had only gone through the third grade." He smiled. "He wasn't all that active in the church! But my mother did graduate from high school. She'd come from a small town to Birmingham for a better life." His eyes narrowed in memory, and his voice was gentle. "She was a moral person, the person I depended on most for an adult perspective. She was a very powerful woman, with a strong position on right and wrong about racism. But she was also afraid for her kids. She didn't want me and my four siblings to get hurt or killed by getting deeply involved in the civil rights struggle.

"In Birmingham, in the fifties, we weren't really encouraged to get involved. You have to remember what that segregated society was really like, Tracy. We had white and colored water fountains, and when I was little, my mother cautioned me, 'White water tastes *different* than colored water!' We went to the white department store, and if we wanted to buy a pair of pants, we couldn't try them on. My mother would have to hold the pants next to me to see if they would fit. That was just the way things were. As long as segregation and that kind of racism were around, young people thought that there was no way to change it, and that we had to 'stay in our place.' Inside, we were wishing that the system wasn't there. But we were wondering, 'Am I the person to make the system change?' And a lot of people made the decision, 'I am *not* the person to make it change. But I wish *somebody* would do that!'"

"What freed you from that, John?"

He looked at me and said very simply, "Howard. In 1961 I left Birmingham and went to Howard University. That was the time of the Freedom Rides and the sit-in demonstrations, and Howard was a very active campus. There were a lot of demonstrations. Action at the Justice Department, and before Congress, to get them to support the fight for civil rights in the South. And I was part of all that. And on campus we heard about the Freedom Summer in Mississippi being organized by Ella Baker and Bob Moses, and they were saying that there was a need to bring more people in from outside the state to work on voter registration. And we got that message. Several of us decided that this was the way to get involved, and volunteered to go. This was a thing I wanted to do. I had

56. Freedom Day demonstration in Cleveland, Mississippi.
"We're not used to seeing pickets here in the Delta."

seen enough racism in Alabama, and my main thought was that this has got to change."

"Did you ever have second thoughts about actually going, John?"

His eyes met mine. "No. But I had questions about myself. 'Can I make a difference by going? Can I be part of making that change? Am I really committed to this?'" His gaze was steady and confident. "And the answer to those questions was yes. I could probably make a difference. I could be a part of it. And I could be committed, because otherwise things wouldn't change. And I knew the commitment was on a deeper level than the Washington demonstrations that were really quite safe. Those were real decisions for me, Tracy. I was going to go to Mississippi. I was going to stay there in Mississippi. And I was going to be in Mississippi for a while."

I smiled, hearing the same determined resolve I remembered from a much younger John Harris. "The first time I spotted you was at the orientation in Oxford, John. I thought at first that you must be one of the SNCC fieldworkers from Mississippi because almost all of the student volunteers were white."

He grinned. "A lot of the kids thought that. The truth was there were not too many black students who could afford to take a summer off if they were going to make enough money for college in the fall. But I was just determined to go, no matter. But it was a big racial adjustment for me. Almost until my high school graduation, when I was eighteen years old, I had never had real contact with *any* white people. Our high school was all black. Our teachers were all black. And I had only seen whites from a distance. And now, at Oxford, I was in this closed situation where I and white kids were *dependent* on each other! Helping each other. Learning from each other. It was very disorienting. I was in a totally different social and political position. And when we left Oxford, and got to Mississippi, we all had to be totally dependent on each other, just to get by. From day to day, we were in it *together,* and we all found that this was different than anything we had ever known. Because after Goodman, Schwerner, and Chaney were killed by the Klan, we knew that they were out after all of us."

"How tough was it to become friends with whites, as well as fellow volunteers?"

"For me, it was an adjustment," he admitted. "The white civil rights workers had their hearts in the right place, but some of them unintentionally brought their chauvinism from the white community with them. For example, we were doing voter registration in the Delta towns, and the black residents were saying, 'Yes, sir' and 'No, sir' to nineteen-year-old white kids. And when I asked the volunteers what they thought about that, they were surprised at my question. They thought it was just 'a southern thing.' And part of it was, but a good part of it was that local blacks were still seeing whites as people a little better than they were. So I tried to get the students to just tell a person in a nice way, 'My name is James. You don't have to be saying "Yes, sir" or "No, sir" to me. I shouid be saying it to you since you are an older person, and I respect you.' We tried to deal with those kinds of things." He smiled, nodding toward Jim Dann. "And some of them, like Jim here, listened."

"I remember those meetings at Williams Chapel, John. And I remember the special way the folks felt about you and McLaurin. They hadn't seen a lot of young blacks willing to step up and take responsibility, because it had been very dangerous to do that, in Mississippi."

John nodded, but looked uncomfortable at the idea that he was regarded as something special. "For me, it was a privilege just to be down there, hoping that I could contribute something lasting. I think it was very important that we were able to bring those folks some hope from outside Mississippi, because they felt so isolated, so hopeless, and so unpowerful. They could see a nineteen-year-old black person who had a message, who had some hope, who could add to their courage and hope. That may have made a difference."

"I saw it, John, the night in Indianola when you were running the first mass meeting in Indianola. I'll never forget that night. In spite of the Klan and the White Citizens Council, that Freedom School was packed with almost three hundred people!"

John's usual equanimity deserted him, and his face flushed with excited memory. "It took so much courage for those people to come out! If you had asked me or any of the other volunteers beforehand, we wouldn't have guessed that could happen. It wasn't like going to a church service, or going to a wedding, or going to a school graduation. It was going to something most people there had never before been to in their life! Just by walking into that Freedom School they were defying *everything* they had learned as blacks in the Mississippi Delta!"

Harris's modesty still made him reluctant to accept personal credit for what he had done for others, but he was very clear on what his involvement had done for him. "It liberated *me*. Before going to Mississippi, liberation was just a theory. It liberated me, Tracy, because I could see that I could make people respond, older people, fifty, sixty years old, who had been so suppressed for years and years. People who had never before been to a mass meeting, who had never gone to the courthouse and said, 'I want to register to vote!' I saw it happening before my eyes! It wasn't something I might see in another three or four or five years. I saw it happening *now!* What I was doing was making a difference *now!*"

Watching John replaying that remarkable night in his head, I saw him in perhaps the ultimate triumphal moments of his young life. There was a joy in his eyes, and his voice was vibrant. "For me to *be* there, running that meeting, was just something you never get a chance to do! What am I supposed to *say*? What am I supposed to *do*?"

He turned to me, and I was struck with the wonder that still remained on his face. Like a patient teacher, he quietly spelled out the lesson. "So you say what you think is right. And," he said to me with astonishment, *"everybody there knew that it was right.* And it wasn't like you were solving a complex problem for them, like getting them to the moon. 'You have the right to vote! Yes! We can help you do that! This is something new you can do! We know you can do it! You have a right to do it! Let's do that!' And, Tracy, people *responded!* It was amazing to me to see that. It was like a revolutionary act."

During the reunion, I was impressed and intrigued by the children who had accompanied their parents. Some, like John Harris's daughter who was filming the occasion, were even older than their parents had been when they came in '64. All the young people seemed eager to hear real stories about the movement that had been so meaningful in their parents' lives. I was curious to find out how politically involved they were.

Harris appeared thoughtful at my question, then responded contemplatively. "I get the feeling that these kids have commitment, that they have a lot of questions, for instance, about whether the Iraq war is something we should be involved in. Questions about whether we should support it or get out. I get the feeling that a lot of these kids don't think we should have gotten involved. They have real good questions they're asking. But when you ask them about the injustice or racism that got us involved when we were that age, you realize that they are committed on civil rights at a very different level. Their focus is different. More of them are questioning about discrimination in sexual orientation, and think that gay people should have the same rights as straight people. A lot of them are concerned about the issue of abortion, and that people should have the constitutional right to choose."

John tilted his head, pondering this new reality. "These kids have two hundred television channels, the Internet, a whole lot of distractions that could let them escape from thinking out those questions if they want to. Distractions you and I didn't have forty years ago." He smiled. "But I have hope, Tracy. The issues have changed in forty years, but I believe these young people are trying to understand as much as possible."

fifty-one

Liz Fusco

There was no way not to recognize Liz Fusco at the fortieth reunion in Indianola. Only two things had really changed. Her name on the name tag was now Aaronsohn, not Fusco. And some very becoming gray was threading through her smart, short-cropped hair. She remained remarkably young and trim, still quietly watchful, but relaxed and seemingly comfortable in the bubbling welcome of old comrades. This chic, smiling woman seemed very removed from the Liz I remembered from 1965, when the young, idealistic educator was feeling very adrift and distressed, pondering what might await her. It was a joy to see her again.

As I made my way to her side, I was remembering clearly that hot July afternoon when I first noticed Liz Fusco. It was the day that the Freedom School teachers arrived in Ruleville from Oxford, Ohio. Short, girlishly slim, and wearing a long, braided ponytail, she looked vulnerable and very young. I had nudged Dale Gronemeier and nodded toward the girl.

"Is that a teacher or a student? She looks like a kid who wants to join the Freedom School!"

Her large, dark eyes seemed to be soaking in every corner of the scene as the chatty, weary, but exuberant women made their careful way among the piles of books that had accompanied their coming. When she caught my eye, I smiled and waved encouragingly. Liz nodded back, smiling shyly, and followed the teachers into the wreck of the building that would become their school. Lord, I thought, that kid looks like she ought to be back in high school. How's she going to make it down here?

It was not the first time that I had misread the age and experience of a young woman. In the days that followed, I learned that Liz Fusco, at twenty-seven, was perhaps the oldest of the Freedom School teachers,

57. Liz Fusco, now a college professor, with Freedom School teachers in Ruleville, 1964.

"We began to learn the most important part of our education. We learned to listen."

and that she was not all that shy. And from the moment she arrived at our fledgling school, students and staff became swiftly aware of the keen intelligence and passion of Liz Fusco.

Now, my arm around her slender shoulders, I steered her through the crowd, finding a quiet corner in an adjoining room. "So when did Liz Fusco become Liz Aaronsohn?"

She laughed. "A long time ago. But I was born Liz Aaronsohn. Liz Fusco doesn't live here anymore!" She cocked her head and smiled. "I was a little Jewish girl from Cincinnati, the daughter of a rabbi. And when I got to be twenty-three (and still not married!), I married a young Marxist whom I met in the Peace Corps. His name was Luke Fusco. Getting married was our first major mistake, and telling the Peace Corps 'You cannot make me have servants if I am to serve in Ethiopia' was the second." She giggled, shaking her head in disbelief. "Just how arrogant can one person be? Well, that was me. And the Peace Corps 'selected us out'!"

"So what happened?"

"Well, it was complicated because it was in the middle of the Vietnam War, and Luke did not want to be drafted. So we stayed married for a year and a half until Luke became twenty-six and was no longer a draft risk." She held my eyes. "I was not good at marriage, Tracy. Flunked twice. But I have a wonderful daughter from the second one whom I adore."

"But we left Cincinnati too fast, Liz. I want to hear what it was like being the daughter of a rabbi. I confess, when I met you I assumed you were Italian!"

She smiled. "No, but a lot of people thought so. But not people in Cincinnati who knew my father! He had been studying for the rabbinate when we got into World War I. And being eager to be seen as a good, patriotic American boy, he dropped out and joined the army." She frowned and looked away. "He was blinded in the service, so he never had his own pulpit or congregation. He would speak for organizations, but for the family it meant real poverty. But what he gave me instead of money was the beginning of a social conscience. What he taught me was, 'Justice! Justice! Justice!'" Her face brightened. "And through his connections I was able to get in Smith College even though they had a very small Jewish quota in the fifties." She said wryly, "It was the beginning of my very upper-class education.

"At Smith College I always had to have a job because I needed the money. And I needed to keep up my grades because I was on scholarship. I never could just hang out with friends at the coffee shop. It was just study, study, study." Her eyes seemed to be seeing a vanished time. She smiled suddenly. "But when I got into interfaith activities at Smith, things got a whole lot more interesting."

Her sudden animation made me smile. "I know you remember the Montgomery bus boycott in '56. Well, some of those Montgomery folks came to talk to us at the Interfaith Council that I was chairing. I'll never forget them! One of them said, 'My feet is tired, but my soul is rested.' *My soul is rested!*" Liz beamed. "I began to hear the poetry of their language, Tracy. And that really pushed me in another direction."

The compass had been reset for her when she went on to Yale for her master's degree. She joined the Yale Russian Chorus and she helped found Challenge. Liz grinned and then orated in a deep, mock-serious voice, "CHALLENGE: STUDENT PROGRAMS AT YALE UNIVERSITY TO CONFRONT WITH REALISTIC CONCERN AND RESPONSIBLE ACTION THE CRUCIAL ISSUES OF TODAY'S WORLD." She exploded with laughter. When she regained her breath, she said, "You bet we were serious! We invited Albert Schweitzer, we invited Camus, hell, we invited the world to come talk to us at Yale. *And some of them came!*" Laughter again simply gushed out. *"They did!"*

"So your upper-class education had some merit after all," I said.

"Of course it had," she said quietly. "For one thing, Challenge got me serious about doing research about really important subjects. Like nuclear proliferation. Like racism. And racism raised a passion in me that led me to Oxford, Ohio, and Freedom Summer."

"Oxford was the whole summer rolled into two weeks," I said. "I was only there for the first one. But what a week it was!"

Liz blanched. "I got mixed up about the dates and was there for both of them. So I was there when Bob Moses declared that Goodman, Schwerner, and Chaney were missing." She was silent for a long beat, then her eyes turned to mine. "Hearing the stories of the SNCC fieldworkers who had come up from Mississippi—Tracy, in my whole life, before or since, I had never been so stunned. I couldn't eat. I couldn't sleep."

"The SNCC kids seemed a breed apart," I said. "The dues they had paid just trying to register voters seemed unbelievable. And during my week at Oxford we were concentrating on voter registration. It was daunting. But what did they have to give you about teaching? Some of them were so badly educated themselves."

Liz looked thoughtful. "It depends on what you call 'education,' I guess. I came to Oxford with all the upper-class-education baggage. I had come out of a tradition where teachers gave tests, teachers did most of the talking, and students did their best to please the teachers. What the fieldworkers taught me, what they tried to teach all of us Freedom School teachers, was that if we were going to be successful, we had to ground our teaching in our students' lives. I had to learn to let them do the thinking, not parrot mine." She paused, frowning. "And that was damn hard for someone like me, who had been socialized to think that citizens needed to be literate and have practice in decision making. SNCC told us what life was like for the people who would be our hosts and our students. So we learned to sing the freedom songs, and we began to learn about the history and the culture of Africans in America. Our test, they said, would be how respectful of the local people we would become. So once we got down to Mississippi, we started attending mass meetings and Sunday services in churches. And we began to learn the most important part of our education as teachers. We learned to *listen.*

"When you met me in the Delta in '65, I was still wrestling with that. SNCC was saying that the success of the movement wouldn't be measured by the numbers of people who would manage to register to vote. It would be defined by the transformation of people's thinking about what was possible for their lives, if only enough of them discovered their voices and got together to speak. By the time I left to teach in the North in 1966, I had learned how true, how necessary, that process was. The permanent effect of the Freedom Schools on many of us who were involved has been to remind us and empower us to teach for freedom with whoever our students are. Wherever our students are."

As we began to fill in the long stretch of years that had intervened, I recognized the focused, alert, and purposeful woman that was Liz, is Liz. Now a Ph.D. who is teaching teachers at Central Connecticut State University, her manner is more measured, and the irresolution is no longer there. This is a woman who has found answers for herself, and I learned how difficult many of the times were when she was seeking those answers.

"In 1966, I tried to take the lessons I had learned to public school teaching in a New York City high school. It was my first job, and I encouraged my predominantly black and Puerto Rican students to write in their own language. I urged them to write about their own issues, and not worry about whether the writing was 'correct.'" Liz's eyes were alight with the memory. "What amazing papers my students wrote when they were given the opportunity to reflect on their own lives! What conversations we had!" She paused, then burst out laughing. "And I got fired from that school in October!

58. Volunteers at Freedom School.
"We turned a wreck of a farmhouse into a school."

"When I left the New York school system in 1971, I went to teach in an all-white working-class elementary school in Massachusetts. And I was challenged by parents who didn't understand my personal methods of teaching. They had no frame of reference to help them understand that when the children and I were reading together, or raising a butterfly, or the kids were writing their own books, it was all 'teaching.' 'How can my child be learning if you're not standing up there in front, teaching?'

"Personally, I felt challenged in a different way. After living for two years in Mississippi, and five years in New York City, with minority people who clearly recognized that they were oppressed, I now had to figure out how to work with marginally employed and barely literate white parents who assumed minorities or people who were on welfare were their enemies. What I had to learn is that when people are really empowered within themselves, they don't need to have power over others. I felt for their kids. It was just as important that they find their voices, their strengths, and their community as it was for the black kids I taught in the Delta."

Liz Aaronsohn's odyssey through American education has taken her from Ivy League beginning to the Mississippi Delta, to rural white America, urban nonwhite America, and finally into the halls of academe, where her student teachers are now the objects of her deepest concern and passion. "I worry about their parochialism, and I try to expose them to multicultural experiences while they're here." She laughed. "They are so like I was when I was a student! I didn't know anything about the world outside. It was all about fitting in, being popular, and boys. And that's all these kids seem to be thinking about. They're still adolescents." She sighed deeply, and a small smile lit her serious face. "Why do I expect so much of them? I guess it's because they're going to be teachers in a few semesters. And that scares me."

"It scares you because you've learned how important education is, Liz. I think it's been your religion ever since you left the rabbi's house in Cincinnati."

"It's all about freedom," she said firmly. "And freedom is so very, very hard."

Chris Hexter

from the corner of the room, there were hoots of laughter, and I could plainly hear the ringing, happy voice of Chris Hexter. Head back, Chris was the consummate storyteller, chortling happily and commenting at full decibel, as delighted with the circle of his old friends as he was by the yarn he was recalling. This was a man who seemed always to find fun and simple pleasure in the ordinary business of human intercourse. Chris had loved the physical give-and-take with the Freedom School kids in a tough football scrimmage, and found equal joy mentoring them, and laughing with them, as they tentatively discovered Huck Finn. All I had learned about Hexter in those early days was that his dad taught at Yale, that Chris loved kids, and that there was a buoyant optimism that seemed to arm him when we got in trouble. No one sang louder, no one seemed more daring, no one seemed more in awe of the quiet but dynamic leadership of Charles McLaurin ("I never saw a man who carried himself with such amazing dignity"). And no one was more surprising than Chris Hexter.

Over a long and delightful dinner with Chris and Alan and Suzie Levine, where the conversation meandered from reminiscence of Hexter's zigzag relationship with his often intimidating father ("He was short, bald, and looked like a bowlegged sailor, and he was a very bright man. And when he got angry, my perception of him as a kid was that the huge scar on his head would light up! It was frightening!") to recalling the black family that took him in ("I can only recall that there was a high degree of politeness. But I vividly remember mayonnaise! In that house, I'm noticing that the mayonnaise was not in the refrigerator very long. And here I am in Mississippi, and I'm worrying about getting ptomaine

59. Chris Hexter, now a labor lawyer, at a football scrimmage with Freedom School boys, Ruleville, 1964.

"Mississippi just sharpened my vision of the possibilities that people can do."

poisoning! Now how stupid is that?"). He would explode with laughter, mostly aimed at his own mistakes and shortcomings.

Memories of Hexter's professor father remain a dramatic influence in his maturation. He turned to Rabbi Levine, who had worked with Martin Luther King, and said, "I remember when Dr. King was arrested in Montgomery, my father said, with warm approval, 'This person is going places.' But when I wanted to go to the Oxford orientation week, I still had to convince my parents to let me go. They were very ready to live with the consequences of how they had raised us, and they were not prepared to tell me not to go. But they were concerned about the hazards there. My father knew something about the reality on the ground because his Yale colleague Staughton Lynd was an architect of the Freedom School part of the Summer Project. I guess it was some relief to my father that I was not going with the first group to Oxford, the ones who were going to work out in the field on voter registration. My group, the second group, would be going to work with the Freedom Schools. And the deal that I made with my parents was that I would not get arrested." Chris paused for a long beat, and then a smile crept over his face. "And I didn't get arrested until my third week in Mississippi!"

"How did a Freedom School teacher get arrested?" asked Levine, smiling.

He shrugged. "Doing what had to be done. I knew my dad was not going to be happy hearing that I was arrested, so my statement to my father was, 'We were going up to Drew as a group to *encourage* people to register to vote, not actually going to *register* them.'" The light gleamed on his glasses as he threw back his head and laughed aloud. "If my father gets furious, I thought, at least I'll have something to say to him if he refuses to bail me out of jail!" His laughter ceased, and he seemed to be looking back in time as his eyes held mine. "My father is Al Capone, Tracy, fronting as a college professor."

I studied Chris. "Having Al Capone as your old man couldn't have been easy. What gave you the confidence to go, Chris?"

"Youthful bravado," he said. "It's youthful bravado that got me through. It's what got you through on D-day. It's what makes a soldier go into battle. It's what makes you do things sometimes that in a cooler, more reflective time you wouldn't necessarily do."

"You were a political liberal in St. Louis, before going south, Chris. Did your political views change there?"

He sipped his drink, settling back thoughtfully in his chair. "No. I don't think so. Mississippi gave me a very strong sense that how wealth, and that means power, is distributed in this country screws a whole lot of people. But Mississippi just sharpened my vision of *possibilities,* of what people can do. Of the power of people when they engage as a group. Of the power of the people to use their government for their benefit. My sense of what's great about America is *possibility."* His usually humorous face was now focused and serious, and he leaned forward, his elbows on the table. "What's bad about America is that our society is so stratified. That disparity invites violence. So people will have to use their power to make that stratification less harsh.

"Maybe that's why I'm now a lawyer for labor unions. It's organized, legalized group activity. I work with the electricians a lot of the time, whose history in the labor-movement building trades was not a good one on race. But my biggest thrill in the labor movement is when I see African American workers working side by side with white workers on issues that are bigger than either of them." His eyes were bright, and he was smiling. "That really excites me, because that's what I saw in the summer of '64, people from different worlds, from different life experiences, finding a way to mediate those differences and doing something bigger than them."

Suzie Levine, who had never been to the American South, was an avid listener. No one at the reunion seemed to savor every moment like the Israeli wife of the rabbi. "What did you do when you left Mississippi, Chris?" she asked.

"When I returned to St. Louis, I got involved with National Neighbors, an organization fighting for open housing." He turned to Alan. "Now I'm active in the first Reformed Jewish congregation to build a temple within the inner city of St. Louis. I called an African American pastor who knew I had worked in Mississippi. And, together, we created a joint venture of the two congregations. We set up a mentoring program in a school where the commitment would always be to have members of both congregations. It was in the poorest section of St. Louis." With obvious pride, he continued. "That mentoring project that we started with two kids now gets some wealthy donors and corporate support. And we have thousands of mentors going to St. Louis schools."

The still youthful enthusiasm of Hexter about his moral commitments made forty years earlier seemed to color and be descriptive of his life today. Diversity, which he cherishes, is reflected in the rainbow of his children. "My oldest daughter, Oleana, is a Hawaiian from three different nationalities. My son Jack is my biological son. Our third child, Kirwood, is Japanese American and Irish American. Our fourth oldest is Anna, an African American, and our fifth oldest is Shelly, who is Irish through and through!"

Alan chuckled. "Now that's an American family! Are your kids political, Chris? Are they committed?"

"They were not very interested at the beginning. But ten years ago I took my three daughters to Jackson, to the thirtieth reunion of the Summer Project, and they loved it. They were thrilled to have been there. The three of them are liberal kids, but they're not politically sophisticated. My son is more analytical, and his perceptions of the world are not mine. But he is living in Israel, Rabbi, and it's a dangerous place. All my kids and grandkids are living in a dangerous world."

Rabbi Levine looked at Suzie, who replied very kindly, "Chris, everybody's kids are living in a dangerous world."

Chris nodded somberly. "I really accept my father's view of how to raise children: 'Hope for the best, and pray that they adopt the best of your views and not the worst of your behavior!'" His face broke into a grin. "And that's from the mouth of Al Capone!"

Alan Levine nodded thoughtfully, weighing Chris's words. "Speaking of behavior," he said, "I thought what I observed on the bus today with Charles McLaurin and the monument to Slim was one of the most extraordinary examples of Christianity that I had ever seen."

"What you saw, Rabbi," said Hexter, "was what we all knew was so special about Mac. His capacity to forgive. The fact that he never seemed to hate people. Slim, after all, is the guy that had come in to that first meeting in Indianola, pulled his gun on you, and wanted to beat the shit out of McLaurin, or kill him, after Mac had faced him down. And here Mac is showing us all the monument to Nathaniel 'Slim' Jack that he talked the city into erecting! What a man! How many of us could have recognized the complexity of the life that black policeman had had to lead!"

Rabbi Levine simply nodded, his eyes moist. "I had never witnessed that kind of capacity for forgiveness before," he said softly.

"I don't think I could ever have been that charitable about Slim," I said. "I thought it was really only a miracle that kept him from killing you and McLaurin that night. A *monument*? Hell, no!"

Chris Hexter was uncharacteristically silent, and when he spoke there was wonder in his voice. "What incredible understanding for a young man to have! Just remarkable!" He gazed at each of us around the table, and his voice rose above the clatter of the restaurant. "When it turned out that Mac, as assistant director of public works, had petitioned Indianola to put up the monument to the policeman that nearly killed him, I thought, `Wow!'"

The following day, I cornered McLaurin, wanting to hear him explain the incident about Slim for myself. "How the hell could you do that, Mac, knowing what he had done?"

He nodded. "Yes, I knew what he had done. But I knew what that time was like, also. How the White Citizens Council killed George Lee over in Belzoni, how the White Citizens Council shot into Jess Court's store in the broad daylight and drove him out of town, what the White Citizens Council did to Dr. Battle when they had him arrested when he was leaving Valley State one night and said he was drunk. And how they used that to take his license to practice medicine away, and break up the NAACP. And I knew, too, what the White Citizens Council did to discredit other blacks in leadership positions and were influential in the black community.

"And I knew that Slim had been hired to maintain law and order on this side of town so that whites would not be blamed for keeping their iron foot on black heads all the time. Even though Slim was the way he was to us, he was a victim of that era. As the only black policeman, he did what he thought the whites wanted him to do. So I took the opportunity to show that I was big enough to forgive him. He was dead, and I was still alive. I thought it was a fitting memorial as a part of the whole thing of forgiving, of the redemption that Martin Luther King talked about, of learning to live together as brothers. I went to the Jack family because they were victims, too, because of the role that Slim had played, and told them what I wanted the city to do about putting up a memorial, and they were very pleased.

"After I went to the mayor requesting the monument, he went to the board and he said, 'You know Charles has been involved with a lot of things about which a lot of us might not have agreed with. But I know him, and it's time we put that period behind us.'"

"That was a beautiful thing to do for the family, Mac. I don't know if I would have had the courage to do that."

McLaurin considered, then smiled. "I don't know if twenty-five years ago I would have done that. I was very angry in those days. I had visions of wiping out all the racists in Washington, D.C.! Getting a job as a cook in the House of Representatives in order to eliminate all the southerners!" He laughed and shook his head in disbelief. "I really did have thoughts like that."

"Well, Mac, you could have saved the country a lot of trouble! There wouldn't have been any racists left!"

"Yeah," he chortled, "and there wouldn't have been any Charles McLaurin left! And my little granddaughter wouldn't even have known me!"

"Yeah," I agreed, "and she wouldn't have ever *wanted* to know you!"

"No. I would have just been a dead terrorist!" He turned serious. "I think what brought me around was when my children were born. I wanted them to realize that we had the capacity to be kind, and to forgive. I had gotten older and better understood God and humanity. And Slim? Slim was just a part of that."

Unsettling Memories

the call from my old friend from Tougaloo College, Susan McClamroch, was, as always, high-spirited and enthusiastic. Her southern-belle voice was tripping with exciting news. "An exhibit, Tracy, and at the Smith Robertson Museum, the first black ethnic museum in Jackson! Not only your drawings from Freedom Summer you gave to Tougaloo, but all the photographs of Freedom Summer you gave to Jackson State! And the 'Unsettling Memories' conference wants to open with your show! Save June 16 to June 20, and y'all plan to come down. We want you to speak at the opening."

"Susan, speak slower. My Yankee ears are struggling to catch up. What is an 'Unsettling Memories' conference? And who is mounting the show?"

"Don't fret, honey. I'm sending you all the material about the conference. And John Sullivan, the head of the Art Department at Jackson State, and I are hanging the show. It's going to be only gorgeous!" There was a brief pause, then the mellifluous voice leaped forward. "And you're speakin' first thing in a long evening program." I stared at the phone as Susan charged ahead. "So you don't have to speak too long. I'm so excited!"

I had come to know and cherish Susan McClamroch when she was working to preserve the rich art legacy owned by Tougaloo College. In the remarkable collection are nearly one hundred of the drawings I had made in the Delta in 1964, the only artist's record of the civil rights struggle in Mississippi, and we felt their permanent home should be in that state. June and I had given the whole folio of drawings in perpetuity to Tougaloo, a college that had played an important and courageous role in the freedom struggle. At a caring, but economically struggling institution like Tougaloo, the capacity to take optimum care of the art was a constant struggle. Susan's fierce desire to save the endangered art and artifacts of the college had led her to a promising relationship with the Mississippi Archives. That august body had been enlisted in her mission, and in 2004 become a partner custodian of the Tougaloo treasures. I was delighted and reassured that my work would now be preserved for generations yet to be. And Susan was the good angel who was helping make it all happen. My gratitude made me grab my calendar and circle the dates she had requested. How do you say no to Scarlett O'Hara?

In short order I received an invitation from the "Unsettling Memories" conference, inviting me to show my work and to participate in the four days of seminars devoted to examinations of the "culture and trauma in the Deep South." Academics from Tulane, Jackson State University, Tougaloo, and the University of Mississippi, as well as veterans of the civil rights movement, would explore the recent tortured history of race relations in the South. I was pleased and honored to be included.

As Gloria and I were packing for the trip, I found my telephone list of old friends in Mississippi. On the list, but numberless, were Lake and Bette Lindsey. Beside their names I had scratched "(Brandon?)." Would I ever see the Lindseys again? On impulse, I called Mississippi Information, plaintively inquiring, "Do you, by any chance, have a listing for a Lake or Bette Lindsey in Brandon?"

"I have a B. Lindsey."

"You *do?*" I spoke so sharply that Gloria paused in her packing and stared at me. "Could you please connect me?"

When the phone stopped ringing, a woman's voice answered, "Hello."

"Bette? Is that you, Bette?" I heard a gasp, a flurry of excited words and laughter, and then "Tracy!" I heard the very recognizable cadence of the woman with whom I had last spoken twelve years before.

"Jesus *does* these things! I do know he *does,* Tracy. Would you believe that when the phone rang just now, I was looking through your book, *Stranger at the Gates?* Where *are* you? Can you come over?"

I assured her that I was in Connecticut, but that my wife, Gloria, and I were heading for Jackson and would love to meet her and Lake in the next few days.

"We will! We will! You said your wife, Gloria?" She hesitated.

"June passed away in 1998, Bette. Two years later I married Gloria Cole, who had been our old and dear friend for thirty-five years. She'll be coming with me."

"I'm so sad to hear about June, Tracy. She was a wonderful woman. But I'm happy to hear about Gloria. I can't wait to meet her! We'll pick you up at your hotel."

I grinned at Gloria as I hung up. "After all these years, the lost are found! You're finally going to meet Lake and Bette Lindsey!"

Gloria said, "Terrific! Was she surprised to hear from you?"

"I'm not really sure she was," I said. "Bette says Jesus does things like that."

"Unsettling Memories" was an ambitious attempt to establish a rational historic perspective on the lingering legacy of the recently apartheid Deep South. Many of the speakers and attendees were too young to have personally experienced the cruel injustices or humiliations of the fifties or sixties, but were eager to explore those times with their academic elders or the now middle-aged veterans of the movement. There seemed to be a shared longing to mine those cruel days in order to shape better teaching tools for today's and tomorrow's students.

If the vanished people and events of the sixties seemed somewhat abstracted in the conference's academic discussions, the show of drawings and photographs that were handsomely mounted by McClamroch and Sullivan contributed an infusion of very real images. In two great rooms of the Smith Robertson black ethnic museum, the conferees could meet the men, women, and children, blacks and whites, who had prevailed through that summer of murder, arson, and unspeakable violence. If the young conference-goers thought that the people who had changed the face of the South were mythic and had somehow been bigger than life, they saw something quite startlingly different. They saw people who looked just like themselves.

There are moments when things seem to fall into place, when you sense an order to things that is usually missing in the business of living. The Jackson conference was one of those moments of grace for me. On the walls of the museum were the drawings I took most pride in, and I was able to show them for the first time to my wife, to my peers, and to so many young and old Mississippians. It was memorable, and I relished the opportunity to share what I had done. And in the immediate aftermath of the exhibit, I was able to reestablish contact with my vanished friends, the Lindseys. Given my credentials and my pedigree, I'm not able to claim that Jesus had intervened to help close the circle. But I am grateful to Whoever had taken the trouble.

For forty years, I have been a "stranger at the gates" in Mississippi. Sometimes I have been a stranger with a sketch pad, a stranger with a documentary camera, or a stranger with a notebook. But regardless of the tools, I have remained an avid outsider, an observer, fascinated by the challenging canvas of this place. As a part of the civil rights movement, my focus has always been on the men and women who have struggled to change a society that seemed unnaturally and irrevocably determined to cling to its past. Those blacks and whites, Mississippians and outsiders, who were willing to bet their lives on the American promise of justice, ensnared my heart. I have tried to capture them in pictures and on pages, and they will remain green in my memory forever.

But what of the Mississippi that almost never appeared in my art, in my writing, or in the documentary films I had created over these past four decades? What of white Mississippi had I learned? Who, really, lived across the highway, barely seen across the cotton patches of black Mississippi? At the fortieth reunion of Freedom Summer in 2004, I asked, "Who among you ever established a trusting relationship with a white family during all your time in Mississippi?" Not a single hand went up. Not one. When I raised my own, they looked astonished. And for the first time, they heard about Lake Lindsey and his wife, Bette.

The Lindseys' generosity of friendship to this "stranger" has been an extraordinary gift to me. Though years have intervened when communication has faltered, the pulse of a trusting friendship has survived over four decades. In candor, what insights I had gained about white Mississippi had come from the long conversations that Bette Lindsey first instigated in 1964. It was the possibility of pursuing our dialogue once again that made the prospect of our evening with the Lindseys so exciting. It was clear to me that Mississippi had evolved over the years. How, I wondered, had change affected them?

Crossing the Highway

We were awaiting the arrival of the Lindseys in front of the hotel when the large black automobile swept up the drive. A tall, sturdy, smiling man left the car and strode up the walk. I was struck by how much a slightly graying Lake Lindsey looked as I remembered him from nearly forty years ago. "Hey there, Tracy! And this must be Gloria! Glad to see you both."

Over his shoulder I watched Bette Lindsey hurry from the car, arms spread wide to embrace each of us. "I'm just so happy to see you!" The vitality of the still pretty woman defied the years that had intervened. She stepped back, cocked her head, her bright eyes probing and searching our faces. "Oh, yes! I want to know *everything*, and I've got a million questions you've got to answer."

I had to smile, for in my head I could still hear that vibrant voice echoing across the gas station in 1964. "Take off your sunglasses," she had commanded. "I've got questions to ask you, and I want to see your eyes."

"We're taking you out of town to a restaurant we thought you'd like," she said. "Besides," she laughed, "it will give us some time to really talk." She took Gloria's hand and led her to the car. "Come in the back with me, hon. The men can talk up front."

As Lake eased the car from the curb, he said, "It's about twenty minutes away. That all right with you folks?"

"Fine with me," said Gloria, easing comfortably back into the seat next to Bette.

"And fine with me," I answered. "After God knows how long, there's so much to catch up on. I haven't talked with Bette for about eighteen years." I turned to look at Lake. "And I haven't talked with you since

1965! I remember Dick Milburn was there. It was hot as hell that morning, and you couldn't stop looking at the sky, wondering if it was ever going to rain again."

He frowned. "I do remember that. That rain never did come. But our old friend Dick is gone. Died some time ago, Tracy." He paused, and then his face lightened. "But I'm the same old country boy," he laughed. "Just a tad older."

As the women began chatting in the back, Lake was orienting me to the new developments visible around Jackson, obviously proud of the changes that had come in the years since I first arrived in the state. "We're a lot less 'country' than you'd remember. Better restaurants now, and newer stores, and the hotels are a whole lot smarter. But I wouldn't recommend that you and Gloria wander around alone downtown after it's dark. Like a lot of cities, there are folks around that take advantage, and there's been a lot of crime in Jackson." He nodded toward groups of young blacks, idling on the sidewalks and corners, seemingly aimless. Their eyes seemed to follow our car as it eased out to the state highway. "Not everything's changed." Lake's deep voice was melancholy. "Still got a ways to go about that down here, I'm afraid."

"Not just down here," I said. "Those kids on the corner look a lot like the kids in Bridgeport, ten minutes from my house in Connecticut. Too much time and too few jobs. Lousy combination, Lake."

As Lake eased onto the state road, Bette was saying, "Used to be, Gloria, I'd go into Neiman-Marcus, and if I found a beautiful pair of shoes I just *had* to have, I'd order them in four colors." Bette's chuckle was flat and mirthless. "But after we lost the plantation, if I wanted a new pair of shoes, I went into Wal-Mart, and bought them on the lay-away plan." When I turned in my seat, Bette's hand was in Gloria's, and she was staring out the window. I turned to look at Lake. He remained silent, busily reading the road ahead.

"You lost the plantation, Lake?" My voice seemed to fill the car in the silence. "How awful for you! What in the world happened?"

Lake's face was flushed as he answered. "I was doing real good, Tracy. Making money every year. Bette and I had married early, and we started farming on the land my daddy had left me, and we did it with great success for a number of years. Things had gone really well." He turned to me. "You remember Ezra Taft Benson? Reagan's secretary of agriculture?" I nodded. "Well, he came out with this policy that we were going to have to feed and clothe the world. 'You need to plant every acre you can.' I was going to really get rich."

"Back in those days," murmured Bette, "the Delta was like Peyton Place! I just wrote checks, Gloria, and Lake wrote checks, and I didn't even know what was in the bank! Insanity! And that's how we all lived. And I became part of it."

Lake's deep Delta voice had a bitter edge to it. "And I made some bad decisions. I doubled the size of my farming operation. *Doubled* it, Tracy! Then it looked like everything I touched just went sour. If I needed a rain, I couldn't get it. I couldn't make a crop."

Bette's sympathetic voice was almost hushed. "We had so many years of drought, and then two years of torrential rain. And we held on too long."

"Then Jimmy Carter came in, and interest rates went to 21 percent. At the time the rains finally came, I had nineteen hundred acres, most of it low land. And it got washed away." Lake's voice broke. "I lost the whole nineteen hundred acres. Before I knew it, I was broke. And you can't borrow yourself out of debt. Things just started to get worse. And we lost our home."

"We had three kids by then," said Bette. "So we both had to do something."

Lake grunted. "It was damn rough. I had never missed having a college education. Until then. And I decided that I had to go in another direction."

"What kind of a job were you able to find, Lake? Your skills were all in farming."

"I got a job up at Parchman Penitentiary," he said quietly.

"What kind of a job?"

His eyes held mine for a long moment. "As a prison guard." He said it simply and without apology. "A prison guard. From four in the afternoon until midnight."

A prison guard! I studied his strong, proud face and the determined set of his jaw. "What guts that must have taken, Lake."

He grinned at my wide-eyed stare. "Somebody's got to do it!" He suddenly laughed and tapped my knee. "Say, do you remember that nice colored gal that we had workin' for us in Ruleville? Used to serve you coffee when you came over?"

"Ora May? Of course I remember her. I remember that first afternoon when we sat around for hours just talking, and Bette told her that I was just 'visiting in Ruleville'!"

We laughed, and Lake said, "You'll appreciate this, Tracy, I'm sure. You know who was my supervisor at Parchman Penitentiary? Ora May!"

I could only stare. "Are you serious, Lake?"

"Dead serious, Tracy. It was Ora May. I was just a corrections officer, and Ora May was my sergeant. I had to work under her. And I had no problem whatsoever with that." He nodded, his eyes reflective. "It opened my eyes in a lot of different ways. She was a wonderful supervisor."

Bette leaned forward, eyes shining, eager to join the conversation. "What I loved best about Ora May being Lake's supervisor was that it was so *right*. I never had a qualm, and neither did Lake. We were so comfortable with it. I just thought, 'This is so *right*.' Kind of the way it should have turned out, isn't it? It was almost biblical!"

"What happened to Ora May?" asked Gloria. "We'd love to have the chance to talk with her."

Bette's voice was soft and sad. "Ora May passed away, Gloria. I wish you could have met her. She was such an excellent mother and wife, and raised a precious daughter."

I glanced at Bette in the rearview mirror and then at Lake Lindsey. Unbidden, the old images of that first afternoon in Ruleville flooded my mind. How embarrassed I had felt then for Ora May, who was ever present when Bette and Lake had been describing the limitations of character and education of the blacks who touched their lives. To a northerner, the Lindseys' words had sounded insulting and insensitive, and I had marveled at the cool equanimity of the black woman in the room. I had even written about it in *Stranger at the Gates*, the very book that Bette Lindsey had asked me to sign.

How complicated we all are! Sketches, I thought, are just sketches. They capture a moment in time. But time just keeps racing ahead. When is the drawing complete?

The big car purred quietly as we moved through the last radiance of the late afternoon. The women's voices in the back of the car were only a murmur. There was a sense of comforting peace in the car, yet I was struggling to understand the extraordinary history that had just been sketched, eager to discern the two Lindseys who had materialized these many years later. How different were they from the impish, provocative woman and boyish, stubborn, racially prejudiced plantation owner I had met when we were all decades younger? I found myself strangely invested in finding the truth.

"Lake," I said, "I'm trying to visualize you as a corrections officer at Parchman. In the movement we heard a lot of stories about Parchman. I'm having trouble imagining you there."

He chuckled. "Well, nothing stays the same. Mississippi doesn't, and Parchman doesn't. My wife can tell you. You remember that when Bette found Christ, and became a born-again Christian, she began working with black women in drug and alcohol rehab at Parchman Penitentiary? She had a long interest in that kind of work."

"I was in my late twenties when I started working there, Tracy," said Bette. "Did it for seven and a half years before they asked me to be a chaplain to the women. I was grateful that God gave me that mission so that I could be involved. I was able to go to maximum security and all over that prison. I like to think that I'm leaving a better place after I've passed through."

Lake added, "Bette got a job at Parchman at the same time I did. And I started to work my way up. I went through several jobs in penology. And during the day I was taking college courses. Got my degree in two and a half years," he said proudly. "I finally became warden over all the maximum security units. In time, I became a superintendent of the Central District Correction Facility in Rankin County. And that's the reason we moved down here to Brandon."

"Is that why I couldn't find you listed anywhere? And why anybody who knew anything about you wouldn't tell us?"

Lake laughed. "Yes. I had to have an unlisted telephone number. I was getting so many phone calls from offenders' wives and mothers. You try to remain unreachable. For more than seven years, it had to be that way.

But now that I'm retired, we're back in the phone book. And I'm glad you found us."

"Do you miss penology? You made a whole career there."

"No. I'm out of the prison system, but I'm not out of penology. I joined a small company, Contemporary Corrections, and now I do consulting work. All the prisons in Mississippi now have to be accredited by the American Correctional Association, and I'm able to help a number of the small prisons to meet new standards."

Bette exclaimed, "Enough, enough about prisons! I want to hear what you both have been doing. Besides, we've arrived!"

As always, Bette had a stream of questions about our marriage, our extended family, Gloria's assignments as a journalist, and information about my work as an artist and writer. And in the process we learned that one Lindsey son is a writer, another has a restaurant, and their daughter is married and has already presented Bette and Lake with their first grand-child. Before coffee had arrived, the four of us had explored much of the personal terrain we had all crossed since the Freedom Summer of 1964. We lingered after coffee, eager, I think, not to terminate the specialness of the occasion. What we had shared forty years ago was a moment in time when any reconciliation of natives and outsiders seemed impossible, yet that was the moment we had found each other, the moment that now bound us. What once poisoned and defined the space between us was now long past, and what graced the evening was the recognition of our common fallibilities.

"When the movement came to Mississippi," I offered, "I think most of us white outsiders felt we were in terra incognita, and that everyone on your side of the highway was 'redneck,' potentially violent, religiously hypocritical, and that you were so *blind because you would not see!* From the perspective of a whole lot of years now, I guess it was not surprising that you thought we were insufferably arrogant and acted like we had a patent on the morally superior truth!"

"You got that right," chuckled Lake.

"That was the number-one resentment of the movement down here," said Bette. 'They don't have a clue!' But what we also didn't know was that neither did we! The blacks that were my friends and whom I did fight for, and truly loved? I didn't have a clue about them! Because I knew my heart was right, and I'd do anything for them, I thought I knew their life. But I didn't have a clue about the depth of it." Bette seemed pensive. "That way of life which you were all so scornful of was all that Lake and I had ever known. It all seemed to be okay." Her head lifted and confronted each of us, wishing somehow to make us understand. "I could never understand how the black race could be so 'satisfied' with their way of life. I was just so ignorant of the situation. So ignorant of the fact that *they had no choice!* I didn't even know that! Lake could tell you—I was always trying to fix things. I wanted to get them married. But I didn't know. I was just so blind! So blind!"

Lake pushed back his cup and tapped the table with his fist. "Bette and I have talked about this. When you don't know any better, and what's around you is all you've known in your whole life, you are partially blind. But when I had some adversity come into my life, and I was suddenly on 'the other side of the highway,' it didn't take long to put things in another perspective."

As we were driving back in the velvet twilight of the Delta, Bette said, "You know, Gloria, when I read Tracy's *Stranger at the Gates,* it was a revelation to me. It helped me to understand in a new way." She leaned forward and touched my shoulder. "Do you remember Mrs. Williams's quote in your book, when she was teaching Sunday school? 'This morning we're going to read why we welcome the strangers at our gate.' That was you and your people in the movement. And Mrs. Williams and the others in the Sanctified Quarter saw the movement as a godsend. And so do I. There was a rightness to it . . . hurting, needy, and weary souls which were reaching forward with hope to their God and the people that he'd sent." She stopped, and the car was silent as it sped through the gathering purple dusk.

"I don't think any of us thought of ourselves that way, Bette. *God's messengers?* I don't think so. The only person whom I knew that thought that way was Fannie Lou Hamer, and she deeply believed it."

"When the movement came to the Delta," reflected Bette, "I do believe my heart was ready to receive the truth, and that my spirit was willing

60. Rennie Williams teaching Sunday school class.
"Why should we welcome these strangers at our gates?"

to change. But it was ignorance that held me back. Ignorance! Ignorance! Ignorance!" She paused, embarrassed by the passion of her words. "I can only speak for myself. Back in the sixties, I thought it would be years before enlightenment and willingness to change could be achieved. I do believe now that I see the light at the end of the tunnel. But I think it will only come together for a generation where families, black and white, are intact. I believe that what is eating Jackson alive today is the crime caused by families that are not intact."

Gloria gently intervened. "Families that are not intact, kids that have no boundaries, and have no predictable love at home, are a terrible problem where we live, Bette. We lose too many of our children, too."

Bette nodded. "It's not a black thing I'm talking about. It's all about losing our children!" The last light had fled when we headed back to

Jackson. There was the quiet pleasure of relaxed time with people you enjoy. In the light from the dashboard I could see Lake, half-smiling, sharing the moment.

"Back in '64, Lake, I remember how distressed you were about the possibility of blacks voting because you questioned their competence to make sound judgments."

"That's true," Lake interrupted. "But if you remember, I was also distressed about illiterate whites voting when some literate blacks couldn't!"

I nodded. "I remember that. But once the Voting Rights Act was passed in '65, everyone had the opportunity to vote. As a result, you now have more blacks in the state legislature than any other state in the nation. Has that been good for Mississippi?"

His fingers drummed on the steering wheel before answering. His eyes narrowed. "I think in a lot of ways it's helped move the state forward. We're starting to appreciate each other on a different level. Where I work, up in Holmes County, which is predominantly black, I couldn't want to work with a better professional group of penologists. Before I started, a friend had told me, 'If you come up here, you're going to enjoy working with this group as much or better than any you've ever worked with.' And it worked out that way. They're fine to work with." The deep voice paused. "I think what we have to do is go back to the word *communication*. I don't think we yet have enough communication between the races. And without communication, it's hard as hell to build trust."

"I do believe you've paid a lot of dues down here, Lake. And from what I see, the state has moved remarkably in the last forty years. I have a lot of respect for that."

"Sometimes we take two steps forward and slide back one and a half. But I do think we're steadily moving forward. There's been a lot of mistakes on both sides. I can't do anything about something that happened a hundred and fifty years ago. I can't be guilty for that. All I can do is do what I think is right now. When I boarded a plane last week to fly back from Chicago, I got on early to get a bulkhead seat. It's more comfortable for my bad knees. This black gentleman came on, and he looked at me, looked at the seat next to me, and hesitated. And I said, 'Come on, sit down.' He did, and we introduced ourselves and started talking. Turned out we had a lot in common, knew a lot of the same people. And we had the finest conversation all the way back to Jackson." He paused, chuckling. "There was another white and black across the aisle sitting together. They spoke to each other when they sat down, and I don't think they ever spoke another word to each other all the way back!"

"They were both cheated," I said.

Lake nodded. "They were. 'Communication' has a lot to do with that."

Before we said good night at the hotel, I told them about the exhibit of my Freedom Summer drawings that was at the Smith Robertson black ethnic museum. Bette declared that they would see it, and she was as good as her word. When we spoke again on the phone after we had returned to Connecticut from Jackson, both she and Lake were eager to talk about their reaction to the exhibit. Lake was ruminative, choosing his words carefully. "I liked your drawings. Made me start thinking back to the fifties and sixties. Particularly that drawing you made of a black perspective of Ruleville, that view of white Ruleville from across a cotton patch on the black side of the highway."

"I'd been living there for a couple of weeks when I drew that, Lake. I realized that looking way over there, where all the nice houses were, was about as close as black Ruleville ever got to white Ruleville."

Lake said, "I realized that that cotton patch was about all that Ruleville was for them. I don't think I ever thought about that. Those things I guess you learn the hard way." His voice brightened. "I liked your drawing of the old gentleman, Mr. Williams, very much!"

"He was a fine man, Lake. Was still chopping cotton at eighty-one and still being deacon of his church on Sunday. I don't think Mr. Williams ever had three years of school. But he was smart as hell."

"But you can be a fool even with an education, Tracy. An educated fool." There was regret in his voice.

"Don't be so tough on yourself," I teased. "You're not an 'educated fool.' You told me Parchman had changed. You told me Mississippi had changed. Do you think you've changed much?"

"Changed much? A meathead like me?" A deep laugh erupted. "Would you believe about 180 degrees!"

Bette said simply, "He has. We have. You wouldn't believe it, but I am no longer the ditzy blonde you once wrote about!"

I hooted. "Who says so?"

"Don't be so smart, Tracy. Just believe me. Besides, I really do want to tell you what happened at your exhibit. I went down to the Smith Robertson, and I truly was transported by the show. I was surprised by the degree it moved me. I knew I would pick up some things and that it would enlighten me, but I was really floored."

"You know how to make an artist happy, Bette. Thank you."

Eager to continue, she moved swiftly to her next thought. "Like Lake, I was most touched by your drawing of Mr. James Williams. I was so moved that I left the room and went out to the desk and asked for some notepaper. And when I came back in to the exhibit, I sat down on the floor to put down my thoughts so I could share them with you. Let me read it to you. 'When I look at Mr. James Williams I see an old soul who is bone-weary, who is down but is not out. He is not defeated! He is bowed, but he is not broken. He is ready to stand for *right*.'" Bette's voice was choked, and she halted momentarily before continuing to read. "'I see many years of oppression in Mr. Williams. But I don't see anything of hate in him. This visit to the museum gives me a powerful sense of transference. I feel a greater understanding, combined with deep, humble feelings of unfulfilled promise. God, please forgive me.'"

I found myself in tears, and quite unable to respond. But Bette had one more gift for me. "When I looked at your writing and your drawings of that summer, I thought, 'Bette, how did you miss that?' And then I had a great revelation. I realized that because of the movement, not only the Mississippi blacks were freed. I was freed."

In my final conversation with Bette and Lake Lindsey, Bette began, "Lake and I have been talking . . . "

Lake interrupted, "It's about trust, Tracy . . . what you and I had been talking about . . . "

Bette's voice now cut in. "And we want you to know that if you are really going to put us in your book, it's okay with us if you decide to use our real names." Bette's chuckle echoed in the phone. "If you still want to call us Cutler, you can. It's okay."

"We leave that decision up to you," Lake added.

I didn't trust my voice, but quickly said, "Thank you both. I have to think about that."

Not a Stranger

for sixty years my life as an artist has taken me to places I could never have dreamed of as a fledgling illustrator who wished only to draw and paint. Syracuse University's College of Fine Arts had given me the tools, but not the reason, to be an artist. But as I sought to understand the carnage and losses that I encountered as a naval officer on the D-day beaches of Normandy, I found the reasons. My drawings could be my compass and my teacher. I learned that my art could be much more than a way to have a career. It could guide me to the truth if I trusted it. And from D-day to the horrors of 9/11, I have traversed my turf and my times, recording in words and pictures what I have discovered.

Of all the destinations I have journeyed to, none has been more daunting, more frustrating, more important, more life-affirming, and more memorable than the state of Mississippi. As an artist and a citizen, I have been most challenged by this most southern of the southern states. Often, Mississippi has seemed like an extraordinary petri dish, a microcosm of southern sensibilities and racial conflict. In six decades of travel and reportage, nowhere in America have I found the riveting personalities and thrilling canvas that have brought me ever back to Mississippi. All the unfinished racial business of America is writ large here. All the moral promise of America can be perceived here. All the tragic flaws that bedevil America can be cataloged here. And much of the nobility, courage, and sacrifice that grace America have been demonstrated here, helping to change the whole nation.

In what other place, and in what other time, in America's long journey from the colonies, did a thousand white kids choose to put themselves in harm's way to achieve justice for their black brothers and sisters? In what other place, and in what other time, did young black warriors, men and women, skillfully, nonviolently, and valiantly dare the darkness and light the way to freedom for so many who longed to follow? Where else in America did one see emerge such an extraordinary cadre of heroic women as Fannie Lou Hamer, L. C. Dorsey, Virginia Gray, and the countless anonymous heroines like Rennie Williams? And where, but in this state, did one watch young black citizens like Charles McLaurin, June Johnson, Hollis Watkins, Jim Foreman, Bob Moses, and Charlie Cobb challenge the establishment, face down the vigilantes, and tear the masks from the racist past?

In the time I have been here, hardly even a blink in history's eye, I have watched a place transformed. Sharecroppers' children who first

61. Jim Foreman, executive field secretary of SNCC.
"Indomitable SNCC pioneer."

found inspiration in the movement's Freedom Schools have gone on to seek real skills in higher education. Some like Cephus Smith, a partner now in an interracial business in the Delta, are free to pursue dreams never dreamed by parents who were bound to stoop labor in the steaming cotton fields. The state that would never yield, never surrender, never embrace its black children as members of the state family has bitten hard on the bullet and slogged ahead. That has taken courage and character by all of Mississippi's children. One can pray, and I do, that the bravery and resolve of Bette and Lake Lindsey have thousands of echoes within the white community. To witness that family's growth and capacity to love, to see them face adversity and embrace change, gives promise to countless others who are struggling to understand their own tilting landscape.

In a larger sense, Mississippi has provided a candid mirror for much of America far beyond Dixie. As Fannie Lou Hamer wisely noted, "The sickness in Mississippi is not a Mississippi sickness. It's an American sickness, and America is on the critical list." For more than forty years, I have been a "stranger at the gates," seeking always to peer inside, to hear the conversation, to understand the truth of the place. For more than forty years it has been a "work in progress," a mission I know in my heart will never be fulfilled. The portrait will never be finished by this artist. But I hope my Mississippi sketches can speak to those who will follow.